D0217076

MARX FOR A
POSTCOMMUNIST ERA

When the Iron Curtain collapsed, capitalism reigned triumphant and the 'end of history' was declared. However, peace and prosperity have been short-lived. In recent years, anti-globalization protests have returned violence to the streets, nations have been ravaged by ethnic genocide, and fundamentalist radicals have intensified their war with the West. In this uncertain climate, *Marx for a Postcommunist Era: On Poverty, Corruption, and Banality* does not doomsay. It does, however, seriously question the ability of market forces to deliver the greatest good to the greatest number. It rejects the class hatred and social engineering that has discredited Marxism in the past and it does argue that Marx's emphasis on social equity, real democracy, and human capital still forcefully resonates in the modern day.

After reviewing Marx's philosophical roots and his twentieth-century reception, Sullivan applies Marx's ideas to three major phenomena—poverty, corruption, and banality—that remain obstacles to freedom in the twenty-first century. Drawing on the 2000 US presidential elections, Russian tax evasion, the mixed success of privatization, the ascent of Hollywood and Silicon Valley, and our fascination with fake theme bars, ethno-chic fashion, and the retro trend in design, Sullivan also highlights the breadth of Marx's legacy both inside and outside the academic world.

Marx for a Postcommunist Era combines a deep understanding of Marxist thought with journalistic engagement in real-world themes. This comprehensive and timely book will be of interest to students and academics in the areas of philosophy, sociology, politics, and cultural studies, and to anyone with an interest in Marx and his legacy.

Stefan Sullivan is the author of numerous articles on international affairs and one novel, *The Final Slum*, which won a Discovery Award at the 2001 Hollywood Film Festival. In 1994 he received his PhD in political philosophy from Oxford University with a dissertation on Hegel and Marx. He lives in Washington, DC.

MARX FOR A POSTCOMMUNIST ERA

On poverty, corruption, and banality

Stefan Sullivan

London and New York

First published 2002
by Routledge
11 New Fetter Lane, London EC4P 4EE

Simultaneously published in the USA and Canada
by Routledge
29 West 35th Street, New York, NY 10001

Routledge is an imprint of the Taylor & Francis Group

© 2002 Stefan Sullivan
Typeset in 11/12pt Garamond by
The Running Head Limited, Cambridge
Printed and bound by
Gutenberg Press Ltd, Malta

All rights reserved. No part of this book may be reprinted or
reproduced or utilised in any form or by an electronic,
mechanical, or other means, now known or hereafter
invented, including photocopying and recording, or in any
information storage or retrieval system, without permission in
writing from the publishers.

British Library Cataloguing in Publication Data
A catalogue record for this book is available
from the British Library

Library of Congress Cataloging in Publication Data
A library record of this data has been requested

ISBN 0–415–20193–4

CONTENTS

ACKNOWLEDGMENTS

I would like to thank Duncan Foley, Gerald McDermott, Marc Pachter, and Miguel Szekely for their insights and critical comments on various chapters. Jonathan Rée, the Ideas series editor at Routledge, had the audacity to suggest that a fresh look at Marx would be a worthwhile undertaking. He has been a valuable sounding board throughout. I also owe a large debt to my Oxford doctoral supervisors, Leszek Kolakowski and John Torrance, for initially nourishing my interest in the Hegel/Marx tradition. The US Library of Congress offered a godsend to the independent scholar in the form of an office space where most of my research was carried out. My wife, Marina, not only assiduously reviewed the manuscript but, as an economist in her own right, was a formidable sparring partner on issues of poverty and development during the evening meal. Finally, my parents, David and Anneliese, are owed special gratitude for their unflagging love and support.

PREFACE

In the course of writing this book, I was subjected to countless sermons by taxi drivers, academics, journalists, and particularly East Europeans who, as schoolchildren, had digested a dumbed-down Marxist-Leninist catechism. They all had an explanation why Marxism failed and why capitalism now reigns triumphant. I realized then that to address a subject that many people consider obsolete is a thankless task. Even more so when it is a subject like Marxism on which everyone claims an expert opinion.

The unseemly associations with totalitarianism, genocide, and unviable economic planning are, indeed, hard to ignore. Yes, even though the euphoria that greeted the fall of communism has since been tainted by the rapacious greed of the ex-nomenklatura, and their carpetbagging Western advisers, few would now invoke a return to Marx. As critics of my project have been quick to point out, the human costs of social engineering have far outweighed the consequences of a capitalist system that, with ruthless logic, simply allocates to each worker the rewards appropriate to his skills on an open marketplace. To read Gulag memoirs, as apparently many communist sympathizers chose not to, or to visit Tuol Sleng prison, the unassuming secondary school in Phnom Penh where Pol Pot's henchmen tortured and killed, is to face the sobering reality that dogma and its reckless certitude are far more dangerous to human freedom than the misery of a subsistence level wage.

But I entered this crowded field not just to say something fresh and readable about Marx, but because I had an intuition that much of what Marx said about capitalism in his day still holds true in ours. This intuition has been borne out. The destabilizing impact of roaming speculative capital, the subhuman conditions in Third World industrial parks, and the corrosive impact of market forces on the democratic process and cultural goods all reflect the unhealthy dominance of the capitalist system. The evidence was too overwhelming to shy away from the common neoliberal challenge that any attempt to expose the flaws of capitalism raises a totalitarian specter. As Slavoj Žižek, a leading contemporary theorist on the left, remarks in some-what heated terms: "liberal scoundrels can find hypocritical satisfaction in their defense of the existing order: they know there is corruption, exploitation, and so on, but every attempt to change things is denounced as ethically dangerous and unacceptable, recalling the ghost of Gulag or Holocaust."[1] Indeed, though individual liberty has a compelling grip on the modern consciousness, I suspected that there was intellectual dishonesty at play among those who misconstrue freedom as the unbridled pursuit of personal gain. The only response can be to argue one type of freedom against the next, the freedom of public safety versus the freedom of gun ownership, the freedom of global health coverage, a living wage and humane work environments versus the freedom of individual preferences (including how personal tax income should be allocated) on an open marketplace. In short, from the perspective of the left, the social allocation of surplus wealth and the intervention of the state in the name of the public good bring far greater freedoms to a far greater number than the neoliberal and conservative alternatives. But to do this, I also felt the need to restore to Marxism its intellectual integrity, one battered by the often appealing counter-arguments of neoliberal triumphalism, the unsavory apologias for the Gulag in the past, and, often, just plain bad writing—either the sweeping generalizations of the pamphleteer, or the jargon-heavy overkill often found in academic studies.

The purpose of this book is to explore Marx's relevance in the post-communist world. I have framed this project primarily in terms of a contribution to a critique of three major obstacles to freedom: poverty, corruption, and banality. They not only encompass the economic, political, and cultural consequences of a society driven by profit and greed, they also give us a fairly comprehensive understanding of the vastness of the Marxian project. For, at its core, it is motivated by a concern no less noble than to expose the impediments to a human life worth living in an alienated world. This implies, in turn, challenging the postmodernist sensibility that denies that there is any coherent world to be alienated from. By claiming that society is fragmented into heterogeneous subjective viewpoints, the postmodernist denies the ideal forms of freedom that afford us our only hope. We may now be wary of rigid notions of the optimal social organization, but we must still strive for improvement in the regulation of the market, in the accountability of states and political agents, and in the aesthetic education of the global citizenry. For to fail to do so will allow unregulated capitalism, disguised as freedom, to continue to impede progress toward a more just and humane society.

But if poverty, corruption, and banality are obstacles to freedom for many countries, at many different stages, Western civilization has now, and rather suddenly, been forced to contend with a more primal threat to the values it holds dear. Until recently this, the scourge of terrorism, seemed containable within the geographic boundaries of the Middle East and the seemingly intractable Palestinian conflict. But with 11 September 2001 the battlefield widened to encompass the whole civilized world. It was not just a revenge attack for US support of Israel but a bitter vindictive strike against modernity in general. Yet to vulgarly equate Western modernity with materialism and Godlessness—as these terrorists have done—ignores all the other freedoms that are integral parts of it: freedom of expression and the press, of the separation of Church and state, of gender equality, of the rule of law, and of open democratic debate. These principles have, at times, been declared more in name than in deed, or have been arrogantly foisted on weaker nations without regard to cultural or historical contexts. And yet, in a very Hegelian sense, they all emerged from a historical struggle which, for the last 200 years or at least since the American and French Revolutions, has pitted the champions of self-governance and egalitarianism against the reactionary forces of feudalism, aristocratic privilege, and corporate wealth. If there is such a thing as humanity's collective wisdom, then at least we can say that ours was secured not through dogmatic assumptions but through hard, and often bloody, historical experience.

All this must be spelled out because the alternative—a vulgar abnegation of political freedom and economic progress—is such a non-starter. Islam, for all its positive qualities as a religion, has done little for the economic well-being of its citizens. Those Islamic countries which have modernized and achieved some economic success, with or without the windfall of natural resources, are those where fundamentalism has had the least influence. Yes, many of these regimes are corrupt and indifferent to the needs of their poor, but those which have fallen under the sway of fundamentalism have fared far worse. There the clerics who preach redemption through hate and who decry the Westernization that undermines the traditional way of life, have proffered no viable economic alternative beyond a murky nostalgia and, for its martyrs, a disturbingly sharp and seductive vision of the afterlife. Given this state of affairs, we can only hope that the conflict ends quickly. For the tensions that color it—apart from those of the Palestinian issue which do warrant a just resolution—are not particularly fruitful or nuanced. Blind vindictive hatred versus self-satisfaction, envy versus indifference—there can be no meeting of minds here; the value systems are too far apart. Nor are there any obvious links between the anti-Western sentiment of radical Islam and Marx's critique of capitalism. In fact, Marx had little to say about radical Islam other than to suggest that history did not treat static, backward-looking societies kindly. He was, after all, a child of the Enlightenment, suspicious of utopias—religious, political, or otherwise. He believed that freedoms, once declared, must also become freedoms which are granted. He also believed that political liberties without economic justice were empty declarations. Ultimately he challenged Western civilization to create a social order adequate to its ideals. This enormous task, despite the current battle with terrorism, must remain at the forefront.

The book is roughly divided into two parts. The first part (Chapters 1 and 2) is an intellectual history illustrating, firstly, Marx's adaptation of the theological and metaphysical questions posed by German philosophy to a rigorous analysis of capitalism (Chapter 1), and secondly, the many and often contradictory forms Marxism assumed in the twentieth century: from Leninist Bolshevism through the postcolonial ideologies of the developing world, to the cultural criticism of the Western Marxists and the Frankfurt School (Chapter 2). The second part presents a sequence of thematic chapters on poverty, corruption, and banality in the postcommunist world. While exploring these topics in their own right, these chapters provide, particularly for the student reader, an overview of Marx's and Marxism's economic, political, and cultural ideas. Chapter 3 addresses the problem of poverty and how it is perpetuated by shortcomings in mainstream economics and the exploitative tendencies at the heart of the capitalist system. Chapter 4 addresses corruption and Marx's critique of liberal democracy based, among other things, on a fundamental distinction between political and human emancipation. It is—the readers should be forewarned—a long and complicated chapter. This is primarily due to the need to clarify, in the course of the discussion, a number of familiar concepts of Marxist political thought that for too long have been saddled with ambiguity and confusion. Finally, Chapter 5 addresses banality—the infestation of capitalism into the sphere of leisure and culture. While the narrative evolves from a discussion of basic to more complex needs, the chapters are also largely self-contained. I have therefore foregone a concluding chapter in favor of concluding remarks at the end of each chapter.

To explore across continents and disciplines will expose me to criticism by the experts into whose territory I have wandered. But any philosopher who is faced with trying to make sense of the real world is faced with only two choices: to abstract from it or stray outside his comfort zone and risk the charge of charlatanism. True to the spirit of Marx, I have chosen the latter path. I have tried to understand the themes of poverty, corruption, and banality in their own terms and disciplinary language, dispassionately and without ideological prejudice. Inevitably, I have not been able to accommodate all the literature and the academic controversies that surround them. But wherever research could not reach, I have drawn upon personal observations from Russia, Thailand, Colombia, and several European countries in addition to my native United States. From this liquid vantage point, I have witnessed poverty both tropic and arctic, corruption, both political and commercial, and banality in all its dazzling forms. Ultimately, I have realized that experience can enrich, but it can also humble. For it reminds us how so many of the big questions elude theoretical frameworks or practical solutions, and how complex and variegated they become when viewed up close. But even in our post-ideological world, the solution of the problems should not be left to the technocrat alone. The left-leaning scholar can expose and criticize a system that on a daily basis affronts human dignity, and cripples our potential. And that is what I have tried to do.

October 2001

1

INTRODUCTION

After the aftermath: the utopian and Dickensian scenarios

The watershed events of the last century—from the Bolshevik revolution through the turmoil of the 1960s to the fall of the Berlin Wall—all reflect the rise and fall of Karl Marx, and his most potent legacy, i.e., that there can be a viable economic and social alternative to capitalism. By now this legacy has been so discredited that any attempts to reassess its value are automatically prejudiced by negative, or at least highly romantic, associations. The whole set of iconic imagery—Politburo apparatchiks reviewing the tanks, Che Guevara in beret and combat fatigues, striking workers in a sea of placards and banners, Left Bank intellectuals in a cloud of cigarette smoke, or the carnage of a terrorist attack—have colonized the modern consciousness to such a degree that any retelling of the story seems well nigh impossible. Even after more than a decade since the fall of the Wall, as unfettered capitalism has left its troubling legacy in the former communist states, and as a vibrant coalition of protest groups has risen to challenge the human and environmental costs of globalization, Marx rarely makes an appearance in the rhetoric. Instead, such groups rally under generic rubrics such as anticapitalism, progressivism, or grassroots activism, sensing, perhaps rightly, that the historical drama of Marxism has run its course.

Evoking Marx can be a liability given his contentious reputation, particularly when the policy prescriptions sought by his ideological descendents, such as a living wage or better environmental standards, can often be defended in terms of broad principles of social justice. But it is also true that by the end of the twentieth century the Marxian legacy had been co-opted by so many political and cultural forms—from African despotism to arcane literary criticism—that it had lost its utility as a unifying mantra for anticapitalist protest.

Furthermore, the socialist experiment as it was applied in the former communist states revealed itself as a perversion of human nature orchestrated by a self-serving elite. It had alienated its citizens from their capacity

1

for initiative, confining them to a life of neither extreme poverty nor extreme wealth but rather a staid lower-class mediocrity. We do not need to dwell on the circumstances that brought down the Soviet bloc and its dependent brood of satellites. There were political and economic realities, personalities corrupted by greed and self-love, and geopolitical dynamics that all complemented the shaky Marxist foundation. The arms race, the superpower conflicts in the southern hemisphere, the cults of personality—Stalin, Ceausescu, Hoxha, Kim Sung—were power games that had little to do with the economic exploitation of the worker.

Nonetheless, there are at least two early lessons that can be drawn from the rise and demise of all these hybrid outgrowths of Marxism. One is that Marxist ideas work best as a set of antithetical ideals aligned against the status quo. Like Christianity, Marxism has been most effective in the midst of sin: exposing injustice, demanding basic rights for the have-nots, organizing the underclass into a political movement. It draws energy from the latent human resentment toward apparently parasitical behavior, the wealthy feeding off the sweat of the poor. But what history has also taught us is that in the aftermath of revolution, when Marxist ideas confronted a clean field emptied of class enemies, either dead or exiled, they lost much of their momentum. The revolutionary leadership turned paranoiac in its search for either internal or external enemies. The populace, once provided with its basic needs, bumped up against a glass ceiling that stunted ambition and the natural material rewards of hard work. In a society in which the medical doctor and the mechanic had to live in the same drab, prefabricated high rise, as was the case in communist Eastern Europe, the natural dream of incremental progress, of constantly improving one's station in life, was undermined. Certainly, there were hidden perks for the educated and well connected—vacation homes, special shops, and trips abroad—but for the most part what remained was a social fabric dictated by the lowest common denominator.

The second lesson is that the socialist ideals have no meaning without adequate economic resources. Indeed, how could an aspiring communist country ever generate wealth if its leadership discouraged competition, entrepreneurialism, and private ownership, scared off or killed off its tax base, and misallocated funds in order to keep pace militarily with economically more advanced countries? On the other hand, socialist polices were not alone to blame. It was also the disadvantageous starting point of those countries which adopted them. For one of the great paradoxes of the communist experiment is that it tended to take root in poor regions—agrarian Eastern Europe, Africa, Latin America, Asia, etc.—with large income disparities, yet it was precisely these conditions that prevented regimes from delivering on their broad promises. In short, those countries most prone to fail under socialism were those that perhaps needed it most. External circumstances also militated against a successful outcome. Beyond the more general point that the Cold War forced communist countries rich in natural resources—Russia and Angola are two obvious examples—to channel social wealth toward military spending, more specific circumstances had long-term crippling effects. In China, just before Mao took power in 1949, his national opponent Chiang Kai Shek fled to Taiwan with all of the country's gold reserves. Likewise, East Germany had much of its heavy industry dismantled by the Soviet occupation, forcing it to rebuild without the Western financial assistance granted its West German neighbor. Cuba, a poor country to begin with, has also suffered from the US trade embargo, even more so now that Soviet subsidies have eroded.

But perhaps the greatest irony is that although our understanding of Marx is now irreversibly intertwined with the fate of the communist regimes in poorer regions, his writings were never intended for them. This is partly due to Marx's own frame of reference, and his historical context, but it also rests on a simple logic intrinsic to his system. The path to communism lies through the redistribution of surplus wealth. If there is no surplus to redistribute, then any poor communist state could hardly satisfy the basic needs of its people. In short, it is much easier to build socialism in a country with a small population and a high GDP, such as Sweden or Finland, than in poor countries, with conversely large populations and a low GDP, such as Cambodia, Vietnam, or even Russia. Indeed, it may well be that the lasting legacy of Marxism will linger longest in the developed countries of Western Europe. Here, the combination of the threat of communism which exacted concessions from the political establishment—to reduce the working day or enact maternity leave—plus the very real political influence of social democratic parties has done more to realize Marx's goals than countless radical insurgencies in the developing world.

What this implies is that, to a certain degree, those who put Marx to rest together with the failed communist regimes missed the continuing relevance of his ultimate goal, one toward which Western society has been gradually moving. For the time being, we might describe this goal as a point at which every citizen, or at least a good number of them, finds satisfaction through their labor, has equitable access to public goods, and has both the time and the material resources to realize their unique potential. This we might call the utopian dimension of the Marxist legacy that continues to inspire progressive policy-makers, activists and critics. But the global spread of capitalism, or perhaps equally our intense awareness of it in the most remote corners of the world, has resurrected another dimension as well. This, the Dickensian dimension of Marx's legacy, has now come back to haunt. Just like in mid-nineteenth-century England, swarms of landless peasants flock to urban ghettos (and more recently, suburban industrial parks) to work long hours for miserable wages under appalling conditions. In the shoe and textile factories of Asia, in the assembly plants on the US–Mexican border, and the slaughterhouses of the American south, these disorganized, unskilled, and uneducated workers have become easy targets for capitalist exploitation.

However, given the skepticism about Marx's legacy, how can these two dimensions offer a framework of analysis in the postcommunist era? Is the utopian ideal too far-fetched and the Dickensian scenario too complex to lend itself to the kind of totalizing vision characteristic of the Marxist idiom? Firstly, in terms of the utopian ideal: even if one can imagine all workers relocated from the din and clang of the factory floor to the carpeted calm of hi-tech offices, there will still be cubicled white-collar wage slaves forced to confront, perhaps now more than before, the futility of their existence. In its own way, the legions of college educated going through the motions in data entry, telemarketing or website maintenance, all under-achieving in a grand way, wasting hours commuting between a suburban ranch style home and an airport access road, all disembodied from any organic sense of community, are a vision as apocalyptic in terms of the sanctity of human life as any Dickensian vision of nineteenth-century factory labor. Furthermore, the guarantee of basic and increasingly complex needs in the modern welfare state now increasingly coincides with the technological displacement caused by increasingly efficient means of production. Automation of the factory floor and the modern office poses the possibility of huge swarms of redundant working-age people. This, coupled with dramatic increases in human life expectancy, invite scenarios of a future dictated by leisure rather than work. "Technological progress," the German Marxist philosopher Marcuse wrote, "would make it possible to decrease the time and energy spent in the production of the necessities of life, and a gradual reduction of scarcity and competitive pursuits could permit the self to develop from its natural roots."[1] The fact that technology may change the relationship between work and play, or may even make traditional human labor redundant, has elicited all kinds of futuristic scenarios from contemporary sociologists.[2] Some of these scenarios can be advanced without appealing to Marx or Marxism, but in those instances where the polarity between work and play, between societies that mandate a shorter work week, generous maternity leave and vacations, and those that do not, is determined by class differences and their disparate levels of political influence, Marx will continue to carry weight.

In terms of the Dickensian scenario of global capitalism, Marx continues to have relevance. The simple fact that many of the conditions that Marx documented and challenged 150 years ago are now quite the norm subverts the triumphalism that greeted the fall of the Berlin Wall. For if the initial rhetoric announced the return of individual enterprise and self-empowement in Eastern Europe, it soon became clear that one system of exploitation merely replaced the next. The party elite became the corporate elite of anarcho-capitalism—in Russia it still amazes the number of former Komsomol (Communist Youth Party) members who ended up in the Moscow branches of Western investment banks—and the socialist worker became the capitalist wage slave but without the benefits, however meager, of a social safety net. The pensioners, orphans, invalid veterans, and, in fact, the average unenterprising worker, all those who could not benefit from the new opportunities found themselves stranded. On a more visceral level, the quality of life of the seamstress in an Indonesian sport-shoe factory is, at the dawn of the twenty-first century, only one notch above the silkworm. Though her product is exported through sophisticated marketing channels, in many ways her working conditions parallel those that Marx gleaned from the so-called Blue Books of English factory inspectors in the 1840s. It is the same old tale of long hours, cramped conditions, and bad food; of the beauty of youth mortgaged to subsistence wages. And because they are subsistence, the idea that these often rural villagers can, after some years at the factory, return home to build a better life, turns out be a hollow dream indeed. The Indonesian seamstress is the face of global poverty, the condition in which the majority of the world's population lives. This is not scaremongering, but a stale statistical fact. The majority of the world's population earns less than three dollars a day. Thus, once we realign the Eurocentric focus of current post-Marxian debates and its arcane jargon, we find ourselves back at square one, in the era of raw capitalism.

The Dickensian and utopian scenarios reflect the wide scope of Marx's legacy. It weaves incessantly between a political economy of oppression and a grander indictment of the troubled human soul seeking deeper meaning in a routine existence. "What constitutes the alienation of labor?" Marx asked in the early *Economic and Philosophical Manuscripts* (EPM).

> First, that the work is external to the worker, that it is not part of his nature; and that, consequently, he does not fulfill himself in his work but denies himself, has a feeling of misery rather than well being, does not develop freely his mental and physical energies but is physically exhausted and mentally debased. The worker, therefore, feels himself at home only during his leisure time, whereas at work he feels homeless.[3]

If we were to take Marx at face value, then his definition of alienation would apply not only to those living in base poverty, but almost everybody who works. Does the insurance salesmen feel any less alienation than the auto mechanic simply because he receives a higher wage? Selling insurance may be just as remote from that person's nature and he may work even longer hours affording him even less time to enjoy his higher wage. Thus, Marx embraces not just the poverty of material existence but also that of human lives, ones freighted with monotony, materialism, and mental debasement. The restoration of one's ownership of labor is then not just a question of redefining the relationship between the capitalist and the proletariat, but of redefining the nature of labor itself. It cannot just be a means to perpetuate survival, or fill the time between adolescence and death, but must be construed, in its ideal form, as a uniquely individuated vehicle of freedom. We express who we are through what we create. We see ourselves through our work. That is our lasting testament.

We might find this grand formulation of labor hard to reconcile with, as Marx proposed, a political process of emancipation. What is more, it seems to throw him right back into the philosophical paradigms he was trying to escape. For Marx's departure from philosophy was dictated by the notion that the antinomies blocking human self-realization are practical in character. They are dictated by particular socio-economic realities that can only be overcome through political engagement. If this conclusion took Marx away from philosophy and toward political economy and socialist agitation, the lofty demands he makes on labor bring him right back again. In some ways, they take him even farther afield from his Hegelian origins, to a radical Schopenhauerian pessimism or classical existentialism. Along these lines, we are all destined to a life of poverty because our will arises from need, from a disequilibrium between what we have and what we desire. Once freed from need, as Marcuse noted, "the natural individuality of man is also the source of his natural sorrow."[4] This radical pessimism underlies much of the Marxist critique of consumer culture, i.e., the fixation on Having rather than Being, the ephemeral nature of commodities, and the sense that—a theme we will take up in a later chapter—global advertising is constantly seducing people to live beyond their means; it also draws attention to the yawning gap between who we are and what we want to be. The gap often eludes a practical reconciliation. Through loans, charity, and public spending, we can judiciously direct our surplus wealth toward the oppressed, reduce infant mortality, increase literacy and life-spans, and earnestly chip away at all the factors that perpetuate a miserable existence. But even when these have disappeared, we are still confronted by a deeper alienation underneath: the more we distance ourselves from poverty, the daily fight for survival, the more freedom we have to express who we are, the more we must confront the even greater challenge of unalienated labor. What would we create if we totally controlled our labor? What if we discovered that we had nothing to express? To paraphrase Marx, if the worker feels himself at home only during his leisure time, the man of idle wealth is at home all the time. In other words, even if the truer picture of Marx's socialism is less about the crude abolition of property but rather increased leisure time under conditions of freedom, then one must still come to terms with this freedom as a potential void. A philosophical conundrum hangs over the whole enterprise.

The German context: from a critique of heaven to a critique of earth

It has been said that, in the postmodern era, it is difficult to speak of alienation from freedom because mankind no longer has a unified vision of the de-alienated Subject. "We can no longer conceive of the individual as alienated in the classical Marxist sense," writes David Harvey, a leading postmodern theorist, "because to be alienated presupposes a coherent rather than fragmented sense of self from which to be alienated."[5] The postmodern onslaught against grand narratives, or against an essentialist vision of human destiny, has fractured the Subject into an eclectic array of gender and racial identities, each pursuing their independent objectives. Furthermore, in the West, the relative security of the worker coupled with the lingering memory of ill-conceived attempts to construct a "coherent self"—the top-down social engineering of totalitarian regimes—have all further eroded confidence in the validity and explanatory value of the "alienated Subject." Yet, it is a central thesis of this book that we must have a coherent vision of freedom, of some ideal of what constitutes a human life worth living. As such, alienation in the classical Marxist sense must be preserved, if not restored. For it represents all the obstacles to freedom that are rooted in the reigning capitalist system. The system's preference for market over human value, its privileging of the monied and powerful in the democratic political process, and its insidious creep into the sacred sphere of culture and leisure, are all more self-evident than ever before. If we abandon any coherent sense of what freedom should be, then the field will be left open for capitalism to shape it for us. We need, therefore, to restore, at least in part, Marx's redemptive vision "of man seeking to attain the mastery of himself and of the external world by means of his creative labor."[6] To do so we must first return to the tradition of grand narratives, particularly to the German philosophical tradition that Marx inherited. For it was here that the ideal of a liberated humanity and its optimal form of social organization emerged from an attempt to secularize the meaning of the Christian drama. Indeed, it is well known that, in the course of its history, Marxism took on many of the attributes of a secular religion, for instance, the rhetoric of historical redemption, the celebration of the propertyless and oppressed, and the whole range of religious imagery that, particularly in the developing world, offered the poor a vision of heaven on earth. But what is less well known is the extent to which these attributes owe much to Marx's German philosophical heritage and its Christian theological influences. It is this heritage that offers greater insight into Marx's grand vision than dialectical materialism or class conflict, the conventional cornerstones of studies on Marx.

No modern study of Marx can limit itself to social costs of modern capitalism, for Marx's philosophy emerged in a German tradition with broader ambitions, one which sought to discover nothing less than the meaning and value of human existence. It was a tradition which combined metaphysical system-building, religious lyricism, and most importantly, a post-Enlightenment quest for God-surrogates or Absolutes, those center pieces of a whole series of grand systems of the German idealists that presented "one of the most remarkable flowerings of metaphysical speculation in the long history of Western philosophy."[7] Whether accessed through mystical intuition (Schelling and Schlegel) or through transcendent reflection (Hegel and Fichte), the Absolute was seen as the aggregate of all human enterprise that ultimately revealed itself in the historical process. This Absolute finally became, in the works of Feuerbach and Marx, man himself, and his eluctable progress toward emancipation. No other tradition invested so much metaphysical grandeur in the historical process as the German. It was the route of fallen man's return to God or the Absolute.

Within the expansive secularization drama that characterizes Germany's philosophical output of the early nineteenth century, Marx played an important, if not defining role. For if the Absolute is a vision of redemption, and that redemption can only take place in the historical process, then at a certain point, as Marx realized, philosophers would no longer have the conceptual tools or language to accommodate the empirical reality of that process. Instead, one must transcend philosophy and harness this utopian vision to new forms of social analysis, ones that directly confronted the human predicament and its daily struggle. As Marx wrote in the "Contribution to a Critique of Hegel's Philosophy of Law," "the immediate task of philosophy, which is at the service of history, once the holy form of human self-estrangement has been unmasked, is to unmask self-estrangement in its unholy forms. Thus, the criticism of heaven turns into the criticism of earth."[8] The criticism of heaven turns into the criticism of earth. And because heaven provides the opiate for the oppressed, and because the more oppressed man is the more he will invest his hopes in the otherworld, announcing the death of God, in Marx's view, is really a call to action. "The demand to give up illusions about the existing state of affairs is the demand to give up a state of affairs which needs illusions."[9] This is the essence of Marx's dictum—religion is the opiate of the people—which has so often been caricatured as vulgar atheism. Instead, it meant only that investing hopes and dreams in an otherworld is a distraction from the real job at hand, to restructure society along more just and equitable lines.

But the theological influences on Marx's thought go far beyond this famous slogan to encompass a number of deeper themes: the redemptive role of the proletariat, the eschatological vision adapted from Hegel's dialectic that freedom for the working class would be realized through historical conflict, and finally, a very German idea about the character of freedom, one based not on the absence of coercion or the individual pursuit of private gain (the classical liberal stance), but on creating an optimal community that would allow the individual to realize his optimal self. In general, Marx's vision of communism is perhaps best described not as theologically influenced but rather imbued with a philosophical heritage in which theology, at critical moments, played a defining role. But this also demands further clarification. For how was it that Germany in particular produced so many philosophers who eschewed incremental measures to improve the human condition in favor of metaphysical dramas and grand theories of radical social transformation? The answer is complex but, I think, at least three ingredients of this particular theological legacy offer some explanation.

Firstly, there is Germany's imperial consciousness, a feeling that it was not just one of many Western nations, but the anointed vanguard of human progress in general. Although many European powers have at times enlisted God to legitimate their imperial exploits, Germany's self-understanding as the one-time center of Western Christian civilization—in 1229, Barbarossa's grandson, Frederick II, claiming sovereignty over all the kingdoms of Christendom and the Vatican crowned himself in Jerusalem—was accompanied by a sense of divine guidance. This, as we know, led to a series of ultimately catastrophic attempts to restore some mythic unity and grandeur of the past. Marx was essentially critical of German, and particularly Prussian chauvinism, but his casting of the social conflict between bourgeois and proletariat as a titanic struggle between two abstract forces betrays a specifically German kind of theological simplification, one which encases its national moral struggles in rigid dichotomies between good and evil.

The second theological influence is Luther. His revolt against papal authority in 1518 had numerous causes and consequences. However, within its immediate German context, it replaced the ritualistic trappings of the Catholic Church with the preached word and Bible reading, turned the focus away from Latin toward the German language, and enabled the individual Christian conscience to establish a more direct relation to God. Through Luther's revolutionary interpretation, the Bible text-based rapport of the believer with God became more relevant to salvation than any external "good works" sanctified by the Church in Rome. Luther's battle against clerical corruption also aimed to recreate the ideal of early Christianity, to find a purer way to knowledge, self-Enlightenment and social justice. Like Jesus against the money-changers, Luther railed against the "Roman bloodsuckers" and the cynical trade in indulgences, drawing upon a long-standing Christian apocalyptic tradition that traces the transition from domination, sin, and oppression toward a perfect, harmonious world. Remnants of this tradition would resurface among Marx's utopian socialist contemporaries such as Wilhelm Weitling, who also saw in the ideal of early Christianity an emancipatory appeal against economic injustice. And in Marx's work, in its disdain for earthly goods and its idolization of the suffering masses, we can also find many of these themes.

Finally, Marx's vision of communism owes something to Germany's collectivist view of freedom. We mentioned above a backward-looking tendency in German history toward some unblemished imperial past, a period of unity and communal solidarity. A corollary to this is the uniquely German understanding of freedom, one which has traditionally defined itself against the liberal individualism of England and France. It ranges from the organicist and folk-based or *völkish* spiritualism of the romantic era, through the more modern controversies of the 1980s generally known as the *Historikerstreit* (the historians' conflict or debate). At the center of all these phenomena lies the question as to how far Germany's collectivist self-understanding has separated it from its Western neighbors. From a historical perspective, this self-understanding rose to the fore in two distinct periods, in the aftermath of the Enlightenment and during and after the First World War. As Hans Kohn remarks in his classic *The Mind of Germany*, "Opposing the individualism and egoism of the capitalistic West, especially of commercial England, the German in World War I spoke for a true socialism in which the individual became part of the community and regarded its growth and strength as his own."[10] The conflation of the individual and the community lies at the heart of Germany's departure from Western liberalism. Although Marx questioned Hegel's glorification of the Prussian state, his debt to this heritage is clearly mediated by Hegelian influences and some vision of an organic community. The theological dimension of these influences is most evident in both the centrality Marx placed on community as the locus of freedom, and the vagueness with which this locus was articulated, as if it were a murky future realm of salvation. This vagueness, in turn, was echoed by the legions of socialist gurus, prophets, cults, sects, salons, and clandestine worker groups which, in the 1830s and 1840s, were all inventing their own terminology to describe various ideals of communal solidarity. In addition to the *Gemeinmensch*, or communal being, of Feuerbach, the immediate inspiration for Marx's communism, a number of other short-lived variants included *communitism, communitarianism, communional, collectism, societaire*.[11] What's more, the terms communism, democracy, and humanism were all used interchangeably,[12] partly because no one had yet given a definite shape to the type of political structure these ideals represented, and partly because their proponents were somewhat lacking in intellectual rigor. On the whole, however, all these varieties of communism defined a general conception of emancipation that sought to distinguish itself from the perceived egoistic worldview of contemporary bourgeois society. That conception gained some concreteness when Marx identified its underlying economic content. As he described it in one of his earliest formulations:

> Communism is the *positive* abolition of private property, of human self-alienation, and thus the real appropriation of human nature through and for man. It is, therefore, the return of man to himself as a social, i.e., really human, being, a complete and conscious return which assimilates all the wealth of previous development . . . It

is the solution of the riddle of history and knows itself to be this solution.[13]

The philosophical basic of communism: Feuerbach's speculative Christology

There are Hegelian currents in this early definition of communism, certainly in the notion of humanity's divided soul and its quest for unity in and through the historical process. However, Marx's more immediate and intimate debt is owed to the Young Hegelians, a school of theological speculation and philosophical experimentation that emerged in the 1830s after Hegel's death. In the annals of German philosophy, the Young Hegelians are not taken very seriously, a mediocre prelude to Marxism, or for those dismissive of Marx entirely, an irrelevant cul-de-sac compared to Schopenhauer or Nietzsche. And yet, the Young Hegelians took an important Hegelian idea— that theology and philosophy have the same content, namely the Absolute, but different forms—and sought to ground it in the arena of human praxis. Fundamentally, the whole generation of Young Hegelians was preoccupied with religion, and particularly one branch of it, speculative Christology, i.e., the philosophical examination of the Christ figure. They asked themselves the question: If the reconciliation of alienation and freedom is the central Christian message, how can this be philosophically reformulated without faith in Jesus Christ, who anyway is a mythical figure? As summarized by David Friedrich Strauss, the theologian whom Marx would credit with initiating "the decomposition of Hegelian philosophy,"[14]: "This is the key to the whole of Christology, that, as subject of the predicate which the Church assigns to Christ, we place, instead of an individual, an idea; but an idea which has existence in reality, not in mind only."[15] By abstracting the central Christian message from the historical figure of Jesus of Nazareth, the Young Hegelian theologians paved the way for a philosophical, quasi-atheistic appropriation of the *idea* of Christianity as opposed to the Christian *belief*.

However, it is another philosopher, one more directly influential on Marx's development than Hegel himself, who rises out of the crowd of his early influences. Marx credited Ludwig Feuerbach with not only adapting the central Christian message and Hegel to the new environment, but also with developing "a philosophical basis for socialism,"[16] a basis which evolved from the secularization of theological, and more precisely, Christological concepts. We should then explore Marx's debt to Feuerbach a little further. For the essence of Marx's utopian vision, to allow man to retake control over his own labor, flows from Feuerbach's secularization of the Christian concept of love.

Although Feuerbach's work encompasses an eclectic array of subjects, he is best known as a philosophical critic of religion. His work can be read as an attempt to salvage from religion, and the Christian religion in particular, the tangible qualities such as love, mutual respect, etc., that could be applied to the modern individual in community. In particular, he developed a theory of alienation based on the idea that mankind has projected its own idealized qualities, its alienated essence, onto its deities. The task was then to reappropriate from Christianity those alienated ideals and ground them in a materialistic context. As a natural starting point, he chose Hegel who, in his view, represented, "the last magnificent attempt to restore Christianity, which was lost and wrecked through philosophy." Hegel had drawn a very clear distinction between the transcendent, abstract God of Judaic monotheism and Enlightened rationalists such as Kant, and the immanent, loving God of Christianity. While philosophers dating back to Aristotle had preferred a God as an absolute, immutable substance, Hegel saw the kernel of Christianity in its embrace of a God who, through his Incarnation in the Son, defiled his own purity in order to engage himself in the historical drama, to show that he was present in and among humanity. Furthermore, Hegel adapted the self-sacrificing Christian God to his own system by claiming that he is not simply a static entity who made one primordial sacrifice of his only begotten Son, but rather that he is the dialectical process itself, the Absolute Spirit, by which humanity realizes its full potential: God eternally begets his Son until that moment, which Hegel vaguely situated in the present, when he recognizes himself in the world. Feuerbach approved of Hegel's ambition to make Christianity philosophically comprehensible, but he felt that Hegel had belittled human agency in the process by making it a mere vehicle of his self-manifesting God-surrogate, Absolute Spirit.

His argument centers primarily on the distinction between the Judaic God, interpreted as distant, authoritarian, and corresponding to a worship of the self (or egoism), and the Christian God who is intimate and grounded in love. Very much along the lines of the apostle Paul, he elaborates:

> The law condemns; the heart has compassion even on the sinner. Law affirms me only as an abstract being—love, as a real being. Love gives me the consciousness that I am a man, the law only the consciousness that I am a sinner, that I am worthless, the law holds the man in bondage . . . love makes him free.[17]

In becoming man, God sacrifices his identity as the projection of egoism and takes the form of Jesus Christ. "As God Incarnate, he shows himself not only as a rational human being, but also as a finite, sensuous, and loving creature." This finitude demands interdependence and the mutual satisfaction of need, which leads Feuerbach to explain how and why love exists among men. Whereas the abstract intellect, the God alone, is self-sufficient, fallible man *needs*, and that need, itself, is love. In this sense, Feuerbach's philosophy "decodes the Christological moment into a dialectical othering"[18] which is driven by the need for humanity to realize itself in community. "Being

Human is the same as the Being of Humanity," Feuerbach stated aphorist-
ically as early as 1835;[19] or, in Christological terms, the *Menschwerdung (Gottes)
ist das Werden des Menschens* (the *Becoming-Man of God is the Becoming of Man*).

In *The Principles for a Philosophy of the Future*, Feuerbach incorporates his
critique of Christianity into what Marx considered to be the philosophical
wellsprings of socialism, by making the human species, not God, the highest being for man. The new anthropotheism makes God nothing more
than object of a new speculative philosophy whose task is to theoretically
reformulate the God that for religion remains otherworldly. This process
of substitution, Feuerbach traced back to the German tradition of God-
surrogates whereby totalizing concepts such as the Ego (Fichte) and the
Absolute Spirit (Hegel) replaced the "divine being" of the old metaphysics
and theology, with the "present, active, and thinking being of man."[20] In
Feuerbach's case, the central character of his metaphysical drama is not ego,
or will, or absolute spirit, but love. The self-alienating God of Christianity,
which creates a being, at once separate from yet a part of thought, "is
himself only an abstraction of human love and an image of it."[21] In turn
love represents "the true ontological proof of an existence of an object apart
from our mind."[22] The synthesis of the heart and the mind that the new
philosophy proposes makes man the focal point.

In preserving yet reconciling the distinction between the Judaic God as a
projection of egoism, and the Christian God as a projection of love, Feuerbach
presents a dual reduction of God to man. Reconciliation can only occur in
community, where thought arises through communication among subjects.
The individual consciousness of truth and reality is underpinned by communality, by the necessity of objectifying one's thoughts and feelings, particularly in conversation: "The community of man with man is the first
principle and criterion of truth and generality. The certainty of the existence
of other things apart from me. That which I alone perceive I doubt; only
that which the other also perceives is certain."[23] This reformulation of God
into community, far from a rhetorical analogy, becomes a starting point for
the new philosophy with love and interdependence at its center. This is
what Marx would consider the theoretical roots of socialism: "The old philosophy said: what is not thought, does not exist; the new philosophy says
on the contrary: what is not loved, what cannot be loved, that does not
exist."[24] Importantly, however, this transition from idealism to sensualism
does not arise independently from thought, it derives from the essence of
Christianity. The path to human emancipation must pass through a speculative reformulation of the incarnate God, for "only the resolution of this
puzzling (Christian) essence, but the thorough *germanic* solution, will ultimately decide the fate of states and peoples when their existence bases itself
otherwise on a heavenly utopia."[25]

We have dwelt at some length on Feuerbach because his work explains
—much more than the conventional links drawn from Marx's Hegelian

inheritance—how in a German philosophical context, a critique of heaven became a critique of earth. Communism in Germany sprang not from workers' movements or class warfare but from the philosophical critique of the alienated communality represented by the self-sacrificing, Christian God. Yet, if Feuerbach now categorized himself as neither an idealist nor a materialist, but a communist, a *Gemeinmensch*,[26] where does that leave Marx, the recognized founder of communism? Is he the Melanchthon to Feuerbach's Second Luther, the disciple who spreads the word, who puts into practice his mentor's theoretical appeal to transcend egoism and realize humanity's communal essence? The truth is that although Marx initially embraced Feuerbach's main accomplishment, he soon emerged from his shadow and, before the age of 30, abandoned German philosophy altogether. In *The German Ideology*, written between 1845 and 1846, and revealingly subtitled, "Critique of Modern German Philosophy according to its Representatives Feuerbach, Bruno Bauer and Stirner, and of its Various Prophets," he declared: "In direct contrast to German philosophy which descends from heaven to earth, here we ascend from earth to heaven."[27] Whereas German philosophy has deduced prescriptions for human behavior from theological concepts, Marx sets out to generalize from empirical observations grounded in humanity's materialistic base, i.e., its means of exchange, its satisfaction of basic need, etc. Marx applauded Feuerbach's salvage operation of the communal ideal from the clutches of religion, but it was only a first step. A materialist starting point cannot simply be declared as an object of contemplation or a *theoretical* tool, it must *practically* negate alienating social structures.

From love to labor: toward a critique of capitalism

As we noted earlier, a variety of Christian-inspired forms of communism abounded among Marx's utopian socialist contemporaries of the 1840s. The followers of Saint-Simon practiced Christian brotherhood by wearing robes that could only be unbuttoned by a partner. In his novel *Icaria*, Etienne Cabet depicted a paradise mingling real democracy with the purity of primitive Christianity. Charles Fourier construed love as a social alternative to reason. Reason would still be required for social engineering but love, "a Divine Flame, the true Spirit of God," would be the main adhesive in his *New Amorous World*. And Wilhelm Weitling, a tailor turned social radical, interpreted Jesus as a revolutionary founder of communism who waged war against money worship and egoism.

But while Marx considered the approach of the early socialists an advance on the abstractions of the German philosophers, he found their ideas for the most part pseudo-scientific and naive. He also found the primitive adaptations of Christianity distasteful, particularly the emphasis on rituals and ceremony symbolizing brotherly love. His objective was not to implement some fantastical vision or ideal community, but rather to craft from existing social conditions a living, historical struggle, a revolution of society. As opposed to this utopian socialism, he advocated a more scientific socialism, one that would criticize capitalism by way of a thorough analysis of its injustices and contradictions.

In doing so, scientific socialism would not only go beyond the bounds of traditional philosophy, it would abandon it altogether. As Marx would demonstrate, the theoretical critique of capitalism would have to take place in the realm of economics, in order to illuminate its contradictions from within. However, even when Marx decided that the most concrete elaboration would come about by abandoning philosophy altogether, his conversion to economic concepts did not come about immediately. It was a gradual process that, at least until the publication of the *German Ideology*, remained well within the shadows of Hegel, Feuerbach, and of a German tradition with a penchant for totalizing concepts such as the Absolute, Love, Spirit, etc.

To illustrate this transition toward economics, we need to review one of Marx's early philosophical text in some detail, particularly to see how he first formulates his concept of labor on the basis of Feuerbach's concept of love. In the *Economic and Philosophical Manuscripts*, a loose collection of essays written in the early 1840s, Marx explored how communism would emerge through the negation of egoism and its socio-economic basis, private property. Through this negation, humanity could recapture its essence and realize its full potential. However, for Marx, Feuerbach's concept of *love* was too vague and emotional to encompass the complexity of man's technical relation to nature and his fellow human beings. Instead, Marx replaces it with *labor*.

Although it was not quite as simple as replacing variables in a mathematical formula, the manuscript on "Estranged Labor" betrays the schematic nature of the transition from love to labor. In it, Marx attempts both to clarify key concepts of classical political economy, and to show how capitalist conditions give rise to human alienation. He initiates his attack by claiming first that political economy, like theology, wrongly begins with certain facts accepted as authoritative. In the case of capitalist political economy, that fact is "private property": "The economist assumes in the form of a fact, of an event, what he is supposed to deduce."[28] Just as the theologian presupposes God's existence uncritically, and then attempts to contemplate God's nature, so too the political economist accepts the existence of private property and then derives economic concepts from it. In contrast, Marx proposes to begin with "an *actual* economic fact" rather than a theoretical postulate: "The worker becomes all the poorer the more wealth he produces, the more his production increases in power and size." Here we find Feuerbach's projection theory applied to political economy, an explicit variation on the theme: "the more of himself man attributes to God, the less he has left for himself."

15

Thus far, Marx has proposed the rough equation: private property = the abstract, theological God. Next, he assesses the nature of alienated labor:

> The *alienation* of the worker in his product means not only that his labor becomes an object, an *external* existence, but that it *exists outside him*, independently, as something alien to him, and that it becomes a power on its own confronting him. It means that the life which he has conferred on the object confronts him as something hostile and alien.[29]

Here we arrive at a central Marxian idea: the process of our labor should be, not what it usually is—a means to sustain our daily existence—but a vehicle for our self-realization. As labor is the fundamental human activity, therefore man is essentially a worker. Man works by virtue of his essence, and for this reason, Marx uses the terms "man" and "worker" interchangeably.

From the assumption that man is a worker, Marx moves to distinguish man from animal by their relations to their productive activity. He has thus far only implied that the object of alienated labor is external to man, in so far as it is used as a means to satisfy external, as opposed to internal, needs.[30] He claims now that the satisfaction of external need as a form of alienated labor corresponds to human-animal activity.[31] In an alienated state, the condition of the capitalist worker, "man (the worker) only feels himself freely active in his animal functions."[32] However, liberation from alienation implies feeling free in his human function, his function as a species-being: "Man is a species-being, not only because in practice and in theory he adopts the species as his object, but also because he treats himself as a *universal* and therefore free being."[33] The species-being objectifies his labor as an end in itself, in which he expresses himself freely, not as a necessary means to sustain life, i.e., animal existence. Alienated labor, on the other hand, makes life-activity, the expression of human essence, into a mere means for existence.

Although Marx's emphasis on labor is suggestive of economic discourse, again his concern here is primarily philosophical, to formulate alienated labor in a way that explicitly echoes Feuerbach's alienated love—the communal love projected onto the Christian God Incarnate. And here we can see how striking the parallels are. In Feuerbach, love means a number of things: "the essential idea," "active realization of the unity of the species," and "key proof that God is Man." For Marx it is labor, rather than love, which is "life activity," "productive life itself." Both Feuerbachian love and Marxian labor fulfill identical roles as foundations of their respective visions as to how to transcend alienation. Both visions depict the unity of man with man in terms of an engagement with nature, with an object outside man that is made his own, appropriated, and, in turn, creating a new object. In both cases, this engagement is the fundamental part of human self-creation. It is only that Marx felt that the ontological foundation was more concretely laid by showing how man *creates* his Being (labor) rather than merely *participates* in it (love). Labor, in his eyes, more scientifically reflected the reality of human self-creation.

What is also remarkable about Marx's early use of terms drawn from economics is the extent to which he broadens them to encompass the whole sphere of human activity. Thus labor defines not only the mechanism of manufacturing material things, but rather the whole sphere of human creation and self-creation. In Marx's scheme, world history, religion, the family, the state, science and art, etc. are all products of human labor. Equally abstract is his definition of private property. Private property represents not just the objects belonging to particular people, it represents the "emergence of an alien reality" in so far as, through the accumulation of material objects, the sense of having replaces all the other physical and intellectual senses. Having denigrates the manifold ways in which humanity should experience the world—tasting, smelling, loving, observing—by reducing everything to the simple act of possession and utilization. Only the transcendence of private property can emancipate humanity from the egoistical character of need and enjoyment. And, finally, money, as a form of private property—or, one might say, its crowning achievement—Marx categorizes as the "alienated power of humanity," which distorts what one *is*. "I am ugly, but I can buy the most beautiful woman for myself. Consequently, I am not ugly, for the effect of ugliness, its power to repel is annulled. As an individual I am lame, but money provides me with twenty-four legs."[34] Marx views money as the quintessential barrier to proper relationships, ones wherein human self-expression would be a function of the unique individuality of the person and respected as such, and not distorted by the purchasing power of material wealth. In his later writings, Marx would thoroughly analyze categories such as private property and money in their narrower economic context. But here, in his early writing, he underscores their deeper philosophical content as obstacles to human freedom.

Finally, communism is defined not so much in terms of reappropriating private property, but rather of recovering humanity's lost essence:

> Communism is the *positive* abolition of private property, of human self-alienation, and thus the real appropriation of human nature through and for man. It is, therefore, the return of man to himself as a social, i.e., really human, being, a complete and conscious return which assimilates all the wealth of previous development . . . It is the solution of the riddle of history and knows itself to be this solution.[35]

No remarks here on workers' communes, union strikes, proletarian revolution, exploitation through surplus value, or the mechanics of capitalism's cyclical crises—all features of his later writings. Instead, Marx laments the collective human soul that has gone astray, a soul seduced by material wealth and the gratification of egoistic needs. Bolstered by a *pot-pourri* of eclectic references—where Luther sidles in alongside Adam Smith, and Goethe alongside Shakespeare—Marx imaginatively construes communism as the antidote to a fundamental human alienation borne of misguided economic relations. No matter how meticulously he later filled in the blanks, no matter how densely and ponderously he later articulated the mechanism by which capitalism would or should implode, Marx never deviated from this starting point.

Marx as the anti-philosopher

The young Marx used the language and concepts of German philosophy to explain economic behavior because the problems which he wished resolved remained philosophical. Humanity was alienated from its true essence, and the task was, as it had been for a number of other German idealist philosophers, how to reunite historical reality with the Idea, with the Truth, or some kind of configuration of the Absolute, in short, how to reunite man with God. Yet Marx believed that the root cause of that essence lay beyond a simplistic atheism, i.e., the negation of God, in an analysis of the means by which man, as a collective entity, interacted with the material, natural world. Therefore, the panacea could only evolve from a critique of those means, i.e., the capitalist system.

Marx's transition from a critique of heaven to a critique of earth had important implications for philosophy, not just in its German context but in general. For, independent of his better known political activism, he challenged the validity of a mode of inquiry which claimed intimate access to the meaning of human existence, yet either lacked or rejected the tools to explore that existence in its empirical reality. Indeed, since the mid-nineteenth century, as the sciences and social sciences have gradually colonized areas of inquiry once reserved for philosophy, its insularity from the so-called real world has only intensified.

> The professional discipline of philosophy [writes one contemporary philosopher] is presently caught in an interregnum; mindful of the dead ends of analytical modes of philosophizing, it is yet unwilling to move into the frightening wilderness of pragmatism and historicism with their concomitant concerns in social theory, cultural criticism, and historiography. This situation has left the discipline with an excess of academic rigor yet bereft of substantive intellectual rigor and uncertain of a legitimate subject matter.[36]

Those academic philosophers who choose to ignore what goes on around them must come to terms with the fact that their area of inquiry is increasingly self-referential and esoteric. Marx, in a trenchant satirical tract of his youth, appealed for a philosophy more engaged in the real world.

18

Up to now philosophers had the solution to all riddles lying in their lecterns, and the ignorant world of the present had but to gape in order that the roasted dove of Absolute Knowledge fly directly into its mouth. Philosophy has made itself worldly, and the most striking proof of this is that the philosophic consciousness has not only externally, but internally as well, been pulled into the torment of the worldly struggle.[37]

Philosophical arguments that pretend to say something relevant about the modern world must be bolstered by experience, the facts and figures and realities that give life to the subject. This is not to say that philosophy should leave the Academy and embark on a kind of learned gonzo-esque journalism. But, at least in terms of respecting social and historical detail, in understanding subjects on their own terms, it could draw some lessons from Marx. Once realizing that philosophy, at least as it was taught in nineteenth-century Germany, was inadequate to understand the forms of alienation experienced by modern man, he embarked on a lengthy study of classical economics to determine concretely the dynamics by which this alienation took place.

Thus, to dismiss Marx as a philosopher, because he left behind no great systematic work on Being and Nothingness, or the Absolute, or the Ego ignores his vantage point. Marx believed himself to be a philosopher in so far as he sought to ascertain and elaborate on the fundamental principles that characterize the human condition. Through his course of study, his journalistic activities, and his engagement with the emerging workers' movement, he gradually determined that these principles should be grounded in more earthly matters. He discarded one by one the abstract concepts of his lofty predecessors and came to the conclusion that man forms himself through his labor interacting with nature. Not spirit but rather matter provided the foundation for the self-realization of the human species. This basic assumption led, in a roundabout way, to a concentration on economic theory, and ultimately, to the monumental *Das Kapital*, on the various aspects of the capitalist system—money, labor, property, and profit—and their impact on human alienation. Yet, no matter how much arcane data he assembled—from the use of gold currency in ancient Rome to the communal property schemes of Peru's indigenous people—to lend support to his economic theories, his research was geared toward philosophical objectives. He wanted to show that an unjust economic system caused human alienation, that is, man's separation from his inner potential, from his Humanity. One may even argue that the rhetoric goes beyond philosophy to religion, that Marx was seeking not only to educate but also to redeem man, and, in particular, its lowest form, the proletariat, by way of an impassioned critique of capitalism.

Marx was also a philosopher by way of a methodological legacy, one that inspired not only generations of disciples but also new forms of analyses in other disciplines. His paradigms have been borrowed and adapted by literary critics, historians, ethnographers, poets, and painters. These paradigms turned the focus away from heroic individuals, a hallmark of bourgeois literature and history, toward the lower classes and their daily struggle. Finally, as a spiritual godfather to the working class, he also inspired militant ideologies and mass movements all around the globe. Although his writings are complex, his basic ideas are simple, easily packaged and consumed. Even the most illiterate factory worker could grasp the injustice of a system in which he worked ten times as hard as the owner yet received one tenth of his wage. Regardless of the fact that Marx's ideas were often contradictory, vague, and vulnerable to over-simplification, the very extent of his influence on not only the intellectual community, but also twentieth-century history, lends support to the notion that he is the most socially-relevant philosopher that ever lived.

2
THE TWENTIETH-CENTURY RECEPTION

In the twentieth century, Marx's thought was subjected to conflicting interpretations, particularly about the operative means to realize his broad objectives. Some sympathizers chose terrorism, others organized revolution, others
parliamentary representation, and still others, cultural criticism. Though
there was a shared view that the exploitative capitalist system was the chief
obstacle to freedom, beyond that, the debate broke down into numerous
interpretations on kinds of capitalism (state monopoly or free market); kinds
of freedom (economic or existential); and fundamentally, as to who were
the chief agents and beneficiaries of the revolution—the urban proletariat, the
peasantry of Third World countries, or, in the case of the later critique of
mass culture, the alienated suburban housewife.

In many cases, historical circumstance and the reticence of the masses
themselves helped to modify the Marxists' ambitions. Lenin hoped for a
world revolution emanating from Russia, but Western Europe, particularly
Germany, disappointed and his successor Stalin concluded it was better to
concentrate his powers closer to home. Castro and Che Guevara equally
hoped to spread insurgency throughout Latin America following their success in Cuba. But when Che was murdered in a hapless commando mission
in Bolivia, Castro retreated to consolidate his revolution on one impoverished island. And the Frankfurt School mandarins who, as exiles, applied
their eclectic critique of capitalism to the United States did not always
understand the emancipatory aspects of American pop culture. Even the
1960s student movement, the one major historical event for which the
Frankfurt School can claim some credit, particularly through the writings of
Herbert Marcuse, imploded from unrealistic expectations and a misreading
of the masses.

The mixed success of the Marxian legacy cannot be attributed entirely to
the fact that no one really knew what a communist paradise should look
like. Not all Marxists were utopians and many of their ideas were eventually
absorbed by the mainstream. But if there is a common thread to Marx's
legacy in the twentieth century, it is the persistent interplay between theory
and praxis, the abstract and the concrete, philosophy and reality, that echoes

from every practitioner. Equally suspicious of both the anarchy of the mob and pure academic theorizing, the Marxist philosopher always had to seek an outlet through institutions such as underground activist cells or bureaucratic organs, through a chosen agent of revolution, whether the peasantry or proletariat, or through a tactical blueprint which could be exported and adapted to a variety of revolutionary circumstances.

Along these lines, to explore Marx's twentieth-century legacy in terms of profiles of its key thinkers, as is commonly done, obscures the graphic interplay between his ideas and historical events. Instead, we will approach our task by addressing three main fields in which the Marxian legacy took shape: 1) the tension between gradual reform and revolutionary violence; 2) the theology of revolutionary struggle; 3) the academic's critical paradigm. The substance of these three categories, covering the gamut from East bloc socialism and postcolonial insurgencies to the Frankfurt School, can be previewed in terms of two dynamic processes, *Embodiment* and *Enlargement*. Both of these processes together transformed his legacy from a collection of texts and pamphlets into a global historical force.

Embodiment refers to the numerous attempts, through revolutions, insurgencies, and coups, to shape a concrete historical reality in accordance with the Marxian agenda. Marx's ideas evolved in response to the particular contexts to which they were applied. These contexts also exposed the limits of Marxian theory as a blueprint for political organization. This came most dramatically to light in the events leading up to and following the Bolshevik revolution. The necessity of a vanguard intellectual elite and subsequently a strong centralized state contradicted much of what Marx had said, but it suited the narrower political purposes of Lenin and his cohorts. Indeed, more often than not, in the aftermath of revolution, it was the threat and use of force rather than the strength of argument that won the day.

But the dynamic of embodiment also taught valuable lessons about the very viability of Marx's most noble aims. The messy transition from *criticizing* capitalism to *implementing* an alternative, a *de facto* Worker's State, opened the theoretician's eyes to the multitude of logistical and administrative problems involved in a structural change of such enormous proportions. As Max Horkheimer, a leader of the Frankfurt School, once cautioned "Marxist science constitutes the critique of bourgeois economy and not the expounding of a socialist one."[1] For when it went beyond critique to expounding and implementing an alternative, complications multiplied. The energy of the masses, it turned out, could not be so easily harnessed, nor their desires so easily divined. Erstwhile compatriots, unified in opposition, clashed once power had been seized. And the monolithic portrayal of a proletarian agent of revolution came to be seen as increasingly naive.

Enlargement refers to the expansion of the Marxian agenda beyond the economic fate of the European proletariat. It expanded principally in three directions which were never fleshed out in Marx's writings but are to some extent implicit in them. Firstly, following Marx's death, Engels took upon himself to narrow Marx's focus on socio-economic developments toward a "scientific socialism." Influenced by currents of the Victorian era, particularly Darwinism, Engels attempted to reinforce Marx's method as a scientific mode of enquiry, particularly by showing that the same evolution from speculation (e.g., alchemy) to empirical analysis in the history of the natural sciences applied to the science of society as well, one which reached its culmination in Marx.[2] While this was initially a laudable attempt to distinguish Marx's thought from the utopianism of his socialist contemporaries, it eventually culminated in the vulgar materialism of the Stalinist era.

Secondly, Marxian ideas spread beyond Western Europe to take root, first in Russia, and then all over the world. In fact, as revolution after revolution failed in Europe following World War I, and the Western proletariat found that the new freedoms granted under social democracy often outweighed the human costs of an uprising, the hope of Marxists was gradually invested in those countries where Marx thought capitalism was least likely to be overthrown. This irony involved a major theoretical adjustment because, according to classical Marxism, the transition to socialism required an established capitalist base. What history testifies to though is that Marxism has appealed most in areas where capitalism was least developed. Instead of a sophisticated mechanism explaining how capitalism would implode, it became a powerful, but more simplistic, polemic against oppression not of the organized proletariat but of the often agrarian *very* poor.

Thirdly, capitalism's penchant for co-opting the anointed agents of revolution, the industrial working class, extended Marxian thinking in a theoretical direction within the original target group, the class antagonisms of Western society. Building on the young Marx's writings on alienation, a number of European thinkers turned their critical eye toward the more insidious by-products of the capitalist system. Borrowing from new developments in sociology, Freudian psychology, and existentialism among others, they addressed the long-term impact of the capitalist system on all members of society, not just the most visibly oppressed. The development of consumer culture, mass leisure industry, technological advancement that created false appetites, the countless slew of gadgets that blinded people to their own existential emptiness, all these trends came under scrutiny by a new breed of Marxist intellectual, the so-called Western Marxist; one less interested in barricades and red banners than in more subtle means of spiritual, or cultural, salvation from capitalism.

Reform versus revolution in the Marxian legacy

Before we trace these themes through the twentieth century, we need to first consider one of the most contentious, yet signature, characteristics of the Marxian legacy; namely, the role assigned to violence as a vehicle for overthrowing capitalism. Indisputably, Marxism is a movement marked by bloodshed and violence. Its critics throughout the twentieth century have regularly raised the specter of the mob and its irrational appetites. Often, among industrial leaders and conservative politicians, such scaremongering was self-serving, to deflect attention from the ends of disenfranchised workers—better pay and labor conditions—and toward their chosen extralegal means. But even astute critics have raised compelling arguments against the futile violence of the masses. Behind the masses' urge for bloodshed, they claimed, lay an array of human weaknesses: an impatience to achieve immediately by force what cannot be achieved with reason, an envy of those better-endowed with material and human capital resources, and a blatant disregard for a central tenet of any civilized society, the abnegation of violence as a means for resolving conflict.[3] Throughout the twentieth century, the Marxist response to these charges has generally followed two contradictory tacks: 1) that violence is the only option when the institutional structures of the establishment give no voice to the marginalized and that the rules of civility are broken the moment that the establishment itself uses violence to secure and perpetuate its hold on power; 2) that violence is *not* necessarily part of the Marxian heritage. Along these lines, it is argued that even if Marx and Engels were enthralled with the idea of revolution in their early years, they later softened their view, and Engels in particular came to regard evolutionary socialism through parliamentary reform as a more effective tactic than revolution in achieving the movement's aims. The great fissure between orthodox and revisionist Marxism generally split along these two lines. But they could only each claim to represent the true Marx because of ambiguities in Marx's own writings, ambiguities most evident in communism's founding and most widely read document, *The Communist Manifesto*. We therefore need to consider it in some detail and primarily its language concerning the advocacy of violence.

The Communist Manifesto

If any budding revolutionary, from Cambodia to Cuba, read anything of Marx, it was bound to be his most translated and influential work, *The Communist Manifesto*. This is unfortunate. For although *The Communist Manifesto* assumed the status of a universal and eternal creed for generations of Marxists, it is in many ways restricted by its immediate historical context. It was, in the words of one noted scholar,[4] "a propaganda document hurriedly issued on the eve of revolution." It is full of incendiary phrases about tearing things apart and asunder; Marx speaks of death and destruction, weapons, battles, revolution, and war. But upon closer inspection, one notices that the violent language is mainly metaphorical in character. Though meant to be rousing, though set against the turbulent democratic activism of 1848, it is the language of an armchair warrior, of a man who wields the pen as a sword. For the militant rhetoric does not necessarily have military implications. Marx writes, for example, "the bourgeoisie has pitilessly torn asunder the motley feudal ties;" "the bourgeoisie has drowned the most heavenly ecstasy of religious fervor in icy waters;" "the weapons with which the bourgeoisie felled feudalism . . . are now turned against the bourgeoisie itself." And yet, in the context of Marx's argument, all these so-called revolutionary processes refer to gradual historical changes, not all of them necessarily violent. His own definition of the "weapons of the proletariat" may provide sufficient demonstration: "The bourgeoisie itself, therefore, supplies the proletariat with its own elements of political and general education, in other words, it furnishes the proletariat with weapons for fighting the bourgeoisie."[5] The proletariat's weapons are therefore not necessarily illegal. It can beat the bourgeois system by educating and organizing itself, by playing by its rules, a conclusion reached years later by Engels in celebrating the success of the social democrats in the German elections of the late nineteenth century.

Marx's ambivalence toward violence is further confirmed when he outlines the proletariat's historical evolution. Though the language is militaristic, the development he charts leads away from violence. He outlines three stages of development. In the first, when the proletariat's protest is geared toward the physical "instruments" of production rather than the "condition," isolated individuals destroy machinery and seek to restore "by force" a golden age of medieval guilds. At this stage, they are still an "incoherent mass." The second stage sees a more industrial and organized proletariat. It forms associations and unions to secure particular freedoms such as improved wages and factory conditions. "Here and there the contest (with the bourgeoisie) breaks out into riots" (p. 46). Finally, the proletariat is organized in a class, "and consequently into a political party," that "compels legislative recognition of particular interests." Admittedly, however, though this evolution follows along social democratic principles, Marx then suddenly changes direction when he notes:

> In depicting the most general phases of the development of the proletariat, we traced the more or less veiled civil war, raging within existing society, up to the point where that war breaks out into open revolution, and where the violent overthrow of the bourgeoisie lays the foundation for the sway of the proletariat. (p. 49)

And he intensifies the rhetoric in the *Manifesto*'s final ringing paragraph: "The Communists disdain to conceal their aims and views. They openly declare that their ends can be attained only by the forcible overthrow of all existing conditions" (p. 77). But as well as reminding ourselves of the propagandistic objectives of the pamphlet, one might well ask here: What is a "veiled civil war," and does not a revolution normally break out into war, rather than vice versa? War, one can only surmise, is used loosely here to define the economic competition between the bourgeoisie and proletariat. On the whole, one cannot deny Marx's call to arms, metaphorical or otherwise, in the closing to the *Manifesto*. But it is so muted and diluted by other militaristic rhetoric that actually refers to gradual socio-economic change, a change that could come about through legitimate parliamentary means.

Even Marx's own attempt to distinguish communists from other "working-class parties" offers little clarity. In the *Manifesto*, he outlines two criteria: 1) that the proletariat transcends national differences in favor of class solidarity; 2) that the proletariat ignores sectarian differences and always acts as a unified front.[6] There is no distinction between violence and pacifism, revolution versus reform. Only that, "the immediate aim of the Communists is the same as that of all the other proletarian parties: formation of the proletariat into a class, overthrow of the bourgeois supremacy, conquest of political power by the proletariat" (p. 51). Again, there is no indication whether this conquest would take place through the ballot or barricades. We can only fall back on Marx's classic dictum that the application of revolutionary principles would depend on given historical conditions.

Eduard Bernstein and evolutionary socialism

The ambiguity concerning the application of violence would fundamentally divide the Marxist movement into those who saw socialism as an evolutionary process of securing greater and greater rights for the working class, and those who saw it as an end-goal achievable through violent revolution. In the former case, most notably represented by Eduard Bernstein, lies the intellectual inheritance of German social democracy and, more broadly defined, the European welfare state. In the latter, lies the intellectual inheritance of Lenin's Bolshevism and the communist struggles of the developing world. It is one of the great ironies of this story that although Lenin propagandized himself as the torchbearer of the Marxist movement, it was, in fact, Bernstein who was the anointed successor. It was Bernstein who was chosen by Marx and Engels to edit *Der Sozialdemocrat*, the leading organ of the socialist movement in Germany, and it was Bernstein, a close collaborator with Engels in his waning years, to whom was bequeathed the Marx and Engels archive.[7] Although Eduard Bernstein was a figure of derision for more radical Marxists such as Rosa Luxemburg and Lenin who saw violent revolution as the only pathway toward socialism, Bernstein was not only the father of German social democracy, he was also a privileged interpreter of Marx's and Engels's intent regarding the highly disputed means to achieve socialism.

Although Bernstein agreed with Marx on many points, he also had his critical differences particularly concerning Western Europe's ripeness for revolution. "The doctrine of Marxism is not sufficiently realistic for me; it has, so to speak lagged behind the practical development of the movement. It may possibly still be all right for Russia but in Germany we have outgrown its old form."[8] In particular, he objected to the "catastrophic theory of evolution" as outlined in *The Communist Manifesto*, that the struggle between the bourgeoisie and the proletariat would culminate in an apocalyptic violent clash after which the proletariat would seize power. By the early twentieth century, not only had capitalism not collapsed, he argued, it showed few signs of doing so. There were few clear signs of increased class antagonism, of increased capital concentration to the detriment of small and medium enterprises, or of a growth in the proletariat's revolutionary consciousness. In fact, the numerous democratic advances propagated by Bismark's enlightened authoritarianism, such as factory safety legislation and universal suffrage, made that collapse less rather than more likely to happen.

To resolve this dilemma, Bernstein concluded that there was still a good degree of utopianism mixed in with Marx's quasi-scientific prognosis. Preconceived theories about the evolution of a socialist movement could not always be reconciled with historical reality. It was therefore better to concentrate on means rather than ends. And from his vantage point at the beginning of the twentieth century, the radical means advocated by Marx and Engels during the 1840s were no longer valid: "No socialist capable of thinking" Bernstein wrote in his major work *Evolutionary Socialism*, "dreams today in England of an imminent victory for socialism by means of a violent revolution—none dreams of a quick conquest of Parliament by a revolutionary proletariat. But they rely more and more on work in the municipalities and other self-governing bodies."[9] The fundamental revision in strategy directed itself toward advancing socialist aims within the parliamentary system. The old insurrectionist rhetoric and banners at the barricades were of little use now that steady progress could be made by more peaceful means.

Bernstein's views were supported by Engels himself who, toward the end of his life, also concluded that "slow propaganda work and parliamentary activity," were now the right way ahead. Citing statistics that showed a growth in the German Socialist Party from 100,000 in 1871 to 1,800,000 in 1895, Engels conceded that, "We the 'revolutionists,' 'the overthrowers,' are thriving far better on legal methods than on illegal methods and overthrow. The parties of order, as they call themselves, are perishing under the legal conditions created by themselves."[10] As his last political statement, made in 1895, the year of his death, Engels here provided a potent renunciation of violent revolution as a means to achieve socialist aims. Indeed, as the Italian Marxist philosopher Coletti later pointed out, the shared hope for parliamentarianism as opposed to revolutionary violence, demonstrates that Bernstein's "revisionism," which would later be much maligned by the more radical Bolsheviks, "was born in the heart of the Marxism of the Second International."[11] It was not a blasphemous accommodation to capitalist democracy, but an outgrowth of the success that German socialism was enjoying as a *legitimate political movement* at that particular time. The significance of this observation cannot be overstated. At the dawn of the twentieth century, Bernstein, the appointed trustee of the Marxian legacy, was strongly convinced that he had found a place for the socialist agenda *within* the establishment. The strategic revision of classical Marxism was to downplay the ultimate aims and concentrate on a gradualist implementation of economic justice through legal reforms.

It is tempting to think that this particular point in the Marxian drama was the crossroads from which it all took a wrong turn; that a pragmatic yet persuasive implementation of the socialist ideals through trade unions, the liberal media, and representative democracy could have fine-tuned the capitalist system to accommodate the rights of the oppressed. If the Marxists had come to a consensus on these means, humanity could have rescued itself from a century of genocides, terrorist attacks, insurgencies, and counter-insurgencies. Bolshevism would not have emerged therefore denying the *raison d'être* of its arch nemesis, fascism. At mid-century, the capitalist establishment would not have reacted as paranoically to the "commie threat"—seeing it only as a well-intentioned movement to improve the conditions of the poor rather than a sinister alien plot—thereby sparing us the McCarthy era, CIA covert operations in support of anti-communist Third World dictators and, on a much larger scale, all the economic waste of the Cold War arms race. In short, if the truth had been acknowledged and properly taught, that the Marxian project was the offspring of classical German philosophy and late nineteenth-century social democratic yearnings, then history would have taken a fundamentally different turn.

Lenin and the rise of Bolshevism

But the strategy of gradually reforming capitalism had little appeal in the turbulent aftermath of World War I. If Bernstein thought that his status as caretaker of Marx's legacy would hold sway with the masses, history, in the form of Lenin, has taught us otherwise. Indeed, Lenin's Bolshevik revolution as the logical outcome of Marxism is so ingrained in our collective psyche, that we can no longer imagine what might have been. All the protests notwithstanding, it was as if the spirit of Marx was whisked away from Western Europe to a new hallowed ground on Moscow's Red Square.

The spectacle is well known. During the May Day festivities of the Soviet era, soldiers, tanks, and trucks pulling cruise missiles would parade underneath three massive banners draping Red Square. They were portraits of Marx, Engels, and Lenin, an intimate triumvirate that symbolized the communist faith. But both Marx and Engels were dead when Lenin rose to power; neither could consent to having their portrait hung high each year on festival day. Nor could either consent to the way that history has judged them, as the undisputed ideological collaborators of the revolution that Lenin carried out in their name. But our purpose here is not to adjudicate on the integrity of Lenin's Marxian inheritance, merely one aspect of it. To what extent is there a justification for violent revolution in the Marxian corpus, and, if so, was it faithfully interpreted by Lenin?

Initially, Marx's ideas arrived in Russia by way of a circuitous route, the radical Russian emigré journals of Western Europe. At the beginning of the twentieth century, the leading figures of the Russian socialist movement, Lenin, Trotsky, and Plekhanov, all found themselves in London editing *Iskra*, the Russian social democratic newspaper. They were far from isolated from the main currents of European socialist theory. On the contrary, they were pan-European, urban intellectuals abstractly plotting a revolution for a nation whose inhabitants—petty bourgeois haplessly trying to follow Western fashion or peasants trapped in folkloric rituals and the superstitions of Russian Orthodoxy—they often held in disdain. And their dialogue with Marx was part of an intellectual exercise, an effort to understand the philosopher *per se* rather than as an instrument of revolution in Russia. But when it came time to act, their revolutionary activities bore the stamp of a theoretical evolution that extended far beyond the core of classic Marxism. That evolution took place primarily in the realm of revolutionary tactics, i.e., political organization and agitation, and debates over the use or abuse of violence. Of these, the legitimacy of violence to achieve Marxian aims emerges as the preponderant theme that would later split not only Russia off from Bernsteinian social democracy but also within Russia itself, the Bolshevik militants from Menshevik reformists.

Marx left many blanks for Lenin to fill, partly because his own revolutionary thinking was formed by conditions of the mid-nineteenth century, partly because he had the sense to realize that historical change would force theoretical and tactical adjustments at every stage. As he noted guardedly in the 1872 preface to a new edition of *The Communist Manifesto*, "The practical application of the principles will depend, as the Manifesto itself states, everywhere and at all times, on the historical conditions for the time being existing, and, for that reason, no special stress is laid on the revolutionary measures proposed."[12] The advances made by organized labor within the parliamentary system, and the contentious legacy of the 1872 Paris Commune's two-month period in power, had forced Marx to realize that there were no shortcuts to socialism via a radical but poorly grounded overthrow of the state, and therefore, that much of the radical rhetoric of the *Manifesto* had become antiquated.

Lenin, however, clearly believed that Russia offered optimal conditions for precisely such a shortcut, and used citations from Marx's texts to that effect. For example, in his foreword to his book, *Karl Marx*, he cites a letter from Marx and Engels noting that the success of the proletarian revolution will depend on "some second edition of the Peasant War."[13] Immediately after this citation, he points out that this is what the Mensheviks have not understood. They have abandoned the proletariat and gone over to the bourgeoisie. They have abandoned revolution. Thus, Lenin could justifiably interpret Marx's qualifying statements as a *carte blanche* for his own advances in revolutionary thinking. Though often opportunistically applied in the process of consolidating power, his appeal to Marx's theory of revolution is authenticated in at least one respect: the actual mechanics of the proletariat's seizure of power, as Marx had stated, must conform to given historical conditions. Faced with ill-informed Russian proletariat and an apathetic peasantry, the Bolsheviks concluded that revolution had to be orchestrated and led by a well-organized intellectual vanguard, followed by the centralization of control in the hands of a political elite.

The justification for violence was applied by the Bolsheviks to distance themselves from the reformist strategies of the Menshevik wing of the Russian social democrats and the Bernsteinian factions in Germany. Later, in the debates of the Third International of the 1920s, which concentrated on the worldwide export of revolution, the willingness to use violence became the deciding criterion in validating the *communist* credentials of the foreign social democratic parties; it became, in fact, the distinguishing mark separating communists from social democrats. The pacifist tendencies of leading German social democrats—all subsumed under derogatory Bolshevik rubrics such as "social chauvinism," "social pacifism," "centrism," and "power sharing with the bourgeoisie"[14]—were criticized as an accommodation with capitalism. A revolution without violence, without the destruction of the bourgeois state apparatus, was no revolution at all. "It is impossible to be a Communist," wrote the Italian Marxist Coletti, paraphrasing Lenin's work *State and Revolution*, "if your aim is not the violent seizure of power."[15]

In retrospect, there was probably enough ambiguity there for the Bolsheviks to exploit for immediate political purposes; and when Marx states that the principles of the *Manifesto* must be adjusted to the "historical conditions for the time being existing," he could be endorsing pacifist reforms or violent upheaval. The ambiguity opened avenues for certain Marxist opponents to stoke middle-class anxieties about anti-capitalist movements of any form. This tactic, in turn, forced social democratic movements to tread carefully in their association with Marx if they wanted also to operate within the democratic system. Others, such as the Fabians in Great Britain, and the socialist parties in the Netherlands and Scandinavia, were able to successfully implement socialist policies with little recourse to Marxian ideas *or* rhetoric. In fact, the pragmatic way in which these countries went about introducing social welfare legislation, without threats of violence, without grandiose theoretical structures, or chiliastic prophesies, exposes the difficulties of defining Marxism if it is not social democracy *plus* violence or the threat thereof.

This ambivalence surrounding violence in the Marxian legacy will create an underlying tension throughout our study particularly when we later investigate the relevance of his ideas in the postcommunist world, an era when many of the previously radical demands of socialists have been incorporated into the mainstream. Still, it is worth bearing in mind that no matter how much the early orthodox Marxists shunned violence in favor of economic determinism—that capitalism would slowly implode—or parliamentary reform—that social democratic parties could achieve their goals through the ballot box—there is still a sense that Marx's philosophy leaves generous space open for violence as a legitimate weapon against illegitimate forces of oppression. Even Herbert Marcuse, who rediscovered the Hegelian and humanist Marx in the 1930s, a Marx totally alien to the Bolshevik variant, could as late as the mid-1960s not exclude the legitimacy of violence under certain conditions. Amidst the student protests of the Vietnam era, and with one eye toward the postcolonial struggles in the developing world, he wrote: "I believe that there is a 'natural right' of resistance for oppressed and overpowered minorities to use extralegal means if legal ones have proved inadequate. Law and order are always and everywhere the law and order which protect the established hierarchy."[16] The last sentence, taken right out of classical Marxist political theory, and uttered long after Stalin's crimes had come to light, forces reflection on whether violence is ever obsolete. Though one may be tempted to denigrate it as a symptom of political immaturity, we can never judge unless we too are faced with an unjust system whose laws favor the established hierarchy.

The Bolsheviks may have felt they were the first to embody Marxism in a historical context, but other claimants to his inheritance sharply disagreed. As Karl Kautsky, a leading Austrian Marxist philosopher and opponent of Lenin's, remarked, "Bolshevism has triumphed in Russia, but Socialism has already suffered a defeat." He then goes on to insist that one make "a sharp distinction between these methods [those of the Bolsheviks] and the Marxist methods, and bring this to distinction to the knowledge of the masses."[17] For their part the Bolsheviks responded that the quietism of the German socialists was naive given the aggressive intentions of the imperialists. In the end, there seemed to be no way to breach the misunderstandings due in large part to the fact that both the European and Russian factions were trying to apply Marx to vastly different circumstances, while at the same time paying lip-service to the proletarian solidarity expressed in the founding creed. Yet, in many ways historical events overwhelmed and outpaced the Marxian theoretical debates meant to justify them.

Particularly in the case of Russia during and after World War I, a series of demoralizing military defeats coupled with indiscriminate military conscription created a mass of angry, armed peasants, all of which hastened the downfall of the Tsarist establishment. In St Petersburg, 160,000 soldiers were garrisoned in quarters that in peacetime were meant for 20,000; and half of these same soldiers mutinied to sway the balance of the February 1917 revolution. At this early stage, Lenin and theory were nowhere in

31

sight. It was but a peasant-worker rebellion, a crude class riot fueled by hatred and envy, and fought over bad food and living conditions (as illustrated in a scene from Eisenstein's film classic *The Battleship Potemkin* where a pompous officer force-feeds a maggot-filled gruel to a defiant sailor). It was only later, after the strategically orchestrated October coup and a bloody civil war, that Lenin structured the newly won freedom and implemented the "dictatorship of the proletariat." This meant in practice, however, a dictatorship by an elite which had arrogated to itself the power to rule; and it meant the establishment of a new bureaucratic apparatus, far more efficient than the Tsarist in suppressing opposition. Though in classical Marxist terms this "dictatorship" was meant to be transitory, in real terms the transition to socialism became a permanent state of affairs. Its fundamental *raison d'être* became the fabrication of a seemingly endless supply of class enemies, both internal and external, who supposedly threatened the precarious existence of the proletarian state.

The rest of the story is well known. The Bolshevik Old Guard was eventually eradicated along with their ideals in the Stalinist purges of the 1930s. Stalin proceeded to build "socialism in one country" and the Marxian inheritance grew fainter and fainter. Though it has been said that Stalinist totalitarianism was born of the Marxian concept of "the dictatorship of the proletariat" coupled with Russia's patrimonial political tradition,[18] Marx's own disdain for Slavic barbarism suggests that, had he fully fathomed the uniquely Russian talent for "dictatorship," he would have chosen his words more carefully.

The revolutionary gospel: Marx in the developing world

The tragedy of the Marxian reception of the twentieth century is that the whole theoretical apparatus—Hegel's dialectics, Feuerbach's speculative Christology, the dense, analytical treatment of capitalism and the economistic theory of history—meant so little to the followers who carried out revolutions in his name. Marx's Eurocentric, if not Germanocentric, philosophizing went over the heads of a desperate mob that simply dreamed of a larger share of the pie. His theoretical apparatus became instead a social gospel watered down to anti-capitalist slogans and tactical blueprints for communist insurgency. And here, Bolshevism played the crucial mediating role. Though but the offspring of a distant theoretical father and earthly Russian mother—more raw, mystical and cruel than anything Marx had ever bargained for—it effectively monopolized the platform of communist revolution under its name.

As noted above, Marx's own admission of the historical limitations of his revolutionary theory gave space to Lenin to fill in the blanks. Not only did this imply establishing a centralized political structure from which to export revolution, the Comintern, but also incorporating the world's anti-colonial struggles to which Marx had given scant attention. Though his many newspaper articles for the *New York Herald* on British rule in India clearly reflected his sympathies with the natives, Marx also endorsed the progressive impact of European modernization on these backward societies. The idyllic village commune was but an archaic expression of Oriental despotism designed to keep the peasants ignorant and preoccupied with superstition and ritual. Europeanization, in the form of new technologies and bureaucratic reform, was considered a necessary component of the transition from backwardness to socialism. Beyond this, Marx had really very little to say on the fate of the developing world. For better or worse, his concerns were fixated on nurturing the socialist movement in the industrialized countries. Thus, Marx's legacy in these countries, though profound and enduring, was nonetheless an indirect one, mediated and packaged by the Bolshevik apparatus. It can basically be broken down into two aspects: 1) Marxist-Leninism: A Revolutionary Strategy; 2) A Revolutionary Gospel.

The centralization of world socialist revolution in the Soviet Marxist-Leninist state can be further broken down into a practical and a theoretical element. The practical element refers to the activities of the Communist International, or Comintern, founded in Moscow in March of 1919. Its two main objectives were to export revolution, and to protect the fledgling Soviet state against anticommunist Western powers. Though technically an independent organization, in practice it was a department of the Russian Communist Party's Central Committee. The theoretical element concerns the interpretation of Marxist revolution, as officially sanctioned by the Soviet Communist Party, and its propagation throughout the world. Though the Comintern payed lip-service to democratic centralism, in fact the Russian leaders—initially Lenin, Trotsky, and Zinoviev—dictated party doctrine. Throughout the 1920s, the evolving doctrine of the Comintern served to consolidate Soviet rule over the export of global revolution, define the criteria for membership in the Communist Party, and establish tactics for supporting insurgencies of member parties, particularly in developing countries.

The Comintern partly consolidated its rule by *narrowing* the definition of communism so that centrist and reformist parties, particularly from Western Europe, would be excluded. That new definition—in contrast to the humanistic, democratic vision of the Young Hegelians—demanded a unified Communist Party centralized in Moscow "endowed with the fullest rights and authority and the most far-reaching powers,"[19] and the advocacy and propagation of violent revolution when necessary. The sovereignty of the national communist parties would henceforth be subordinated to the discipline and unity of one Communist Party. As such, the Comintern patented a new definition for communism, and became its self-professed institutional embodiment. All the other socialist groupings that did not sign on to the new doctrines were discredited as traitors to the communist cause. At the same time, the Comintern *enlarged* the Marxian agenda by exporting it to the developing world. As noted by Lenin, "The Communist International once and for all breaks with the tradition of the Second International, which recognized only white-skinned people. The aim of the Communist International is the liberation of working people of the *whole* world. In its ranks, the Communist International unites white, yellow and black-skinned working people in brotherhood." [20]

Both the Moscow-centered Party apparatus and the new multi-racial ethos of the Comintern extended far beyond the realm of Marx's original corpus. In fact, in so far as much of the developing world lacked the conditions necessary for a revolution of the Marxist type—an educated elite, an urban proletariat, a capitalist industrial base—his theory was reduced to fragments and slogans, selectively invoked. And, in so far as the majority of his writings had nothing to do with plantations and peasantry and colonial overlords, these fragments were largely drawn from the inspirational rhetoric of *The Communist Manifesto*. As the *Manifesto* spoke only vaguely of restoring justice to the oppressed, it was but a short step to apply Marx's demands for the European proletariat to the even greater misery of the African, Asian, and Latin American peasantry. "The peoples of the Third World," declared a group of radical Catholic bishops in 1967, "form the proletariat of mankind today. They are exploited by the great and threatened in their very existence by those who, because they are more powerful, assume the right to be the judges and policemen of the less fortunate." [21] In plain speak, the meek shall inherit the earth. Almost like the proverbs of Jesus from the New Testament, a revolutionary gospel laying claim to man's most basic material rights replaced all the technical analysis of nineteenth-century capitalism which Marx had made his life's work.

Theories of imperialism

However much the *Manifesto*'s faintly-sketched visions of redemption suited religious purposes, it would be misleading to limit Marx's Third World legacy to a beacon of hope for marginalized peasants. That was but one aspect that worked in tandem with a more sophisticated attempt to update his critique of capitalism with particular reference to the colonial empires. Hilferding's *Finance Capital* (1910), Rosa Luxemburg's *The Accumulation of Capital* (1913), Lenin's *Imperialism: the Highest Stage of Capitalism* (1917) all testify to an earnest taking-to-heart of the Marxian dictum that the critique of capitalism must at each stage correspond to existing economic conditions. Thus, in the early twentieth century, the new dynamic of imperialism—particularly the export of financial capital to the colonies as both an outlet for surplus and a source of new profits—to a large extent replaced Marx's nineteenth-century focus on exploitation in the industrial process. The new emphasis also provided correctives on what little Marx did have to say on imperialism. For example, one delegate, Kuusinen, at the 6th World Congress of the Comintern, went against the grain of classical Marxism by arguing that because it encouraged collusion with local feudal elites, colonialism could no longer be considered a progressive force. In the postwar period, Paul Baran's classic study, *The Political Economy of Growth* (1957), elaborated on Kuusinen's thesis: "Far from serving as an engine of economic expansion, of technological progress, and of social change, the capitalist order in these countries has represented a frame-work for economic stagnation, for archaic technology, and for social backwardness."[i]

These studies on imperialism, particularly the earlier ones, were closely intertwined with factional debates over the "breakdown theory" (*Zusammenbruchtheorie*)—the idea that capitalism's insatiable quest for new markets would eventually reach a saturation point culminating in crises, stagnation and finally collapse.[ii] Along these lines, imperialism could be read as either a last gasping attempt by Western industrialized countries to feed off non-capitalist markets, or a sign of capitalism's renewed resilience, each argument sup-porting a different interpretation for the "breakdown theory." Nonetheless, this controversy, however much it preoccupied early twentieth-century Marxists, was somewhat contrived from the be-ginning in the sense that it tried by more sophisticated means to imbue one of Marx's fundamental, yet vaguest and most problem-atic, assertions with scientific credibility. Namely, that capitalism would and should implode.

Although the European theorists largely viewed the colonial world as a distant abstraction, preoccupied as they were with trying to prognosticate capitalism's doom, their studies on imperialism had a more poignant impact. Firstly, the theme of class conflict, of the exploitation of proletariat by capitalist, became one of colonies by colonizers. In turn, this rift drove and was driven by local nationalist movements whose members were drawn from across the class spec-trum. The reasons were partly economic. Northern finance capital invested mainly in government-guaranteed loans for infrastructure projects—railroads, mining, etc.—with an eye toward the repatria-tion of profits. And the imperialists had little interest in promoting a local manufacturing base that would compete with their low-priced commodity exports. The bourgeois insurgents were, in turn, also motivated by political and cultural sentiments centered on the patriotic defense of nascent national sovereignty. Thus, proponents of the Marxist theory of imperialism had to take a position on the legitimacy of the alliance between bourgeois and proletariat in anti-colonial movements. At the Second Congress of the Comintern, Lenin, in fact, overruled the protests of more radical revolutionaries in advocating solidarity with these bourgeois insurgencies in the early stages.[iii] From this a distinct North/South polarity emerged which would, throughout the Cold War, define relations between Western "imperialist" powers and the Soviet-sponsored Third World insurgencies.

i Paul Baran, cited in, C. Oman and G. Wignaraja (eds), *The Postwar Evolution of Development Thinking*, London, Macmillan and OECD, 1991, p. 207.
ii For a review of the various schools of the breakdown theory, see P. Sweezy, *The Theory of Capitalist Development*, London, D. Dobson, 1946, pp. 190–213.
iii See Carlos Rafael Rodriguez, "Lenin and the Colonial Question," *The New International*, vol. 1, no. 1, 1983, pp. 119–28.

While the Bolshevik-led Comintern strived to create a unified doctrine of global revolution, major adjustments were needed to make orthodox doctrine palatable to local conditions. Asian revolutionaries—Mao in China, Ho Chi Minh in Vietnam and Pol Pot in Cambodia—focused their theoretical work on a radically idealized peasant commune. Latin American revolutionaries, on the other hand—Castro in Cuba, Sandino in Nicaragua and Guzman in Peru—also transformed class conflict between the rich and poor into a David and Goliath battle between Latin America and the imperialist United States (and its colluding local elites). In much of this, Marx was but a distant inspirational voice. As one Cuban theorist wrote, "Marx did not write directly for us; he looked upon us from afar and viewed us as part of a totality, one in which—in a very Hegelian but already quite Marxist sense—he assigned historical primacy to the Europe that was close at hand."[22] Lenin, in his revolutionary tactics, in the priority given to the seizure of power, and the leading role played by a disciplined party elite, provided much more of a blueprint. But, overall, the Eurocentric stigma of both Marx and Lenin often made it more expedient to replace them with agrarian Maoist paradigms, or with local heroes entirely. The founder of Nicaraguan socialism, Sandino, we are told by one Nicaraguan revolutionary, "grasped the class character of the revolutionary movement, the class struggle as the motor of history" and that "armed struggle was the only road to lead the revolutionary transformation of society." Though both are classic statements of Marx and Lenin, respectively, neither philosopher finds any mention in the revolutionary's speech.[23] Likewise, in much of the Cuban literature, it is Castro, not Marx or Lenin, who theorizes, wins, and implements the local revolution. This need to lionize a native prophet who translates the Europeans' theoretical corpus into the local parlance touches again on the uncanny religious dimension of Third World socialism. The more undereducated the audience, the greater was its attractions to evangelical icons and local hero-worship.

Furthermore, whatever influence Marxist theory may have had, it was often overshadowed by the power-driven priorities of local leaders and age-old ethnic and geopolitical rivalries. The early turf battles between Mao and Chiang Kai-shek in China of the 1920s and 1930s, and the never-ending rivalry between Hun Sen and King Sihanouk in Cambodia, the one an ex-Khmer Rouge supported by Vietnamese communists, the other an early founder of Cambodian socialism backed by Chinese communists, owe more to competing ambitions in a localized historical context than grand theory. Likewise, as with the Indians in postcolonial Burma, the Chinese in Thailand, and the Vietnamese in Cambodia, the theme of class struggle was often tinged by nationalistic sentiment toward wealthier (and commercially more savvy) immigrants concentrated in urban areas. In this respect, the rhetoric of envious nationalists and communists was often virtually indistinguishable. The Thai King Rama V, who always held the loyalty of the peasant class, railed against Bangkok's Chinese merchants, labeling them "'the Jews of the Orient' who like so many vampires steadily suck dry an unfortunate victim's blood." And Pol Pot in Cambodia held an obsession with thwarting the influence of neighboring communist Vietnam—in turn, a corollary of centuries of Khmer–Vietnamese distrust.

Finally, the piecemeal manner by which Marx's ideas were transmitted to remote areas had important consequences for their application. In these areas, Marx's legacy was distorted by faulty and incomplete translations, the editorial doctoring of the Soviet propaganda machine, and the uneven schooling of those revolutionaries, such as the Paris-educated Ho Chi Min and Saloth Sar (the later Pol Pot), who claimed to have absorbed and transcended Western ideas. As a result, much of the Third World Marxist literature is appallingly bad, mired in a mix of dogma and crude sentimentality, platitudinous, repetitive, and irritatingly bereft of detail. As much of it was intended for the party faithful, this should not surprise. Far more damning, however were the human consequences of such amateurism ruthlessly applied; Pol Pot's twisted vision of a neo-primitivist utopia, a New Man and a New Time, being only the most graphic example—graphic because the bones of its victims are still on display outside Phnom Penh.

Nonetheless, beyond the pamphleteering, some important Third World studies eschewed simplistic interpretations in favor of localized critiques of capitalist injustice. One such example is Frantz Fanon's *The Wretched of the Earth*. Dubbed "the Communist Manifesto of the Third World" by Jean-Paul Sartre, Fanon's work was based on his experience as a psychiatrist in Algeria during its war with France in the 1950s. It is an eloquent polemic against the insidious and subtle legacies of colonial rule. Where Marx used economics, Fanon applies psychology—in particular his personal case-studies on post-torture trauma of Algerians and on the marital and family problems of the French police officers etc.—to paint a portrait of violence and mutual hatred between colonizer and colonized. He shows not only how hatreds evolve and nourish themselves, how violence festers and breaks out in spontaneous eruptions, but also how, in the aftermath of World War II, the French police employed psychological techniques of oppression to manipulate the masses. Given this state of affairs, namely that the colonial regime owes its legitimacy to force, Fanon's response is unequivocal: "the colonized man finds his freedom in and through violence."[24] The levels of hatred and anger are so high, and the democratic means to channel them so scarce or corrupt, that the only form the struggle can take is violent rebellion.

Although Fanon defended the use of violence, his stance toward the native revolutionaries was by no means uncritical. He particularly chastised the dictatorships that had taken power following anti-colonial uprisings for their cronyism and power-broking along tribal lines. He worried that the poor quality of the local bourgeoisie, "a sort of little greedy caste . . . only too glad to accept the dividends that the former colonial power hands over to it,"[25] would hamper the development of an autonomous and honest local technocratic cadre. And, on the cultural level, he worried about the crisis of self-esteem that local intellectuals confronted as they attempted to fill the vacuum left by the withdrawal of Mother Country culture. Perhaps, Fanon's most important contribution—one, however, which Marx never considered— was his frank assessment of the aftermath of revolution; that when tempers settle, peasants realize that "hatred alone cannot draw up a program,"[26] that the slogans of independence provide little guidance on economic policy, and that when the vanquished colonizer withdraws, he always takes his money and expertise with him. Thus, a revolution that only rides on hate and anger without the human and material resources to manage the aftermath is doomed to failure.

No survey of Marx's Third World legacy would be complete without some mention of Cold War rivalries. After all, in the postwar era, fear that have-not nations would fall into the hands of communists kindled a flame of "compassion" among the Western powers. Point IV of the Truman Administration's 1949 foreign policy program, the UK's 1950 Colombo Plan, Kennedy's Alliance for Power in Latin America, the creation of the OECD's Development Assistance Committee (DAC), and the World Bank's turn toward fighting global poverty were all, or in part, directed toward countering Soviet and indigenous "Marxist" influence in the developing world. Into remote battlefields like Angola, the USA, Cuba, China, South Africa, and the former colonial overlord Portugal all stretched their self-interested tentacles. The Soviet Union gave technical advice and arms—gave in the sense that many credits were never paid back—to dictatorial regimes such as Ethiopia, Libya, Iraq, and Syria. And the USA, through the covert aid of the

CIA, countered by sponsoring assassinations of left-leaning politicians such as, it is alleged, Salvador Allende in Chile and, with mixed success, numerous anticommunist insurgencies and operations. This litany of superpower proxy wars often owed more to geopolitical considerations than ideological imperatives. The seemingly arbitrary set of bedfellows they spawned—such as the USA and socialist Iraq against Khomeini's extremist Islamic Iran, the USA and the extremist Islamic Afghani mujahidin against the Soviet occupiers, the Russian-backed Vietnamese against the Chinese-backed Cambodians—shows clearly enough that the major powers, and their Third World allies, were willing enough to set their core values aside in the name of political and military expediency.

None of this has much to do with Marx or Marxism, yet the extent to which his name has been attached to Third World socialist revolution, by sympathizers and detractors alike, and usually in its hyphenated Marxist-Leninist form, has forced us to explore this ambiguous paternity. In general, one can say that Marx's Third World legacy was based on a highly selective and overly literalistic reading of a complex set of ideas whose application was not always relevant to backward societies. This is not an apology for Marx. The militant rhetoric of the *Manifesto* coupled with a distinct lack of pragmatic thinking as to the consequences should that rhetoric ever be taken to heart lend themselves to easy abuse. Furthermore, the obscurities of his thought—Did proletarian dictatorship imply an abolition of democracy or its truest form? Did his notion of the family as a bourgeois contract suggest that it should be eradicated, or that it would be restored once poor parents and children no longer had to work 12-hour days?—could, in the wrong hands, invite cruel and crude applications. Finally, Marx's teachings betray Hegel's iron faith that history would slowly unravel its virtue and goodness irrespective of the petty whims of egotistical demagogues. In terms of his Third World legacy, this was perhaps his greatest oversight; namely, failing to see that the masses were just that, a herd either lifted up or broken down by the decisions of a small group of individuals. An elite of mediocre intellect and adolescent arrogance, armed with appetizing propaganda and modern weaponry will, as fallible humans do, build a revolution in its own unflattering image.

Western Marxism: the academic's critical paradigm

> The totalitarian universe of technological rationality is the latest transmutation of the idea of Reason.
> H. Marcuse, *One Dimensional Man*

The fractured global spread of Marxism, filtered more often than not through the Soviet ideological apparatus, and selective translations of his work, broadened the critique of modern capitalism to a more generic and flexible indictment of wealth and power in general. Its religious dimension in the developing world arguably grew from this broad application, a vague yet materialistic vision of hope, and its potent militant imagery of destroying the old and ushering in the new. But these developments are somehow remote from Marx's thinking which was geared fundamentally toward reforming modern industrial society not primitive agrarian ones. In other words, Marx was a German philosopher whose objectives, in terms of both human and social capital, were of a higher order. In his Eurocentric view, revolutions geared toward killing the white and/or rich man were non-starters; the victors would still be faced with their own dismal administrative and technological limits, not least because, as the purges of Stalin, Pol Pot, Mao, etc. demonstrate, when the financiers, free-thinking writers, artists, diplomats, and the cultured upper classes are dead or in prison, one is left with less not more. In that sense, a successful communist revolution, such as in Cambodia, has always been an incredibly regressive and destructive act.

The twentieth-century European thinkers who fell outside the Soviet sphere of doctrinal influence started out with this given: If Marx had anything to say at all, it had to do with a revolution of consciousness within the Western industrialized world. It was neither about the Soviet Union nor the developing world, both of which had hand-tailored and distorted Marx to suit their backward conditions. Instead, it concerned the comprehensive impact of capitalism and technological progress on human society. This was more than just Eurocentric arrogance. If the West was the most culturally and technologically advanced, it also posed some of the most worrying questions about the nature of man and progress in general. For the faith which the Enlightenment had vested in reason—the faculty that would liberate man from ignorance and superstition, that would shape and tame natural forces—came increasingly under scrutiny at the beginning of the twentieth century. But the thinkers who professed this line of thought also set themselves the task of returning Marx to the European philosophical tradition, thereby, hopefully undermining the monopoly on his legacy which Soviet ideologues so jealously guarded.

This tendency has often been categorized under the rubric of Western Marxism. In opposition to Eastern, or Soviet, Marxism, it arose in the 1920s partly as a response by West European Marxist philosophers to counter the heavy-handed tactical approach of the Comintern toward nationalist parties, and partly to retrieve the humanistic, philosophical Marx from the dogmatic scientism of the Soviet ideologues. Along these lines, Marxism became not just a critique of the economic base of capitalism, but, very much in line with the writings of the young Marx, a critique of the alienated human essence under capitalism. This, in turn, once again created space for the philosopher, as opposed to the ideologue. Ultimately, Western Marxism took Marxism away from the Bolshevik-style practicalities of revolution and utopia-building, and toward a more idiosyncratic application in many fields outside of economics. Its wide scope, ranging from Merleau-Ponty, Sartre, and Althusser, through Gramsci, to the Frankfurt School, eludes any kind of systematic review here. The interested reader would be better served consulting the vast primary and secondary literature on each of these thinkers.[27] Instead, I intend to focus on those thinkers who not only had the most unmediated link to Marx's German philosophical tradition but also provide a framework of analysis that can endure post-1989; that is, after the political expressions of Marxism or variants thereof have been discredited. For these reasons and others that will be addressed in later chapters, the Frankfurt School will occupy the bulk of our inquiry in this section.

Before we turn to the Frankfurt School, we must consider briefly Gyorgi Lukács, one of the founders of Western Marxism, and most influential reclaimers of Marx's German philosophical, and specifically Hegelian, heritage. Though his reputation is somewhat chequered by his later sycophantic allegiances to Stalinism, he provided the first impetus for an appropriation of Marx's broader humanist mandate. Furthermore, his story illustrates yet again the idiosyncratic manner in which Marxism wove its way into the fabric of European high culture. For Lukács, in a sense, inaugurates a trend that would be the hallmark of the Frankfurt School. Namely, he initially had little interest in the gritty political activism—the pamphleteering, stump speeches, even terrorism—that characterized the communist movement in Europe during the early part of the century. Instead, like many of the later Frankfurt School theorists, he came from a cultivated leisure class whose interest in Marxism was born primarily of a *fin-de-siècle* malaise and romantic anti-capitalism. It grew less from a critique of economic exploitation than of modernism, of the loneliness and futility of existence in an alienating, shallow, and rapidly industrializing world. Born into a prominent Budapest banking family in 1885, he first developed these themes as a literary theorist, and briefly and unsuccessfully as a writer. But it was a series of personal upsets that led him to a quasi-religious conversion to Marxism. Following the suicide of his first love, and divorce from his first wife, a convicted Russian terrorist with liberal sexual proclivities, Lukács appears to have experienced a modernist crisis of his own. Contemptuous of the self-indulgence of his own life, and that of contemporary Western literature as expressed in the works of Kafka and Joyce, frustrated with the egotism associated with the prevailing concept of freedom, and frustrated with his own inability to love, he converted to Marxism in the hope that his creative efforts could have beneficial human consequences. It was his attempt at reconciling one of the key and most profound antinomies, particularly for a sensitive intellectual: namely, the yawning gap between thought and action, between the lofty aims of the "chattering classes" and the reality outside. Simply put, he felt a need to do good. Immediately after his decision, he moved from his family villa and joined a sect of "Franciscan" communists.

This biographical vignette not only typifies the guilt and alienation that motivated many bourgeois children to embrace Marxism, it also suggests how alienation—or in Lukács' vocabulary, reification—would become one of the main themes of Frankfurt School Marxism. In his first major work, *History and Class Consciousness* (1924), Lukács establishes reification as the central underlying concept of Marx's work. Drawn from Marx's concept of commodity fetishism developed in *Das Kapital*, it implied simply the lack of unity between an individual and the objects he creates. Because of given socio-economic structures, these objects appear alien to the producer; their human subjective content is subverted by their value as a quantifiable commodity of exchange. Though Lukács also made important contributions in re-Hegelianizing Marx and reinforcing a viable understanding of philosophy as praxis, it is through his theory of reification—that is, by shaping Marx's concept of commodity fetishism into a paradigm of cultural criticism—that he earns his place as the Godfather of the Frankfurt School.

In the hands of Lukács and the Frankfurt School, reification was shaped into a kind of philosophical pessimism that, crudely phrased, follows these lines: The emancipatory quality of reason unleashed was gradually discredited as man, huddled in urban ghettos, lost touch with nature and the agrarian traditions modeled after its cycles, as his individuality was reduced to a numerical value in the industrial process, and most dramatically, when the weapons of mass destruction were turned against him. In turn, the havoc wrought by the twentieth-century's two world wars, not just the millions of lost lives, but also cities and civilizations, confirmed, it seemed irreparably, that technocratic efficiency lay at the very root of modern evil. "When even the dictators of today appeal to reason," wrote Max Horkheimer, the founder of the Frankfurt School, in his seminal 1941 essay "The End of Reason," "they mean that they possess the most tanks."[28]

The Frankfurt School

Pessimistic, angst-ridden, moody, and often morose, the Frankfurt School challenged the feel-good rhetoric of capitalism and middle-class complacency at every turn; most importantly, it took Marxian theory away from crude economic determinism and Leninist dogma, and applied it to the broader sphere of mass culture and the cultural consequences of modern technology. Founded in Frankfurt in 1923 as the Institute of Social Research, the School eschewed both the blueprints for a rosy socialist future and the tactical measures to get there in favor of an incessant and interdisciplinary critique of the capitalist system. "Marxist science," said Horkheimer, "constitutes the critique of bourgeois economy and not the expounding of a socialist one."[29] At the heart of that critique lay Reason's complicity with technological processes that alienated man and destroyed his individuality. In short, co-opted and subsumed by the establishment, it had lost its critical faculty. As Marcuse, another prominent member of the School, summarized: "Reason has found its resting place in the system of standardized control, production and consumption. There it reigns through the laws and mechanisms which insure the efficiency, expediency and coherence of the system."[30]

The new disenchantment with rationality was shared by many twentieth-century philosophers and schools but the Frankfurt School stands out in its persistent identification of reason's wrong turn with specific social, economic, and cultural institutions and structures of domination. With some exceptions, members of the School had little patience for, or interest in, left-wing political activism, let alone violent revolution. But they were consistent in their animosity toward the bourgeois establishment, not as a monolithic caricature, but as the aggregate of countless, and seemingly harmless, systems of oppression. Adorno provides a typical example in his reflection on "easy listening" music: "It inhabits the pockets of silence that develop between people molded by anxiety, work and undemanding docility."[31] The strength and, equally, the fatalism of the Frankfurt School lie in its tendency to see the enemy everywhere. There is no capitalist swine or proletarian hero. It is modern society in general, rotten to the core, that fills these silences because its population has lost the ability to exchange ideas. This existential malaise was the hunting ground of the Frankfurt School theorist. Often when pure philosophy proved an inadequate weapon, they crossed over into other creative media and disciplines—Lukács and Benjamin to literature, Adorno to music, Marcuse to psychology, Horkheimer to sociology—and linked them in a pioneering way to their broader social implications.

But such a general definition can hardly accommodate either the eclectic range of the School's output or the varying affections for Marx held by the individual members. As Wiggershaus, who has published a monumental study on the subject, concedes: "To start with, it [The Frankfurt School] described a critical sociology which saw society as an antagonistic totality, and which had not excluded Hegel and Marx from its thinking, but rather saw itself as their heir. The label has, however, long since become more vague and all-embracing."[32] Because of the heterogeneity of the school's output, it makes some sense first to review the common strands that united the various members before turning our attention toward their specific accomplishments. In such an exercise, biography plays a larger role than is normal in the study of philosophers because their work is particularly colored by a turbulent historical context from which, as academic theoreticians, they were not able to isolate themselves. On the contrary, as persecuted Jews during the Nazi period, than exiled intellectuals in America, then reluctant gurus of the 1960s' student movement (with the exception of the more enthusiastic Marcuse) following their return to Germany, their theoretical framework was fortified by the empirical substance of complex, vagabond lives. In this respect, as intellectuals outside of mainstream academia devoted to putting philosophy into practice, they are indeed true heirs to Marxian philosophy.

Of the biographical data that unite the group, their common Jewish heritage is the most important. As the offspring of wealthy, often extremely wealthy Jews—Lukács' father was the president of Budapest Kreditanstalt, Hungary's leading bank; Adorno's an established Frankfurt wine merchant; Horkheimers's a Stuttgart, textile manufacturer; Marcuse's a Berlin construction magnate; Benjamin's a shareholder in a Berlin art auction house, Felix Weil's a multi-millionaire Argentinian grain trader and later Frankfurt property speculator, etc.—they were at once products of the bourgeois system, yet its most trenchant critics. This ambiguity gained import as anti-Semitism festered and spread in depression-era Germany. The dilemma of the German Jewish bourgeoisie—that one could have enormous knowledge and wealth, that one could be perfectly cosmopolitan and liberal-minded, and still have no power; in fact, still be totally vulnerable against the sinister pact between the primitive anger of the mob and modern systems of domination—fed into their more general theoretical enterprise. It created a set of contradictions that intertwined the fate of Jewry with the fate of the Enlightenment.[33]

The persecution of the Jews culminated in the Holocaust, yet by that time, the members of the Frankfurt School were safely exiled in America, either working for the OSS, the precursors to the CIA, or under contract to organs of the US establishment like the Rockefeller Foundation. To ingratiate themselves with their American hosts (for example for grant applications), they had to keep their Marxist leanings secret, particularly the links they suspected between fascism and monopoly state capitalism. But this was not just the emigré's calculated attempts at assimilation. More authentically, their previous Marxian sympathies for the proletariat seemed at odds with the theoretical confusions generated by the Nazi regime. For National Socialism was a populist movement that confiscated the property of a class, the Jews, identified with excessive wealth, yet it did all this in collusion with major capitalist enterprises. It spoke in the name of the worker and created massive infrastructure projects—such as the *Autobahn*—for the benefit of Everyman; yet at the same time, the main victims of its racist zeal were the poor Jews of Eastern Europe—the workers and peasants, and disenfranchised who, when war broke out, suddenly found themselves in an occupied zone. The wealthy middle-class Jews of Germany—ironically, the main targets of Nazi anti-capitalist propaganda—with their means and information access had far better chances to secure a passage to freedom. One can only speculate on the sense of guilt which wealthy Jewish Marxists in exile must have felt at this irony. But what is clear is that, during the war, the classic Marxian dichotomy between capitalist and proletariat lost much of its force when set against the far more pressing and topical conflict between German and Jew. "It often seems to me that everything we used to see from the point of view of the proletariat," Adorno mused in a letter to his chief collaborator Horkheimer, "has been concentrated today with frightful force upon the Jews." And in another letter from the same period: "Anti-semitism is today really the central injustice."[34]

Horkheimer, Adorno and The Dialectic of the Enlightenment

Germany's systematic annihilation of the Jews, capitalists, communists, and East European peasants alike became, in the eyes of Horkheimer and Adorno, synonymous with the crisis of the Enlightenment, of modernity in general. In short, the Jews, the most ardent supporters of liberalism and cosmopolitanism in Germany were fundamentally betrayed by the Enlightenment. The first sentence of their wartime classic, *The Dialectic of the Enlightenment* (1944), dramatically sets the pessimistic tone: "In the most general sense of progressive thought, the Enlightenment has always aimed at liberating men from fear and establishing their sovereignty. Yet the fully enlightened earth radiates disaster triumphant."[35] The opening salvo gives way to a high-culture diatribe of intense, if unsystematic, lyricism, where Marxian references to commodity fetishism jostle alongside Leibniz, Bacon, and Greek mythology, all extemporizing on the leitmotif: that Enlightenment, as a weapon of freedom and disenchantment, has been reduced to a paradigm of domination.

Though the few references to Marx are subsumed under their diatribe against the degenerate Western category of reason, the work essentially modernizes the Marxian theoretical apparatus by liberating it from its narrow economistic framework. The proletariat as the agent of rebellion is broadened to a wider definition of social disillusion with the Enlightenment. The Western system which stole the mantle of Enlightenment, reducing knowledge and culture to a functionalist and technology-driven manipulation of the masses, was challenged by the Frankfurt School Marxists and exposed as a fake. Given the grandeur of this theft, which is really man turned against himself, the machinations of one exploitative class seem trivial in comparison.

Instead, in the era of late capitalism, the dichotomy between bourgeois and proletariat was transformed into an all-pervasive tension between the culture industry and the consumer. In its assembly-line character, its illusory promise of happiness to the small man, in its commodification of fantasy, the culture industry has stolen tricks from the advertising industry. In fact, as Adorno and Horkheimer argued, the two are all but indistinguishable:

Advertising and the culture industry merge technically as well as economically. In both cases the same thing can be seen in innumerable places, and the mechanical repetition of the same cultural product has come to be the same as that of the propaganda slogan. In both cases the insistent demand for effectiveness makes technology into psycho-technology, into a procedure for manipulating men. In both cases the standards are the striking yet familiar, the easy yet catchy, the skillful yet simple; the object is to overpower the customer, who is conceived as absent-minded or resistant.[36]

In targeting the oppressive forms of mass entertainment that narcotize empty lives, that market the cheap fantasy of a "more exalted life," Horkheimer and Adorno broadened the debate from alienation at *work* to alienation at *play*, the remaining sacred space for human self-expression. In his pursuit of profit, the capitalist had invaded the home. The always fragile hope that man could have some space and time to recreate himself by force of his imagination, the *Bildungsideal* of the German romantics, had been subverted by an industry that force-fed imagination to a numb and dumb populace. Man's most secret yearnings had been surveyed, standardized, and reproduced to save himself the effort of articulating them in an individuated form.

> The most intimate reactions of human beings have been so thoroughly reified that the idea of anything specific to themselves now persists only as an utterly abstract notion: personality scarcely signifies anything more than shining white teeth and freedom from body odor and emotions. The triumph of advertising in the culture industry is that consumers feel compelled to buy and use products even though they see through them.[37]

The metastasis of late capitalism to the sphere of leisure has fully co-opted the individual. The message of Adorno and Horkheimer was resigned and fatalistic. They extemporized on the symptoms of a sick society yet offered no cure, certainly not a political one. Tactical insurgencies, labor strikes, revolutions, all these recipes—however much they may appear as palliatives in the developing world and backward Russia—had no place in America, the most advanced capitalist state. There, the proletariat had become complacent wanting nothing more than to be recognized as bourgeois. Seduced by the culture industry, it sought only the accoutrements of bourgeois status; it contented itself with chasing the trappings of success. "Here in America there is no difference between a man and his economic fate. A man is made by his assets, income, position, and prospects. The economic mask coincides completely with a man's inner character. Everyone is worth what he earns and earns what he is worth."[38]

Against this state of affairs, Adorno offered only the vaguest of utopias grounded in securing the individual's freedom of imagination in a sea of mass-produced cultural goods. To liberate the individual from bourgeois norms—material fulfillment in the land of plenty—is the job of the critic and the artists, the ones who persistently expose the falsehoods fed to the

46

eager consumers. But the exit from the unhealthy society was not a clear path. It was fragmented by the utopian, anti-functionalist, anti-utilitarian visions of creative intellectuals. "Perhaps the true society will grow tired of development and, out of freedom leave possibilities unused, instead of storming about under a confused compulsion to the conquest of strange stars."[39] The vision suits the artist and aesthetician. It complies with what Adorno, in a later work by the same name, called *negative dialectics*, an incessant critique of the given without synthesis or sublation, a form of thinking that, in the vein of his beloved atonal music, eschewed neat resolutions, resolving chords, and happy endings; a destruction of beauty and the ephemeral to make way for transcendence. In particular from Adorno's elitist, high-culture vantage point, it seems that the only art that could lead the way must be highly unpopular, highly individualistic, and slightly obscure.

If the Marxian legacy in Adorno is somewhat overshadowed by his aesthetic bent, particularly toward music, he nonetheless fruitfully extended the critique of capitalism to new frontiers. Furthermore, his work reflects the Frankfurt School's closer affinity to the earlier Marx than the later, resisting the impulse to ossify utopian ideals in a specific political program. Unfortunately, this resistance turned against him during the student movements of the 1960s when his rarefied utopian individualism found little resonance among impatient radicals seeking theoretical sanctions for their violent acts. The elderly Adorno came across as quietistic, contemplative, and aloof. He could only look on with disdain as students took to the streets burning cars and waving placards in the name of some ill-defined liberation from the establishment. His narrow interest in the emancipatory potential of aesthetics came to be seen as overly self-involved, as such, a betrayal of the revolution, and in some sense anti-Marxist.

Marcuse and One Dimensional Man

One might also say that Adorno's quietistic aesthetics were a betrayal of critical theory in so far as it abandoned praxis. His criticism of existing conditions was so purely negative without offering constructive alternatives or the means to achieve them, that it could not hope to have any particular mass appeal. Herbert Marcuse, another member of the Frankfurt School, was perhaps a less eclectic and erudite thinker than Adorno, but he never lost sight of the practical imperative that underlies any authentic Marxian thinking. In *One Dimensional Man* (1964), trumpeted on the cover of its paperback edition as the "most subversive book published in the United States this century,"[40] Marcuse wrote that critical theory was based on the judgment that "in a given society, specific possibilities exist for the amelioration of human life and specific ways and means of realizing these possibilities."[41] At least initially, Marcuse's interest in "ways and means" had no grounding in a radical politics. Instead, it evolved from a highly theoretical search for a "concrete philosophy" that grew, surprisingly enough, out of disenchantment with Heidegger. Much like the young Marx's farewell to Hegel, Marcuse, who had been Heidegger's assistant in Freiburg in the late 1920s, found that "concretion" was lacking in his mentor's thought. Though Heidegger, through his category of *Dasein*—"being-there"—had retrieved for philosophy the pre-eminence of human existence in this world and had attempted through such motifs as anxiety, alienation, and death, to establish criteria for authentic or inauthentic living, he, like Hegel, had not sufficiently theorized "the concrete historical conditions under which a concrete *Dasein* exists." Instead, Heidegger had fallen back on a philosopher's idea of *Dasein* in terms of a lonely, contemplative existence.

The publication of Marx's *Economic and Philosophical Manuscripts* (*EPM*) in 1932 provided Marcuse with a concrete philosophy, an ontology rooted in historical conditions. Unlike the doctrinaire, economistic Marx who fortified contemporary socialism, Marcuse discovered in the *EPM* a philosophical discourse on alienation that was grounded in concrete historical conditions, i.e., an indictment of capitalism. Marx, according to Marcuse, had determined correctly that the human essence could no longer be separated from its facticity, its unique rootedness in a specific, concrete context. When, as Marcuse wrote in *One Dimensional Man*, that facticity or existence does not serve to further the realization of its guiding essence, then man reaches a state of alienation:

> If essence and existence move apart in this way, while at the same time the reunification of both of them as an actual achievement is the truly free *task* for human practice, then, where facticity has progressed as far as the complete *reversal* of human essence, the *radical abolition* of this facticity is the supreme task. The unwavering vision of the essence of man becomes, precisely, a relentless impetus towards radical revolution: the fact that in the actual situation of capitalism it is not merely a question of economic or political crisis, but a question of catastrophe for the essence of humanity—this discovery condemns every mere economic or political *reform* to failure from the outset, and demands unconditionally the catastrophic abolition of actual condition by means of *total revolution*.[42]

The passage typifies Marcuse's derivation of revolution from a philosophical, rather than an economic, problematic. The *radical abolition of facticity* is not born of hatred toward the bourgeoisie, or political activism against social injustice, but rather of the need to liberate the human essence from constraining historical circumstances. Marcuse found in the young Marx a model for "concrete philosophy" in so far as it posed the liberation of essence from capitalism in practical terms, yet terms above and beyond the mechanics of the capitalist system. When, in the era of late capitalism, class antagonisms had receded, when the proletariat wanted nothing more than to be bourgeois, the task of the critical theorist was then undermined by the complacency of his audience: "All liberation depends on the consciousness of servitude, and the emergence of this consciousness is always hampered by the predominance of needs and satisfaction which, to a great extent, have become the individual's own."[43] According to Marcuse, man's consciousness of his alienation is obscured by "system preconditioning," an array of "false needs" that masquerade as true ones. These false needs—"to relax, to have fun, to behave and consume in accordance with the advertisements"—are characterized by a mass conformism dictated by the prevailing whims of the culture industry. But they are so threatening and powerful precisely because they are not recognized as false; they are made out to be an extension of the individual ego, their satisfaction is thus a form of empowerment. Borrowing from Freudian psychology, Marcuse terms this fulfillment of false needs, repressive satisfaction. In a state of repressed satisfaction, the consciousness of servitude is hampered by the persistent propagation of a myth, namely that liberty is synonymous with the vacuous choice between various brands and gadgets.

More ominously, the illusory communality created by the shared pursuit of these commodities masks a dysfunctional society and its underlying inequalities:

> If the worker and his boss enjoy the same television program and visit the same resort places, if the typist is as attractively made up as the daughter of her employer, if the Negro owns a Cadillac . . . then this assimilation indicates not the disappearance of classes, but the extent to which the needs and satisfactions that serve the preservation of the establishment are shared by the underlying population.[44]

In advanced capitalism, the lower classes not only produce but also *consume* for the establishment. What is more, the semblance of freedom that this consumption generates obscures their own predicament. For Marcuse, this illusion of freedom constitutes a "more progressive stage of alienation" because it invades man's most intimate space, his soul. One can no longer posit one's inner yearnings against an alienated existence. Instead, the "false sense of unmediated association between his private subjectivity and the objective world" has created the One Dimensional Man.[45]

For Marcuse, the culprit of advanced capitalism is no longer class antagonisms or belching smokestacks of the Industrial Revolution; it is rather the psychologically destructive illusions of freedom created by the culture industry. For the critical theorist, whose job it is to expose this illusion, it nonetheless proved difficult to problematize an exit: "If the individuals are satisfied to the point of happiness with the goods and services handed down to them by the administration, why should they insist on different institutions for a different production of different goods and ser-vices?"[46] Given this subtle form of brainwashing, the critical theorist who harps on about those who "find their soul in their automobile, hi-fi set, split level home, kitchen equipment,"[47] could only strike the repressively satisfied consumer as a shrill irritant. In short, if no one feels alienated, how can one have a revolution? The radicalism of the 1960s partly answered this ques-tion. Marcuse's *One Dimensional Man*, published in 1964, fueled the social unrest by venting rage on an unseen enemy. With the exception of the civil rights movement which battled against social and political inequalities, most of the causes embraced by the student rebellion emerged from the more subtle anxieties and repressions of middle-class America. Very much like *One Dimensional Man*, it was a broad revolt against consumerism and complacency; against sexual puritanism and conservatism, against the Sys-tem, writ so large it became an all-embracing arch-nemesis to the point that any attack upon it could be justified as an act of liberation.

It is beyond the purview of our survey here to judge the quality of the 1960s indictment of the System. Nonetheless, Marcuse, as one of the stu-dent movement's anointed gurus, must bear some responsibility for foment-ing rebellion without coherent objectives, for fomenting a negativism that ultimately hardly extended beyond inter-generational warmongering. In short, he gave theoretical substance to what some disenchanted radicals now call the era's "transcendental conviction that there was something apocalyptic lurking behind the veil of the ordinary."[48]

We know now that the only thing lurking behind the ordinary was a mirror image of the radicals' future selves. The hormonally-charged era of the love-in gave way to the everyday concerns of family and career. Marx was just one of many icons jettisoned along the way (e.g., Lenin, Mao, Che Guevara, Timothy Leary, Jimi Hendrix, Ravi Shankar), and all the other posterboys of the '60s youth rebellion. But the Frankfurt School lost its influence in America not only because its audience grew up or moved into the more separatist and exclusionary activism of the 1970s—feminism, gay rights, environmentalism—but also because its demonization of popular culture, to some extent, had missed the mark.

The misreading of mass culture

The German-Jewish mandarins of the Frankfurt School had neither respect for nor understanding of the potency of the ordinary in American popular culture, a potency which was not apocalyptic but liberating; not barbaric or crude, but cathartic; cathartic in the most basic sense, sensual, spontaneous, erotically charged, and fun. For example, Adorno's highly dismissive com-mentaries on jazz reveal a startling prudishness toward the folk idiom, one that wholly ignored the rhythmic power of syncopation, the unmediated spontaneous energy of improvised performance, the ecstatic synergy between musician and audience. Yet, ironically it was this same culture industry, in the form of the mass-production of vinyl records and radio airplay, which gave obscure musicians trained in the folk idiom, whether negro spiritual, hillbilly or southern gospel, a massive nationwide following. In the 1950s, this complicity between authentic folk culture and the culture industry launched the era of rock and roll, one of the most original and influential pillars of American popular culture. This example only illustrates that the culture industry is not so much an instrument of establishment manipulation, as an instrument of massification whose value must be judged on a case-by-case basis. Equally, when Marcuse compares making love in a meadow to making love in a car, he claims that "the mechanized environment (i.e., the car) seems to block self-transcendence of libido."[49] Yet the distinction is culturally not universally conditioned. Whereas Marcuse may well have had a sexual experience in a meadow, it seems that, unlike millions of Americans, he had never made love in an automobile, that mechanized arena of 1950s' teenage liberation, let alone with a steamy slow rock ballad playing on the radio. The archaic and fusty, in short, old world, link between authentic cultural experience and natural, untainted surroundings could not, and does not necessarily need to, ring true for a society for whom a mechanized environment had already been seamlessly integrated into the fabric of human experience. Particularly in the form of the automobile, that mechanized environment was a symbol of independence and, in terms of teen culture, an island of privacy distant from the repressive sexual mores of the parental home.

Instead, the Frankfurt School imposed a blend of high-cultural pessimism and modernized Marxism on American leisure society without intuitively understanding its language. That language—of erotically-charged popular music, of the uncomplicated heroics of sport, the risqué humor of bar room banter—they often dismissed with a heavy philosophical rancor, as opiatic crumbs tossed down by some omnipotent establishment; and all this for the simple reason that this group of Jewish-German exiles had no organic link to it. It was alien to their autobiography, their memories of an idyllic and pampered childhood, their own culturally conditioned and rather bookwormish idea of what constitutes a good time. In many ways, they used their own alienation, the self-exclusivity of the Central European aesthete, as an absolute standard for an authentic existence which, in the end, had little relevance to their adopted homeland. What is more, there were many other theorists such as Veblen, Ortega y Gasset, Bell, Jaspers, McCluhan and Anders, who made eloquent indictments of mass culture without the baggage of Frankfurt School pessimism. Among their works is often a more refreshing tendency to treat the marriage of technology and the masses as an irreversible, historical given and to find space therein, without necessarily advocating violent revolution, for an authentic existence. In particular, Anders' idea of "solo mass culture"—that is, reproduced commodities geared toward intensely private enjoyment, such as slot machines, posters, television—may be more relevant to our cybernetic age than neo-Marxian ideas that see in all technology the unfettered suppression of individuality.[50]

The three obstacles to freedom: poverty, corruption, and banality

The weaknesses of Marx's twentieth-century offshoots—from Soviet bureaucratic centralism through revolutionary amateurism in the developing world to the Frankfurt School misreading of mass culture—were evident long before the so-called fall of communism in 1989. As early as the 1930s and 1940s, as the atrocities of the Stalinist era became known, respected Marxist intellectuals such as Lukács or Sartre compromised their integrity by publicly defending the ugly Soviet reality that spoke in Marx's name. Later, during the era of decolonization, the Vietnam War, and Pol Pot's crude attempts to create a New Man, such apologias seemed more and more marked by naiveté and denial rather than intellectual rigor. In the aftermath, many left-leaning intellectuals retreated from polemics and political causes into a more academic world. There they reinvented Marxism not as a discipline in its own right, but as a modifier to existing disciplines, e.g., history, anthropology, or sociology, where it retained its oppositionary status by seeking out contradictions and underlying class bias in the orthodoxy in whichever discipline it was applied. Though discarding its insurrectionist tone, it, at least originally, preserved its progressive methodology: to uncover power structures, often money-based, that hid behind a façade of neutrality and normality. Along these lines, the era of political correctness and, to a lesser extent, postmodernism reflected a "mainstreaming" of once subversive notions, i.e., that the whole set of Western cultural icons and values, in which minorities, women, and the underclass had been historically under represented, were but the off-shoots of obsolescing, white male-dominated power structures. But by the early 1990s, these paradigms had also been exhausted. The defense of so-called oppressed groups became caricatured as victimology, the act of defending and elevating oppressed groups simply because they were oppressed. This tendency has been particularly acute in the field of literature where writers—irrespective of their literary merits—are celebrated simply because they have "given a voice" to previously silent minorities.

This then brings us to the present. One might easily conclude that Marxism is now irretrievably dispersed among a wide spectrum of institutions and subcultures, its underlying utopian premise thoroughly discredited, and that the genuinely populist dismantling of communism following 1989 gave an enduring credence to the view that the free market guided by an enlightened democratic state is, in fact, the natural and best order of things. Indeed, if much of the twentieth century was colored by clashing ideologies and utopian schemes—from worker states to free love communes—the twenty-first century seems to be an extremely pragmatic age. Solutions to society's problems are now advanced with technocratic caution, usually context-specific, and often guided by a mix of state and market-driven mechanisms. There is a renewed faith in technology to prolong human life and democratize information access. And non-governmental and non-profit organizations are increasingly influential in the political process.

On the other hand, if the abuses of capitalism which Marx challenged and exposed still persist, if the corruption and hypocrisy of the ruling power structures is still evident behind the faint veil of democratic legitimacy, and if rampant commercialism continues to threaten culture and leisure, in short, if there are such widespread imperfections in the economic, political and cultural sphere, then the attempts to lay Marxism to rest alongside the communist states, are premature. As long as there are grounds for a broad-based pessimism, in the present as well as the future, there are grounds for the study and application of Marxian ideas. In the modern postcommunist age, this set of problem areas can be formulated in terms of three major obstacles to freedom—poverty, corruption, and banality—all of which are rooted in the capitalist system that now reigns supreme. To explore these obstacles, as we will do in the following three chapters, is an exercise in philosophy in a Marxian vein. But not in the sense that conventional wisdom might have it—that it betrays a class bias, or an economic determinism which crowds out other important social, political, and environmental factors from its analysis; or that its conclusions are prejudiced by a conception of capitalism as inherently evil. It is primarily Marxist in its totalizing scope, one that fleshes out the intimate connection between theory and data, anecdotes, and observations drawn from the real world. In this respect, our conversation in the following three chapters will be less with other theorists than with the variety of circumstances that either contradict or lend support to Marx's theories.

Given the many works which base their critique of modern capitalism on an eclectic range of real world sources—from motorcycle factories in China to agrarian reform in Colombia—such a method is so common-place as not to bear mentioning. The difference however is that our exploration of these three themes also has a philosophical agenda. For poverty, corruption, and banality are not only topics which can and should be explored by means of the raw data of contemporary life, they also form a comprehensive set of obstacles toward realizing the philosopher's end-goal: the meaning and nature of freedom. Freedom, in the Hegelian vein, is the march of historical progress, the application of accumulated reason to the ills of society. And, while it may be utopian to hope for it everywhere, it is certainly not utopian to identify and address its obstacles. To make philosophy worldly, as Marx claimed, we need to pull it into the "torment of worldly struggle," but in doing so we also need to keep this end-goal in our sights. We need to remind ourselves that, whatever its other meanings may be, philosophy aspires toward a totality, an aggregate of observations on the complexity of life, and on the interdependence of seemingly disparate phenomena. For any of these themes studied in isolation would lead to inconclusive results. Poverty cannot be studied without addressing corruption and the political system that distributes society's surplus wealth, and both categories remain empty and static without addressing banality, the unhealthy and commodified leisure culture under capitalism that distracts rich and poor alike from realizing their freedom. Marx and the Marxist legacy, at least in a skeletal form, unite these three themes in a totalizing vision of the insidious nature of capitalism. Finally, it is worth mentioning that all true philosophy is colored by a kind of sadness and pessimism. The contrast between the reality of the human condition and the philosopher's ideal weighs heavy on the soul. For Marx, this sadness was transformed into anger and outrage, and ultimately an optimistic political plan of action. However, today, faced with the lessons of totalitarianism and the Cold War, it is harder to share that same faith in a political solution. Thus, the conclusions of this inquiry will invariably be more ambivalent and circumspect, more heterogeneous in their ideological debts, and less sweeping in both their condemnations and their praise than many studies of the Marxist variety.

We might still ask ourselves why we must necessarily appeal to Marx in the course of our study. After all, there are numerous critical inquiries into the nature of capitalism and its global scope which operate freely outside of specifically Marxist paradigms. This is not a purely tactical exercise on their part as if they were forced to disguise their Marxist beliefs behind more benign paradigms of grass-roots activism or civic protest. It is that they genuinely, and at times rightly, feel that although they might share Marx's condemnation of capitalism, they do not share the same faith in the communist alternative. Therefore, before we continue, we need briefly to outline Marx's ideas on poverty, corruption, and banality, for these three themes will serve as leitmotifs throughout the rest of our study. These themes are, in my view, general enough to lift Marx out of the stale, sectarian struggles and polemical simplifications that have characterized his work over the last century. But they are also specific enough to Marx's intellectual contribution and that of his followers to structure an attempt at illustrating his contemporary relevance.

On the subject of *poverty*, Marx's contribution can be broken down into four central points. Firstly, Marx provided an analytical framework for the study of poverty. He did not accept it as preordained by the natural order of things, but rather showed how it derived from the specific dynamics of the capitalist system, in particular, the quest for maximizing profit. He demonstrated in graphic detail, drawing extensively on official government records such as the Blue Books of English factory inspectors, how the exploitation of the worker took place, and why it was a necessary function of capitalism's self-sustaining mechanism. Secondly, he demonstrated how it was in the

interest of the ruling class, i.e., those in control over the means of production, to perpetuate the poverty of the underclass. From this emerged a
theory of class struggle as expressed in the famous opening words of *The
Communist Manifesto*, "all history is the history of class struggle." Thirdly,
through his propaganda activities, he provided the first comprehensive guidelines for mobilizing class consciousness. As a theory of revolution to eradicate economic injustice, these guidelines drew upon the premise that, given
the conspiracy of the upper classes against them, the poor could only rectify
their fate by forming an opposition from below. In short, it provided the
poor with an organizational strategy for their revolution against poverty.
Finally, Marx offered a quasi-religious doctrine of hope and optimism to the
impoverished. This latter point, while the least scientific and rigorous, may
nonetheless have been his crowning achievement. His impassioned rhetoric
crystallized the dreams of the poor for a better world in the form of a
communist paradise. However vaguely formulated, the ideal of communism
provided an enduring standard against which the oppressed could judge and
transcend their current plight.

On the subject of *corruption*, Marx applied a healthy cynicism to the
widespread faith in the power of democratic ideals and institutions to effect
real change. This attack—which, one should add, was conditioned by the
legacy of the French Revolution and the transition from monarchy to bourgeois liberalism—can be broken down into three components. Firstly, in the
essay "On the Jewish Question" (1843), where Marx most cogently outlines
his political theory, he contended that the state's becoming free through the
acceptance of democratic ideals does not yet imply human freedom. He
draws explicit parallels between Christianity and democracy to illustrate
how the truth of either ideal was still far removed from their declared
reality. This is the core of Marx's attack on legal forms of emancipation, and
particularly on those espoused in Enlightenment liberalism. The liberal democratic state is criticized along Feuerbachian lines, that is, as an affirmation of
an alienated Christian spirit. In order for the religious Christian spirit to be
secularized, its corresponding historical stage must be constituted in a secular form. That form is the democratic state where each man is sovereign to
himself. Importantly, "Not Christianity, but the *human basis* of Christianity
is the basis of this state."[51] However, while an advance in the right direction,
this does not go beyond the shortcomings of bourgeois individualism. The
solo, self-interested man—and here we find again echoes of Feuerbach—"is
not yet a REAL species-being."[52] The Rights of Man of the French Revolution, the lofty ideals of liberty, equality, and fraternity, only served to
validate the egoistic individual; thus, "the practical application of man's
right to liberty is man's right to private property." Likewise, equality only
validates men as "self-sufficient monads."[53] In short, "none of the rights of
man . . . go beyond egoistic man, beyond man as a member of civil society."[54]
Still alien to his true human essence, the egoistic man cannot be free even

when fitted out with political rights that legitimate him as free citizen. In short, all the formal trappings of democracy—a legislature, popularly elected leaders, the rule of law—are meaningless institutional shells if they cannot realize the ideals they supposedly represent. Secondly, in a more particular sense, the state can never be true to these ideals if its component parts are beholden to specific groups motivated by economic self-interest. The interests of self-preservation of the ruling class are such that, no matter what formal declarations this class makes about its disinterestedness, it is still corrupt in its exercise of political power. Likewise, for the self-centered bureaucrat, the temptation of careerism subsumes the aims of the state under his own private aims. Thus, corruption is not only a symptom of a weak, or formal democracy, it is its necessary complement as long as the ruling socio-economic interest groups hold the reigns of power. Lastly, and this was perhaps Marx's most controversial idea, the state as an instrument of the ruling class could and would never adequately represent the interests of the masses and thus must wither away and be replaced by more democratic forms of political organization. Such a hypothetical dynamic, Marx conceded, could only take place in conjunction with a radical overhaul, if not overthrow, of the capitalist mechanism that sustained the ruling class.

We need not consider here whether or not history validates Marx's cynicism regarding the democratic state. To be sure, some of it seems misplaced given that in every complex modern polity there are a number of checks and balances to ensure a viable function of its democratic organs. Nonetheless, as we shall see in the chapter on corruption (chapter 4), there is an increasing realization that many of the systemic causes of poverty in both developing countries and Western society derive from abuses of power of special interest groups, tribal structures, and financial conglomerates even in—and perhaps because of—openly democratic societies. In many cases, the fragmentation and weak authority of democratic institutions provide little more than a green light for rampant corruption by cynical politicians. Therefore, while Marx may have exaggerated the state's accelerated path toward implosion, his tenacious, critical challenge for political institutions to realize what they profess to represent retains its relevance.

Lastly, the theme of *banality* ties in directly with Marx's enduring relevance in Western society. Banality, though not a word Marx ever used, describes the cultural and spiritual alienation he identified in the capitalist system. Rooted in the humanistic tradition of German idealism which affirmed the total self-realization of the individual, both in the mind and the heart, Marx's attack on banality follows three interrelated strands. Firstly, as touched upon in the discussion of alienation in chapter 1, Marx distinguishes between *having* and *being* in order to illustrate the corrosive impact of materialistic desires as a means to self-fulfillment: "Private property has made us stupid and partial, that an object is only ours when we have it, when it exists for us as capital or when it is directly eaten, drunk, worn, inhabited, etc., in short utilized in some way."[55] Instead, we realize our true human potential not through the possession of material objects, but through productive, creative activity, through the expression of our unique individuality by which we achieve recognition and spiritual satisfaction. While the observation that money cannot buy happiness is an old common-place, Marx's originality lies in his analytical dissection of the culture of *having* as a fixture of modern capitalism. It infected not only human work, but more importantly for the modern day, human leisure, that sphere where man ideally carved out a slice of freedom in which to develop his unique inner self. Secondly, Marx, again in the tradition of German philosophy, lays much emphasis on dynamism and movement in the process of self-creation. Life and self-development is a constant learning process. In his attack on banality, these are contrasted positively with the passivity in which the modern masses, numbly and dumbly, absorb the manufactured products of the leisure industry. Thirdly, and here Marx deviates from the tradition of German idealism, banality as the by-product of a morally dysfunctional economic system could only be transcended by overthrowing the ruling socio-economic structures. Without this structural transformation, individuals will never find the spiritual autonomy to fulfill themselves.

In a purely static sense, the conditions of poverty, corruption, and banality correspond to the economic, political, and cultural scope of the Marxian legacy. But more dynamically, they also mirror social priorities at different levels of social development. There is an evolutionary matrix at play here which can be seen as society's increasingly sophisticated attempt at realizing the goal of freedom. Thus, in the nineteenth century, the earliest labor standards were designed to alleviate the misery caused by basic deprivations or *poverty*—subsistence wages, excessive hours, and dangerous work conditions. In the twentieth century, the modern states assumed a greater and greater responsibility for social welfare. Income taxes were introduced to redistribute wealth and enhance public services. The definition of basic needs grew more complex to include free education, and in certain countries, subsidized health care and cultural institutions. Often in the early stages of this growth, there were opportunities for widespread abuse of the public trust, either by higher-income individuals evading taxes, or by government officials helping themselves to the fiscal trough. In short, the era of *corruption*. Finally, as these needs were satisfied by modern, well-functioning institutions, as the urgency of popular revolt subsided, there arises the specter of *banality*—how our leisure time, our freedom to develop ourselves, is threatened by the commodification of culture.

While this crude sketch roughly corresponds to the evolution of modern Western society (and Marxism's contribution to it), today these three stages co-exist in different countries to differing degrees. In some countries, they might even exist to disproportionate degrees. Thus, in low-income countries such as Bangladesh, North Korea, or Cambodia, the main issue may be widespread hunger and poverty. Here corruption is less of an issue because, perhaps cynically, there are fewer fiscal revenues, beyond foreign assistance, to exploit. However, in medium-income countries, such as Brazil or Thailand, the potential to alleviate poverty is often thwarted by the corruption of government and self-interested elites, even though there is considerable wealth available. Finally, in the wealthiest nations with relatively efficient and transparent governments, such as Japan or Germany or the United States, more nuanced questions about the development of the self come to the fore. Here, in addition to lingering problems of poverty and corruption, we are confronted with the threat of banality. Banal societies are close cousins with decadent ones where boredom sidles alongside sex tourism, existential malaise alongside internet addiction, and careerism alongside consumerism. As is all too often said, in a stable democracy where everyone can have a house and car, many people have trouble finding a higher purpose.

Together these successive, or at times co-existing, obstacles to freedom are fruitful arenas for a postcommunist discussion of Marx. Though they might not all lend themselves to Marx's radical prescriptions, they all reflect one of the central points of Marx's theory of capitalism. Namely, that capitalism generates its own contradictions, and these contradictions are either radically challenged, through revolution, or, in those advanced societies where class antagonisms are more subdued, they mutate into less visible, but no less destructive, forms of alienation.

3

POVERTY

Introduction

In its heyday, Marxism appealed to the wretched of the earth, the poor and poorly skilled desperate for any form of work to survive another day. Wherever the contrast between the haves and have-nots was particularly stark, wherever a corrupt elite rode on the backs of the poor, Marxism had widespread appeal. It then disappeared, not because the conditions that nourished it disappeared as well, but because the revolutions carried out in its name subordinated individual freedom to the dictates of an elite, or turned economically and politically moribund. However, while capitalism now thrives on an ideologically uncontested field, the dimensions of poverty have broadened dramatically, in their volume, complexity and, perhaps most of all, their geographical scope. Our new global awareness fueled by 24-hour news coverage and an industry of academic surveys, working papers, and monographs on every imaginable form of poverty—whether the hazards of coal mining in Russia, shoe manufacturing in Vietnam, or flood damage in Bangladesh—militates against any kind of insular complacency. And yet now, when close to three billion people, or half the world's population, lives on two dollars or less a day,[1] we are confronted with an embarrassing contradiction. Though we, as a global society, have both the financial resources and the know-how available to mitigate poverty, for one reason or another, we have not applied them. In short, the persistence of poverty represents a dismal failure of human self-governance.

Poverty defined

Absolute poverty

In order to delineate the human responsibility in alleviating poverty we need to distinguish between its two basic forms, absolute and relative. For though we might say that poverty is the deprivation of material wealth, it is also, on a much broader field, the deprivation of skills and resources necessary to acquire that wealth. This deprivation may at times be due to human failure or greed and the unfortunate tendency of the strong to exploit the weak, but it may also be due to the set of attributes which fate has dealt a particular individual or whole groups of individuals—illness, an abusive or dysfunctional family, or a drought, disease-ridden, or hostile political environment.

What fate has dealt lies at the root of absolute poverty. It refers to the lack of means to satisfy basic needs, "the minimum necessaries for the maintenance of merely physical efficiency."[2] It is poverty's most tragically photogenic face. Encompassing the victims of famine, drought, or plague, those people on the brink of starvation in Africa or Asia, the glue-sniffing street urchins, the swollen-bellied toddlers, the AIDS-inflicted prostitutes who live only to live another day. At this elementary level, poverty is measured in terms of physical welfare such as caloric intake, incidence of disease, and infant mortality. Those who fall into this category have little sense of their human potential, and even the most basic activity of life-forms, the act of reproduction, is threatened. But not entirely. The instinct to procreate is so strong and its motives so complex that parents often ignore the fact that they have not the means to provide for their young. Although it may be politically insensitive to call such reproduction irresponsible, at the very least, it represents an unrealistic assumption of an added financial burden. Along these lines, absolute poverty perpetuates itself independent of the natural scarcities that contribute to it. Perhaps then, it should not surprise that the two most populous nations, China and India, have the largest share of the world's poor. Equally unsurprising is the fact that those who have studied the problem of absolute poverty in-depth, from classical economists such as Ricardo and Malthus to modern institutions such as the World Bank and the United Nations, have focused on population control as one of the central means of alleviating absolute poverty.

In Marx's critique of capitalism, absolute poverty—whose causes are more natural than man-made—is not a major factor. Nonetheless, there are at least two points at which it converges with the dynamics of the modern capitalist world. Firstly, the desperation of the absolute poor—whether Irish peasants migrating to nineteenth-century England, or, in the twenty-first century, poor Mexican workers smuggled across the US border—guarantees that capitalist industry is secured a constant supply of cheap labor. The very volume of this supply ensures that when it comes to determining wages, the employer can basically name his price. The desperate man or woman, often with extra mouths to feed, will work for any wage. This factory labor pool, which Marx called the "Industrial Reserve Army," was only partly fed by the cyclical or systemic poverty of agrarian life. The other part stemmed from the process of mechanization intrinsic to capitalism. Increased efficiency with the introduction of new technology would perennially displace unskilled workers to the unemployment pool from which new industries would draw. Both components of the Industrial Reserve Army are very much evident today, a phenomenon we will address in more detail later.

The second link between capitalism and absolute poverty is the disinterest of wealthy countries and corporations adequately to allocate their surplus wealth to the absolutely poor either in the form of debt relief, financial aid, or the supply of basics such as medicine and health care. To give just one current example: faced with an AIDS epidemic in developing countries, global pharmaceutical companies could either sell their product at a price local markets could afford, or even better, license their product cheaply so that it could be locally reproduced. Yet, although the anti-viral HIV drugs are available in Western markets, corporations withhold them from poor countries on primarily financial grounds. There are, of course, complex issues of intellectual property at play here and even critics must concede that the high price at which these companies sell their products also include substantial research and development costs.[3] Nonetheless, "medicine withheld" provides a particularly graphic example of the amoral nature of capitalism. Faced with an epidemic of plague-like proportions, yet in the absence of profit incentives, capitalist corporations have little inclination to provide assistance. Such examples suggest that while capitalism does not directly cause absolute poverty, it can perpetuate it by refusing to correct the natural downward pressure on wages exerted by a cheap supply of labor, or by refusing, in the absence of a profit-motive, to allocate surplus toward the poor.

Relative poverty

Whereas absolute poverty refers to life at or below a subsistence level, relative poverty refers to "the failure to meet the basic requirements of a 'decent life'"[4] where the meaning of "decent" has a highly relative character depending on societal norms. As these norms become more sophisticated as the quality-of-life standard evolves, so too does the understanding of what it means to be poor. Along these lines, relative poverty refers "to the position of an individual or household compared with the average income of the country."[5] Thus, the standards for measuring the minimum income and consumption necessary for subsistence, usually in the form of poverty lines, vary from country to country. A poor man in Denmark will have an income equal to if not higher than a middle-class doctor in Bangladesh, but in terms of his income in relation to the mean income, he will consider himself, and be considered—for the purposes of statistics and welfare support—poor. As such, consciousness of poverty depends on the ability to contrast one's condition with the standard of living that prevails in a given nation. As the statutes of the European Community define it, the poor are "persons, families and groups of persons whose resources (material, cultural and social) are so limited as to exclude them from a minimum acceptable way of life in the

Member State in which they live."[6] In other words, the poor are those who occupy the lowest level of any given social pyramid. Because the poor define and assess their condition in relation to that of their fellow-citizens, we can only conclude that relative poverty is the recognition of deprivation, not only of income, but of any number of goods that enable one to lead an acceptable and meaningful life. As Amartya Sen, one leading poverty expert, notes, "Being relatively poor in a rich country can be a great capability handicap, even when one's absolute income is high in world standards. In a generally opulent country, more income is needed to achieve the same social functioning."[7] Marx makes a similar point when he argues that the value of labor must not only satisfy the basic necessities, it must also satisfy "certain wants springing from the social conditions in which people are placed and reared up."[8]

Non-income aspects of poverty

Even if one acknowledges the injustice perpetrated against the poor in the form of subsistence or below-subsistence level wages, one may still wonder why they do not take initiatives to improve their skills. Quite logically, the new skills would allow them to earn higher wages, and move them out of poverty. Yet, although there may be a connection between skills and income, in many societies there are, in addition to financial constraints, cultural constraints, or non-income barriers, which impede the poor from enhancing their skills.

The most common examples cited refer to the treatment of women in orthodox Hindu and Islamic societies where the low literacy rates of girls compared to boys are particularly staggering. Discriminatory barriers imply lower education levels which in turn imply lower incomes. More importantly, these cultural values often over-ride the letter of the law. The constitution of Bangladesh, for example, ensures equality of the sexes, but this is all but irrelevant when it comes to questions relating to marriage, divorce, child custody, etc., that are dictated by community and religious laws. In these societies, the woman's reproductive role remains centerpiece of her socially determined existence.[9] Other non-income aspects of poverty would include the whole range of psychological and social knock-on effects, resignation and fatalism, defiance of authority, apathy, etc., that perpetuate poverty, in short, the culture of poverty itself. In ghettos across the world, the common pattern is surprisingly regular. Because of social failure and lack of hope for the future, the poor seek out deluded forms of self-fulfillment, mainly by men making babies, and women having them. Perhaps this is what Marx had in mind when he wrote that in an alienated state, "man (the worker) only feels himself freely active in his animal functions." For the men, sexual prowess soothes the self-esteem, for the women nurturing the young assigns purpose to an otherwise empty life.[10] The tendency to use reproduction as a surrogate form of empowerment is exacerbated by a host of poverty-related symptoms: domestic violence, alcohol and drug abuse born of frustration and hopelessness, the sheer boredom that accompanies ignorance and the absence of intellectual curiosity, and the lack of any sense of deferred gratification.[11]

Over the last fifty years, particularly in the field of development economics, various paradigms have emerged to better accommodate these and other non-income and cultural aspects of poverty. These would include the so-called Basic Needs School, based primarily on the writings of Streeten ("A basic needs approach to development," wrote Streeten in 1977, "starts from the objective of providing the opportunities for the full physical, mental and social development of the human personality, and then derives the ways of achieving this objective"[12]), to more recent attempts, such as the Human Development Index of the United Nations, to quantify more broadly quality-of-life standards beyond income indicators. Finally, there are even "Happiness Equations" put forward by economists in advanced societies that attempt to measure human welfare independent of economic wealth. These use highly sophisticated models to make rather obvious points, for example, that loving partners and job satisfaction often contribute more to happiness than high levels of income.[13] But they do highlight a problem present in any research into poverty and the means to alleviate it. For even if we see poverty as an absence of opportunity, we have to acknowledge that there is an enormous variety of opportunities, not all of which can be provided by either the market or an enlightened state.

We must therefore concentrate on those forms of poverty which may lend themselves to a Marxist analysis. As we turn now to study Marx's economic thought in more detail, we will notice that he restricted his focus to that form of impoverishment caused by man-made structures of power and exploitation as opposed to some static or sporadic condition of destitution caused by nature. Because the category of labor is central to his thought, it is the proletariat, the working class, and not the *lumpenproletariat*—the beggars, vagrants, and invalids who were not able to work—that became the main focus of his inquiry. Most simply put, in the context of an exploitation theory that lies at the center of Marx's economic thought, the beggar, or cripple, or blind widow have little role to play. If they cannot work, they cannot be exploited. Their deprivation is of a natural sort, not caused by the capitalist system and therefore falls outside the range of Marx's concerns.

Marx's economic ideas

We need first to outline two distinct strands in Marxist economic thought which, in his study of capitalism, however, are often intertwined. The first strand would include his thorough analysis of the various characteristics of capitalism such as money, credit, profit, and competition, all presented in a

63

way that accents the dynamic character of the system. Not all of Marx's work has withstood the test of time. He considered, for example, that capitalism's dynamism, and its relentless drive to accumulate and overproduce, was the source of its cyclical crises and eventual downfall. But during periods when capitalism appeared inherently stable, Marx's more pessimistic theories such as the falling rate of profit—the tendency for profits to decline with increased competition—were discredited or subjected to critical scrutiny. At the same time, new studies on the falling rate of profit,[14] coupled with recent signs about the inherent instability of capitalism (the Asian economic crisis, and the dot.com boom and bust are the most notable examples), suggest that Marx's pessimistic economic analysis will continue to merit consideration. On the whole, however, we might say that this first strand—his general economic thinking—was already seriously challenged by early criticisms, some as early as Böhm-Bawerk's late nineteenth-century work, *Karl Marx and the Close of his System*, or simply outpaced by the subsequent evolution of capitalism itself, as expressed in the rise of investment banking and capital markets. A vast literature has already covered this terrain thoroughly—from critical condemnations to reverent textual exegesis; the reader may consult the works of Ernest Mandel, Louis Althusser, Joseph Schumpeter, or Joan Robinson for more detailed analysis (see Bibliographical essay), but this is now all primarily of historical interest. What is more important for Marx's modern relevance is the second strand, namely, the manner in which Marx imbeds a moral indictment of capitalism in a sophisticated economic critique.

This indictment is imbedded principally in two ways. Firstly, in the manner in which Marx applied philosophy to the economic system. Not only did Marx philosophize (or Hegelianize) capitalism by setting the system in motion, revealing it in a perpetual state of flux, but also by constantly questioning its underlying premises. As Althusser has observed, this distinguished the philosopher's reading from the economist's. Whereas the economist analyzes in relation to a supposedly immutable object, capitalism and the free market, the philosopher questions the very validity of that object, and its legitimating discourse.[15] In doing so, Marx uncovered the tendency of so-called bourgeois economists to disguise the historical and transient aspect of economic relations behind a veil of immutability, one that assumed that the exploitation intrinsic to capitalism was a natural functioning of a free market and could not or should not be altered.

Secondly, the moral indictment emerges from certain economic facts intrinsic to capitalism rather than from an emotional response to its injustices. These would include such familiar Marxian concepts as the industrial reserve army—the perpetual supply of cheap unskilled labor which capitalism secures from the surplus provided by either rural-urban migration or technological displacement; the surplus value of labor—the difference between the value of the commodity which labor produces and the wages paid for that labor; and what may be called the implosion theory—the notion that capitalism, by virtue of the exploitation of surplus value, would generate its own rebellious underclass, the proletariat, who would lead the way toward socialism.

While Marx was not alone among his contemporaries in condemning the abuses of capitalism, the manner by which his moral indictment emerges from economic facts distinguishes him from the sentimentalism of early socialists. Even those socialists who grounded their views in the economic theories of the day, and particularly Ricardo's theory of value, were, in his view, wrongly applying a moral argument to an economic fact. Marx agreed that the Ricardian theory of value—that the value of a commodity was solely determined by the quantity of labor invested to produce it—served as a useful basis for socialism because it appeared to demonstrate that a significant portion of the value produced by the worker was wrongfully expropriated by his employer in the form of surplus, or profit. Socialism was then the process of reappropriating the surplus which rightfully belonged to the worker. But in his view, it was a misplaced moral argument simply to condemn this relationship and *a priori* posit socialism as the necessary alternative. Instead, Marx intended to demonstrate how the moral consciousness of exploitation would, in a very Hegelian sense, *become* a new economic reality. As Engels formulated it in his preface to Marx's *The Poverty of Philosophy*,

> If the moral consciousness of the masses declares an economic fact to be unjust, as it has done in the case of slavery or serf labor, that is a proof that the fact itself has been outlived, that other economic facts have made their appearance, owing to which the former has become unbearable and untenable.[16]

In other words, the moral consciousness of capitalist injustice could not just be posited statically against an economic reality, as the utopian and Ricardian socialists might have it, it must galvanize the victims of that injustice to shape history and positively change it. This then leads directly to Marx's understanding of poverty. Poverty was not simply a static condition of destitution, it contained within it the seeds to transform economic reality. These seeds of poverty had a "revolutionary subversive aspect which will overthrow the old society."[17] Marx's curiously dialectical explanation, i.e., that in the bad there is good if properly understood—also explains why the famous warning of *The Communist Manifesto*, "the spectre of communism is haunting Europe," is something more than rhetorical scaremongering. Rather, it is grounded in an analysis of capitalism which, among other things, says that its parasitical tendency to feed off surplus value will galvanize the poor toward a socialist revolution.

The critique of mainstream economics

The Marxian approach to poverty incorporates structures of power, class relations, and exploitation which mainstream economics could not or did not want to accommodate. And many of the weaknesses he exposed have still not been addressed in the modern day. (For our purposes, we will use "mainstream economics" to refer to both nineteenth-century classical political economy and contemporary neoclassical economics. Although imprecise, the technical differences between classical political economy and neoclassical economics—the latter introduced marginal analysis and placed a greater emphasis on supply and demand than labor in the determination of value —carry less weight, at least in a study on Marx, than what they share in common: a faith in the self-regulating free market, and economic reasoning based on the preferences of individual agents rather than societal pressures or group dynamics.) It was Marx's contention that mainstream economics, as inaugurated by Smith and Ricardo, was trapped in a romantic eighteenth-century notion of the natural individual, the isolated hunter/gatherer who reaps as much as he sows. To this day, modern economic textbooks still adopt this Smithian idea of perfect liberty—the assumption that employer and employee are free agents on a level playing field who negotiate a price for that labor, the wage. In this view, the wage, like the value of any commodity, depends not only on the objective laws of supply and demand, but also on the amount of labor invested to acquire these skills. Thus, different skill levels will command different values on the labor market. Professions that demand large and long investments in education, such as medicine or law, will command higher wages than professions that do not. In this sense, education becomes a form of capital.[18] In general, mainstream economics assumes that individuals, similar to firms, think in free-market terms, that they make autonomous choices based on their preferences and a calculated assessment of the costs or benefits of these choices. Yet, beyond such indisputable logic lie a number of ambiguities concerning the determination of value. For example, one popular microeconomics textbook used in the United States declares matter-of-factly that "one reason why teacher's salaries are so low relative to those of many other college graduates is that teaching jobs have few dangers and offer long vacations."[19] Setting aside the fact that most jobs for college graduates have few dangers, there are a number of jobs with long vacations such as professional athletics which pay far higher salaries. Likewise, there are numerous professions for college graduates which involve far less preparation than teaching, such as stockbroking or real estate, that offer far higher renumeration. Conversely, there are dangerous jobs, such as a foot soldier in the army, that offer little financial reward, often even less than teaching.

For Marx, capitalism was full of such mystifications in which the market values of commodities hid underlying structures of power, hype, expectation, or any number of intangible determinants which are often divorced from the value of the labor invested in it. He exposed what lay behind this façade of harmonious agents negotiating in the marketplace, and how capitalism together with mainstream economics disguised unequal bargaining positions between employer and employee based on socially-determined power structures. "The size of wages," Marx wrote,

> is determined at the beginning by free arrangement between the free worker and the free capitalist. Later it turns out that the worker is compelled to allow the capitalist to determine it, just as the capitalist is compelled to fix it as low as possible. Freedom of the contracting parties has been supplanted by compulsion.[20]

By disguising inequalities of leverage behind a seemingly harmonious movement of agents toward equilibrium, mainstream economics rightly merits the label of "an apologetic ideology,"[21] in that it throws a veil of equality over unequal bargaining positions between labor and capital in the marketplace. Such a veil lies equally over more modern economic advances such as equilibrium theory, developed by Kenneth Arrow in the 1950s, which tries to explain market behavior on the basis of complex mathematical models, but ultimately can only do so by making unrealistic assumptions: that rational agents on the marketplace operate in a framework of perfect information and perfect competition. In short, mainstream economics is an apologia for capitalism not necessarily in the strong sense of a discipline beholden to corporate or upper-class interests, but in the weaker sense that its paradigms can simply not accommodate the web of unequal relationships, unequal bargaining positions, and unequal levels of skill that dictate economic decision-making in the real world.[22]

Whatever weaknesses Marx may have had as a classical political economist, this rather simple discovery—that economic relations are based on mysterious determinants of value and varying degrees of leverage in the marketplace, both of which mainstream economics cannot accommodate— still has widespread application. And the more that a particular context deviates from the standard assumptions of mainstream economics—a pure unregulated market, perfect competition, institutional neutrality, legal transparency—the more pronounced these mysterious determinants of value become. Today, such determinants are particularly acute in developing countries where entrenched power structures dictate the distribution of wealth, in countries with an abundant supply of cheap labor, in short, in countries whose conditions are similar to those that gave rise to Marx's critique in the first place.

The exploitation theory

Although Marx is often caricatured as hostile to capitalism, he made many ideologically neutral contributions to the study of its behavior. He was the first to capture comprehensively its dynamic character, its tendency to innovate constantly and to renew and reshape itself. He was the first to develop a theory, however crude, of capital concentration, the tendency for corporations to merge in the name of greater efficiency and larger market shares, and the third volume of *Das Kapital* contains, according to Lawrence Klein, "probably the origins of macroeconomics."[23] But it is his theory of exploitation which has no real analogues in mainstream economics. It was his contention that the driving force of capitalism was its exploitation of unpaid labor which it appropriated in the form of profit. Reclaiming that surplus between what the worker is paid and what the capitalist received for the commodity produced by that worker, would, he argued, not only liberate the worker from that ugly equilibrium, from a subsistence wage, it would also eliminate the capitalist who cannot survive without that surplus. Thus both worker and capitalist feed off each other. Each seeks to rob the other of his existence.[24] The worker, in the Marxian system, sees the surplus as his lost wage, whereas the capitalist sees it as the return on his investment.

Within this snapshot of Marx's exploitation theory, one can already identify a number of problems. Critics have made the basic point that the level of exploitation which Marx attributed to capitalism is so difficult to measure because unskilled manual labor is but one of many components that add to the final value of the product. Research and development, packaging, advertising, in sum "the unpaid contribution of mental effort,"[25] as Simmel, the late nineteenth-century sociologist, observed in *The Philosophy of Money*, all add to the final value of the product, and often, much more than the initial labor. If anything, it is advertising, not the manufacturing labor, which allows a basic product to sell at such a high price. It creates the illusion of specialness, it fosters brand identity and allegiance among customers, and that allegiance is sustained by fostering an association between the customer and the sponsored celebrity. And it is primarily this illusion which allows for a shoe which costs five dollars to manufacture to retail for over seventy. The other reason we cannot properly measure the rate of exploitation is because there are, in fact, two processes which determine price: one, the production process—the chain of capital inputs and labor which combine to make the commodity, and two, the circulation process—the market forces of supply and demand, entry barriers, competitor behavior, and consumer preferences which determine the final price. Finally, we cannot determine the rate of exploitation because there is no rule determining what percentage of the profits are retained as surplus, and what percentage are reinjected as capital to expand the business or to service debt. One would think, for example, that the management board's salaries would be an obvious target to tap into for reclaiming surplus. But again these salaries are determined not only by their contribution to the final price of the product, but also by the circulation process, the supply and demand for highly skilled labor. The job of the executive is to develop new products and find new markets for them. If he fails, he will be fired. If profits are low, or non-existent, he will lose his bonus, or even face a salary reduction. In general then, executive pay is tied to performance in an erratic and unpredictable marketplace, and therefore, it would be difficult to measure precisely which percentage of the surplus generated by the worker that ends up as part of the executive's pay should be returned.

It would be safe to say then that Marx's theory of exploitation cannot accommodate very well the complexity of value generation in a capitalist society. But in Marx's defense, his main concern is not how surplus value is generated, but rather how it is taken away, how it, in many cases, reduced the worker to a state worse than slavery. Worse, because whereas both slave and worker are paid for their subsistence costs—the slave in terms of in-kind maintenance, the worker in terms of his wage—at least the slave is not subjected to labor-market fluctuations. He does not have to withstand periods of unemployment, or underemployment. He does not have to take desperate measures—crime, prostitution—to ensure his survival. The slave, in this grim comparative framework, actually does not have it that bad.[26] In short, the emancipatory rhetoric of exploitation theory is rooted in a cool logic. "If the worker," Marx writes, "resigned himself to accept the will, the dictates of the capitalist as a permanent economic law, he would share in all the miseries of the slave, without the security of the slave."[27]

While the analogy may seem overwrought, it has gained a new resonance in the era of global capitalism and free trade. When highly mobile capital moves freely around the globe in search of the cheapest labor supply, an eclectic consortium of human rights advocates, nationalist politicians and labor unions interested in protecting their wages, all now draw comparison between a fair wage and slave labor. "Money and jobs are going overseas," says Jimmy Hoffa, the high profile head of the 1.4 million-member US Teamsters Union. "U.S. workers can't compete with slave labor."[28] What he means is that countries with low labor and environmental standards, little or no taxes imposed on corporations, and an almost unlimited supply of desperately poor people, can provide far better conditions for profit maximization than countries which have such constraints. One does not need to be a Marxist to acknowledge this new reality. High wages, and high labor and environmental standards are the price of civilization, the stage at which we have arrived after a long evolution. Along these lines, to regress to a more primitive level, the level of raw capitalism of nineteenth-century Europe, can only be seen as a return to barbarity and wage slavery.

For a good deal of the twentieth century, it was fashionable to argue that Marx's writings were rooted in an antiquated Dickensian vision of raw capitalism that no longer applied. Even Marxist economists such as Paul Sweezy, writing in the 1970s, prematurely conceded that "the trends which he (Marx) stressed and projected on to the future—flooding of the labor market by women and children . . . abasement of living conditions etc., reached their maximum intensity in the first half of the nineteenth century and had already been checked or reversed before the publication of the first volume of *Capital*."[29] But this view has, in turn, become antiquated and outpaced by the advent of globalization. In fact, some of the most primitive imagery of global capitalism that the most ardent Marxist could fabricate— as a voracious beast, a spreading fire, a contagion—seems to take on new life in the new postcommunist era when corporations can move their production base to wherever the highest degree of exploitation is married to the lowest labor and environmental standards. Not only that, such corporations have an incentive to keep these countries from evolving toward a more humane treatment of their workers. As noted by one researcher investigating labor practices in Southeast Asia:

> The authoritarian conditions that prevent workers from organizing and making demands, are an integral part of the calculus that makes relocating capital and production facilities to Indonesia appealing in the first place. Closing the freedom gap (the gap between the current and a living wage) would deprive transnational investors not only of the opportunity to produce cheaply in postcolonial states, but also of the leverage they have with labor back home when they can make credible threats to relocate to places where the workers are cheaper, more pliable, and more intimidated.[30]

These systemic flaws, driven by the addictive quest for "comparative advantage," higher profits, cost-efficiency, etc., are what Marx and socialism intended to address. Of course, such a categorical condemnation ignores the technological benefits and managerial skills that Western corporations impart to developing countries. But, within the narrower paradigm of the exploitation theory, these same corporations clearly benefit from the lack of regulations concerning worker wages and safety that are now the norm in Western society. In short, the same ingredients that gave the idea of a worker revolution such inspirational value during Marx's day, are as prevalent once we expand our scope of observation beyond the industrialized West.

The Marxian theory of exploitation goes to the root of global capitalism's parasitical tendencies, ones which feed suburban and urban factories with the rural chronic poor, and which make every effort to sustain wages at the lowest possible level. Throughout the 1990s and the 2000s, a resurgence of anti-capitalist activism has highlighted the human consequences of so-called "sweatshop" labor and appealed for Western corporations to force their local subcontractors to offer higher wages. Pro-capitalists, free-trade advocates, and defenders of globalization have countered, however, that either Western corporations generally pay higher wages than local counterparts, or that wage increases, in general, would lower the collective welfare of workers by disincentivating corporations to invest. But from a Marxist perspective, the most fundamental issue in this whole debate is that of surplus. If the influx of Western industries into these poor areas does pay comparatively higher wages, then one would assume this would also lead to a higher standard of living. But this is often not the case. Potential surplus is often offset by higher living costs at the industrial parks where these workers are forced to live. Although collecting data on worker savings rates is notoriously diffi-cult, entailing, as it does, nothing short of household surveys on consump-tion patterns, a non-governmental organization investigating Nike labor practices in Indonesia found that a female employee earned only two-thirds of the amount necessary to cover basic living expenses. The negative surplus, as is usually the case, was addressed by working overtime.[31] In other cases, such as the Mexican *maquiladoras*, the massive industrial parks for low-skilled labor, the problem of insufficient wages is compounded by the lack of basic services such as sewage disposal and running water because these tax-free zones often fall out of the local jurisdiction and fiscal responsibility. As a result, the foreign companies feel little obligation to provide any services beyond subsistence level wages, services which normally would come from local tax revenue to which they are not contributing. Whatever services investors do provide—a new kindergarten, free transport—are, for the most part, token and piecemeal.[32]

Even if we feel compelled to condemn these abuses on moral grounds, the cynic, pragmatist, or capitalist apologist can always draw attention to the rural misery these workers left behind. As Paul Krugman, a well-known mainstream economist asks rhetorically: "Why does the image of an Indone-sian sewing sneakers for 60 cents an hour evoke so much more feeling than the image of another Indonesian earning the equivalent of 30 cents an hour trying to feed his family on a tiny plot of land—or of a Filipino scavenging on a garbage heap?"[33] Krugman argues that the reason lies in a misplaced righteousness, that these people's suffering for our benefit, i.e., the shoes we buy, somehow makes us feel unclean. But, from a Marxist perspective, such moralizing is irrelevant. Instead, the source of the outrage lies in the distinc-tion between paid and unpaid labor, the root of the theory of surplus value. Whereas the subsistence-level farmer is merely working enough to feed his family, and creates only enough value to do so, the laborer sewing sneakers creates value *far beyond* the cost required to possibly sustain him or her, i.e., the wage. Thus, the reason why we are troubled by these conditions is due not to the absolute but the relative misery of the poor and, more importantly, a relativity not based on simple contrasts in income between the employer and the employee (that would be a moral argument), but by the fact that these contrasts directly evolve from the labor process in which both parties share.

In fact, eschewing the moral argument, Marx applies capitalist logic against those capitalists who would deny the worker a living wage. If, as he argues, labor is a commodity like any other then its production costs must be lower than its market price in order to thrive. Since the production costs of labor are the costs of living—the basic needs required to sustain labor power—when the market price of labor, i.e., the wage, is near or below these production costs, no worker can be expected to survive, at least not for long. Any capitalist would then recognize that the only answer is to keep production costs at a minimum even if such costs, in the case of labor, refer to the livelihood of human beings. This then leads us to Marx's subsistence wage theory: *"The general tendency of capitalistic production is not to raise but to sink the average standard of wages, or to push the value of labor, more or less, to its minimum limit."*[34] In this axiom is imbedded a moral indictment and a condemnation of human practice. It is not natural scarcities (the scourge of absolute poverty) that provoke our concern but rather that, given a regular supply of cheap labor, capitalism deliberately sustains wages at a subsistence level even when it has the surplus available to raise them to a more humane level.

Every capitalist knows that his success depends on maximizing profits and minimizing cost, but it is precisely in the space between these two poles where the confrontation lies. And, in defense of capitalism, it is not a question of absolutes, that he should be denied his profit entirely, but rather a question of degree. In this space, which we will call the profit buffer, lies the potential for compromise, a compromise ignored most by those who have the power to make it. Even if labor cannot *de facto* claim a higher share of profits simply because it desires them, at the very least it can claim an increase in wages as profits rise, as the value of labor's creation increases. But because profits and wages are not often, as they could be, related, the determination of wages is frozen in an autonomous matrix driven by the continued supply of cheap labor. Indeed, as in the earliest days of capitalism, the determination of wages responds to the variable of relative labor supply rather than value which labor generates. What is more, not only is surplus value in the form of profits withheld from the worker, the factory owners make no concessions to the fact that their profits and the workers' wages are even related. Instead, they fix a value based on the minimum necessary for the worker to sustain his existence. Depending on his desperation, the worker will stay or seek better opportunity elsewhere.

The profit buffer and wages: three cases

A recent *New York Times* undercover investigation into the Smithfield corporation, a major player in the US pork industry, found that though the firm's profits had doubled in 1999, wages remained flat. More troubling, in the 1970s, when the meatpacking industry was based in the northern areas of Chicago and Omaha, Nebraska, unionized labor was able to secure an hourly wage of $18, more than double what is now paid in North Carolina.[i] At the non-unionized Smithfield plant wages are held down by the continued supply of Mexican migrant workers—many of them illegally hired with false documents and saddled with debts to the middlemen who smuggled them across the border. Their desperation ensures that there will be little pressure to raise wages even though, in terms of its profits, the firm is certainly able to do so.

A more glaring example comes from the handgun industry. The Lorcin L-25 semi-automatic pistol, a so-called "junk gun" and one of the staple tools of violent crime in America, costs only $10 to manufacture yet retailed in 1997 for $69, still the least expensive firearm in the country. It is astoundingly simple to make. A tool and die shop cuts out the low-grade metal parts and ships them to the firm for assembly. At its Los Angeles plant, workers then assembled the parts for $6.60 an hour, but the owners, who in a space of six years were able to turn their $100,000 investment into $8 million in annual sales, paid themselves each close to a million dollars in annual salary. During legal proceedings (the firm recently filed for bankruptcy to avoid lawsuits by injured customers), a defiant owner defended the huge discrepancy between his and his workers' earnings: "As measured by its return on investment and risk-reward ratio, it offered the best opportunity . . . I'm a capitalist. I enjoy making money."[ii]

But still the most egregious examples of exploitation come from the developing world. In one example cited on Mexico, a man's casual shirt that retails for $32 in the United States, costs $4.74 to manufacture locally. Of that, $0.52 goes to the workers and $0.52 goes to the supervisors. With a retail price set at seven times the manufacturing cost and more than 30 times the labor cost alone, there is a considerable buffer to enable a modest wage increase without significantly affecting profits or the final retail price.[iii]

i Charlie LeDuff, "At a Slaughterhouse, Some Things Never Die," *New York Times*, 16 June, 2000, pp. A1, A24–5.
ii Sharon Walsh, "The Cheapest Handgun Was Loaded with Profit," *Washington Post*, 26 August 1999, p. A1.
iii Liza Featherstone and Doug Henwood, "Clothes Encounters: Activists and Economists clash over Sweatshops," *Linguafranca*, March 2001, pp. 27–33.

All this would not matter if the jobs created by investment at least provided a better life for low-skilled workers who previously had no employment at all. And it is precisely this term, "better life," which so often eludes consensus. For how can a Marxist uphold his claim to defend the poor if the defenders of the neoclassical view include not only economists, but also the governments of developing countries who need investment and resent the imposition of foreign morality and standards, as well as the poor themselves, who need to work at any price? Imposing punitive standards on poor countries will not feed hungry mouths. In response, from the Marxists and anti-globalization activists comes the grand appeal to create a universal system of standards. But such an agreement is a long way from reality. In the meantime the poor will gravitate toward the industrial parks, and the capitalist investors will exploit them. In the meantime, the poor will ignore the fact that not only is their income marginal to begin with, the abysmal working conditions and the long hours ensure that whatever dreams they are saving up for will have to be savored by their children. In short, they will ignore the tragedy of their existence. Like a race in which all the runners have very short legs, they will expend an enormous amount of energy just to reach a mediocre standard of living at a mediocre speed. For a Marxist, or any social progressive, it presents a conundrum. If he eschews the radical solutions—the mass protests, the threat or use of violence, or the grand transformation of society on new terms—all he can do is stand on the sidelines and condemn the illusory hope which the poor invest in their miserable jobs. The hope is an opiate because savings will not accrue, the debt to the smuggler who snuck them across the border will not be paid off, life will be short. In such instances, one can only conclude that the benefits of employment only make sense if they lead to a better life. And the criteria by which that life is measured must, by all accounts, take into consideration not just the income earned, but also the happiness (understood as the capacity to live a "decent" life) that is forfeited. As such, the relatively higher wages paid by the multinational subcontractors are meaningless when set off against the higher living costs and lower quality of life at the industrial parks. And they are unjust if they could be raised to a living wage without significantly impacting the firm's profit buffer.

Marx on poverty alleviation

Popular texts that predate Marx's turn toward economics in the mid-1840s also acknowledged that due to the capitalist's need to maximize profits the worker could rarely rise above a subsistence wage. "As the capitalist will always keep wages as low as he can," wrote the Rev. J. K. Black in *Conversations on Political Economy* (1828), "the laborer and his family can seldom command more than the necessaries of life."[35] But Marx distinguishes himself in at least three respects. Firstly, it was his conviction, right or wrong, that poverty could be eliminated with the demise of capitalism. Whereas bourgeois economists viewed poverty as "merely the pang which accompanies even childbirth, in nature as in industry,"[36]—a view still shared by a few economists to this day—Marx viewed it as a transitional and socially-determined function of the capitalist order. Along these lines, the cause of poverty was not natural, but a product of a system which denied the masses the full reward for their labor power.

Secondly, Marx argued that not only was it possible to alleviate poverty, capitalism was moving in this direction anyway, due to its self-contradictory nature, its tendency, through the immiseration of the proletariat, to create its own gravediggers. Unless addressed, class antagonisms would reach a crisis point, i.e., revolution, which would reconstruct society on a more equitable basis. Thirdly, the working poor were not just condemned to become passive victims of exploitation. Once they became aware of their power by means of political organization and a free, critical press, they could accelerate the move from capitalism to socialism.[37] Whereas even the most compassionate of the early critics of capitalism saw the poor as passive victims of a wretched fate, a fundamental tenet of Marxism is the potential for self-empowerment among the masses, based on the conviction that they can bring about change.

The fact that so many of the same particularly capitalist causes of poverty which Marx identified in the mid-nineteenth century still apply today does not necessarily imply that the radical strategies he proposed or inspired are equally valid. These strategies were more vaguely formulated than commonly assumed (such as the organization of a future communist society) or they were associated with specific contexts whose historical limits were often forgotten once they entered the Marxist canon (such as the call to violent insurrection based on the events of the 1848 revolution and the Paris Commune). But even if we grant that there has been a tendency to attribute certain historical developments wrongfully to his ideas—whether the communist states of Eastern Europe, the guerrilla insurgencies of Latin America, or the leftist terrorist factions of Western Europe—we might still conclude that the level of generality with which he approached the solution to poverty also left far too much latitude for abuse. This generality is most evident in his somewhat monolithic portrayal of the masses. It could not always accommodate the heterogeneity of poverty, and the diversity of worker interests and concerns. If, as Marx claimed, poverty contained a "revolutionary, subversive aspect which will overthrow the old society," we can recognize now that *how* the masses will respond to their so-called exploitation is far more important and far less self-evident than the *why*.

Violence and mass movements

As we have noted above, Marx did not condemn exploitation in moral terms. Rather, he attempted to show that this exploitation would eventually lead to growing immiseration until the proletariat would revolt, until capitalism would implode from its own contradictions, until socialism emerged from the ruins. In short, capitalism's exploitation of the worker would eventually lead to its own demise.

Since the beginning of the twentieth century, the upward growth in wages in developed countries (albeit a trend which has stagnated, at least in the United States, since the 1970s) has made the proletariat, to the chagrin of many committed Marxists, complacent and quietistic. Violence as a revolutionary strategy in the West, and particularly since the failure of the 1968 student movements, and 1970s terrorism, has become obsolete. In retrospect, the aspirations of the students were too utopian for a working class whose own aspirations at the time tended toward incremental improvement in their quality of life. However, in the developing world, where the majority of the world's poor now reside, the weapon of protest, terrorism or insurgency is still a very real threat to the capitalist status quo. When the avenues of political expression are blocked—due to the machinations of a self-interested elite, the weakness of unions and collective bargaining, or to the simple apathy and resignation of the poor—then the potential for unorthodox correctives presents itself. In Indonesia, in May of 1998, popular grievances resulting from the Asian financial crisis broke out into an all-out rebellion that eventually brought down the corrupt Suharto regime. In Colombia, during the 1990s, Marxist guerrilla groups, however morally repellent their fundraising tactic—from kidnappings to cocaine exports—gained a following in rural areas due to the widespread income inequalities, lack of land reform, and a government with little popular support. At its worst, violent revolution is a quick remedy peddled to an ignorant and poor populace with often horrible consequences. But it also reflects desperation reaching a critical breaking-point. Even when the threat of revolution is not carried out, the threat alone is often enough to force the government and ruling elites to address the concerns of the poor.

Short of violence, mass movements—sit-ins, strikes, demonstrations—have a long pedigree in the Marxist tradition. In the heyday of organized labor in the first half of the twentieth century, they were the prime vehicle by which workers exacted improvements in their living standards, particularly when voluntary concessions on the part of the employer were not forthcoming. More recently, after a long period of complacency, the grassroots protests against the World Trade Organization (WTO) and the World Bank/International Monetary Fund (IMF) in the fall of 1999 and spring and fall of 2000, respectively, and the recent American student activism against the use of "sweatshop" labor to manufacture apparel with college logos, all suggest the resurgence of direct action against the logic of capitalism. Yet, as in the past, much of the street violence, vandalism, and provocation of authority brings little direct benefit to the causes which its perpetrators advocate.[38] For corporations are rarely bothered by sit-ins and protests. They only respond if the protests threaten their corporate image among consumers, and thereby, their profit buffer.

The new breed of anti-globalization activists would also benefit from a more rigorous defense against the often compelling arguments of free-trade advocates and mainstream economists. As some have noted, the movement lacks the support of high-profile economists who could provide theoretical and analytical legitimacy for their cause.[39] Despite their passion and obvious outrage about exploitation, they have so far failed to articulate clearly a response to the most common mainstream defenses, i.e., that the wages paid by multinational corporations or their local subcontractors are generally higher than those paid by local independent firms. Consequently, any actions forcing divestment would make these countries and their people suffer more economically. In this chapter, I have outlined two possible responses to this defense:

a   to refocus the debate away from relative wages to relative savings to determine whether the relatively higher wages paid by the multinationals generate higher savings (particularly given the higher living costs at the industrial parks). Even given the complexity of collecting savings data, a body of evidence suggests that the wages often fail to meet basic needs.

b   to refocus the debate away from relative wages toward comparisons between a firm's profit buffer and the wages it pays. In cases where wage increases have little or no noticeable impact on sales or profits, but would have a significant impact on the living standards of the worker, a strong case can be made for offering workers a living wage. Although not legally obligated, corporations who fail to absorb these nominal increases—assuming they have the profit buffer to do so—are guilty of gross exploitation and are legitimate targets for protesters.

The utopian determination of value

A living wage exacted from multinational corporations, through a combination of mass actions, awareness-raising campaigns, consumer boycotts of sweatshop labor and dispassionate, well-reasoned argument, would go some way toward alleviating poverty in the developing world. But would it lead to a durable reform of capitalism? If the reform of capitalism is best achieved not through violence, but through targeting mechanisms intrinsic to the capitalist process (labor's generation of surplus, i.e., the profit buffer) are we then not regressing to the era of Bernsteinian revisionism, a strategy of piecemeal complacency? Any reconstructed Marxism, even one that renounces violence, must never lose sight of the utopian objective to make human social relations less dependent on market forces. Along these lines, we propose as a starting point that there is enough surplus wealth to subsidize public goods which would not legitimately survive in the free market. There is enough surplus wealth to pay wages above a subsistence level. There is enough surplus to invest in projects that fall outside the profit-oriented matrix of the market even in cases where the volume of revenue does not justify the expenditure, such as rural hospitals and transport. All this is perfectly feasible under optimal conditions of surplus wealth redistribution.

Underlying this observation, is a deeper human consideration about the nature of value. All public goods toward which surplus is directed have, of course, a market price. "Free" education still includes the salaries of teachers, the construction and maintenance of facilities, the purchase of books and materials. And the government that pays for it must act like any other agent—albeit a powerful one—when it contracts from the market to make its purchases. But the return on its investment is not formulated in terms of profit but rather in terms of its social benefit. This formulation applies not just to education but to all public goods—affordable health insurance, public libraries, and even prisons. The whole point then of surplus value—and herein lies its utopian dimension—is that its public distribution operates outside the framework of free-market decision-making.

This leads us then to a working postcommunist definition of communism. So far we have cited two definitions of communism. Marx's original formulation, "the abolition of human self-alienation," a definition which, as we argued, owed much to the Christian theological currents prevalent in German philosophy at the time; and Lenin's formulation which, in order to separate communism tactically from West European social democratic parties, argued for an authoritarian centralized apparatus and the violent overthrow of so-called imperialist states. Our third formulation is not original—it was coined by the French Marxist philosopher, Althusser—but its great strength is that it cannot be rendered obsolete, either directly or by association, by the historical failure of communist states. It states simply that communism is *the absence of relationships based on the market.* Althusser called this the "only possible definition of communism."[40] He went on to say that it is a definition true to the spirit of Marx, that aspects of it already exist in the modern world and, most importantly, that the Soviet state could never serve as an example of this definition. Beyond the Soviet state, beyond vulgar caricatures of communism that still inhabit the public consciousness, it is a fitting definition for the modern era in which market relationships continue to damage human relationships, and perpetuate poverty. The absence of relationships based on the market implies the presence of relationships based on values that are not dollar-denominated but socially determined. They may have a market price, but they need not deliver a financial return on investment. Investments in culture, health care, schooling, transport, public buildings and parks deliver not a financial but a human and social return. They are good in their own right. We may say that it is impossible to realize this goal fully, but it is not utopian to approximate it.

Finally, we may consider the individualistic corollary to the above definition of communism, one which lends itself less readily to a technocratic solution. This is the theme of self-realization through labor. The grand theme underlying Marx's economic analysis is the recuperation by the majority of mankind of its own capacity for creation. What this implies is not only that a greater part of the surplus generated by the worker should be returned to the worker—allowing him means beyond his daily subsistence—but also that job satisfaction be intrinsic to a happy life. In other words, every human being has the right to meaningful work. Mainstream economics—with its restrictive focus on growth rates and quantitative measures of utility—cannot accommodate more elusive criteria such as meaningfulness or happiness. Instead, it has a tendency to equate economic growth with some greater good as if prosperity were the sole indicator of communal well-being. The mantra of full employment, or, at least, jobs for the greatest number, generally ignores what kinds of jobs these people are fully employed in. Even when it makes distinctions between low-skilled and high-skilled labor, it tells us nothing of the highly skilled work. A data entry specialist in a software company may have a more sanitary work environment than a meatpacker, but in terms of the repetitiveness, and lack of scope for creative thinking or individuation, it represents an equally alienated form of labor.

Of the two utopian elements in Marx—that value should be tied to its social, not monetary, profit and that work should be personally fulfilling—the latter is clearly more elusive. While we expect that enlightened government can value goods whose provision is based on certain non-economic criteria, and subsidize from the surplus wealth generated by the capitalist system, it is much harder to envision a society in which everyone, or even the greatest number, expresses their unique inner selves through the labor process. It would imply a leisure society in which work were analogous to hobbies or other creative pastimes. It would imply a society in which the distinction between work and leisure disappears. Nonetheless, this utopian demand placed on labor—that it be individualized and spiritually fulfilling—is a useful standard against which the majority of the world's population must measure their own job satisfaction. In the Marxian system, happiness, defined as dealienated labor, remains the *sine qua non* of social reform. But just below that lies the more modest goal of reappropriating the surplus generated by the capitalist system. To have means, whether measured in terms of time or money, to enjoy beyond the labor sold to subsist, is the more immediate challenge that faces theorists, policy-makers, and activists looking to temper the severity of the capitalist system.

The utopian ideal advocates the right of the worker to a life worthy of a human being. Such an ideal can be contrasted with the animal-like existence of the many (willing) victims of global capitalism. Because such victims are deprived of the surplus created by their labor, because they only earn enough to re-create their dismal existence for yet another day, this ideal still has tremendous potency in the modern world. Furthermore, we can categorically dismiss Marx's radical communist alternative, not just in the facile sense that it did not work in practice, but in the more, in my view, truthful sense, that it was a function of his disenchantment with nineteenth-century politics. After all, with the benefit of hindsight, we now know that modern democracies can legislate on behalf of the have-nots. The motives for these reforms may not be entirely altruistic, nor are they necessarily initiated by those, the capitalists, whom they benefit least. Nonetheless, instruments of leverage, persuasion, or coercion can carve from the capitalist system certain spaces or arenas that are governed by human as opposed to market values. The absence of relations based on the market—Althusser's definition of communism— need not be, nor will it ever be, comprehensive. But it can develop in pockets largely fed by the judicious allocation of social surplus in the interest of social equity. The crucial point, from a Marxist perspective, is that these subsidies are not charity but a product of the surplus that exploited labor generates.

Poverty alleviation without Marx

It may appear that the global exploitation of low wage labor coupled with the continued presence of mass poverty and destitution in the developing world, particularly in rural areas, has created fertile ground for a reinvigorated Marxism. Nonetheless, once one strips it of all the theoretical baggage that has been invalidated either by subsequent economists or historical events themselves, one might well question what contribution it can make to alleviating poverty. Yes, Marxism can condemn the systemic and institutional causes of poverty, it can incite riots and strikes, it can sketch out a utopian synergy between the worker and his output, and it can demand that every human being receive a just share of the social surplus. But now, because the communist alternative has proved untenable, because the world is skeptical of radical social transformation, any postcommunist inquiry into poverty must make some compromises with the free market. This implies, firstly, that it must accommodate, very much along neoclassical lines, the motives and preferences of individual agents in the marketplace. It cannot, for example, just condemn exploitative wages outright without considering whether or not the worker has alternative employment opportunities, or how these wages compare with his or her previous ones. Just as peasants in medieval Europe or slaves in the post-Civil War south often voluntarily subjected themselves to serfdom (or sharecropping) rather than risk starvation as small farmers,[41] so today the rural population of developing countries often gravitates to the factory as a last resort. Secondly, a postcommunist Marxist critique must in certain cases take into account the criteria of market efficiency even as it condemns the moral abuses of the market. When, throughout the 1990s, striking Romanian coal miners regularly threatened violence and thereby gained concessions from the government, they were artificially sustaining a sector that the market had already determined to be inefficient and obsolete. Or, in the case of the welfare state, if high labor and tax costs in the name of social justice chase investment overseas, then the ideals become self-defeating. Not only does the state lose its critical tax revenue, it must also cope with the fiscal responsibility and the social costs of unemployment that results from industrial flight. As we noted earlier, there *are* arguments and strategies against the mainstream economic resistance to wage hikes but these should be advanced cautiously so as not to antagonize investment to the point that it withdraws entirely.

Even if the Marxist critique works within the parameters of a market economy, that is, rests content with its critical role—to move gradually toward a reduction of market relationships—it must still legitimate itself next to a host of policy prescriptions which share its ideals but not its tactics. There are, for example, interventionist strategies which share the goal of minimizing market relations and/or empowering the poor, such as redistributive taxation, microcredit programs, philanthropic contributions, subsidies on health and education, and private/public partnerships. All these, in various ways, help alleviate poverty yet have little in common with Marx's radical demands for social reform. And while most economists would agree that some level of government intervention is critical for addressing poverty, the recommendations vary widely from using state marketing boards to foster export-led growth, to more precisely targeted subsidies for social safety nets. Overall, the modern approach is technocratic, country-specific and value-neutral, refreshingly hesitant to apply blanket measures to a problem whose complexion varies enormously from case to case.[42] The question then becomes whether in these debates between, on one end, free marketeers who feel that poverty is alleviated by creating jobs and empowering individual agents and, on the other, advocates of statist and redistributive measures which do not, however, accommodate Marx's radicalism, there is still legitimate space for a Marxian contribution.

Job creation and income growth

Before we can reach some provisional conclusions, we need to review briefly some of the alternative strategies to poverty alleviation. Of the many arguments put forth by conservatives and free-market advocates on the problem of poverty—that it is an unfortunate but necessary by-product of the early stages of capitalism, that it is perpetuated by the irresponsibility of the poor (reckless procreation, laziness, alcohol and drug abuse), and that public programs for the poor are overly-bureaucratic—none is stronger than the argument that the best means to alleviate poverty is through fostering income growth. At least until the early 1980s, it was a general fixture of mainstream economics to link poverty reduction directly to high growth rates. The theory was that income generated through investment and the expansion of the industrial capacity would, through job creation, "trickle down" to the poor. The "trickle down" theory has been subjected to much derision by critics but, in its defense, it assumes only that man is happiest when self-empowered, when he can directly benefit from the fruits of his own labor. Along these lines, private investment that fosters job creation leads, in the long run, to a more satisfied populace, satisfied because its income is not dependent on charity or state welfare, but only on its own labor. Thus mainstream economics has tended to view increases in per capita GDP—the gross domestic product divided by the population—as positive indicators of economic development.

However, besides the fact that growth in per capita GDP reveals very little about how the new wealth is distributed, and often masks large income inequalities, it has been found that it had little overall impact on poverty alleviation. In 1983, at the height of the Reagan/Thatcher eras, Frances Stewart, a leading development economist, concluded, "The trickle-down strategy has been effectively demolished as a way of tackling poverty by the fact of increased poverty despite growth in income."[43] Even in those countries which have reduced poverty amidst high income growth rates, the connection between the two is tenuous at best. In the cases of Taiwan and South Korea, two countries often cited as models of income growth-led poverty reduction strategies, interventionist governments actively pursued policies such as rural industrialization and large investments in education and human resources (Korea, in particular, also benefited from the expropriation of large Japanese-owned landholdings after the war). And even when economic growth is accompanied by rises in income among the population, the income gains are often unevenly distributed not just among the classes but among different geographic sectors of the population. For example, Brazil experienced a spectacular doubling of its real GNP between 1967 and 1974, but the rises in income generally favored the urban educated. If one might still imagine that rises in income would enrich the state coffers from which the poor could draw public benefits, Mahbub ul-Haq, an adviser to the United Nations Development Program, again with reference to Brazil, provides a sobering corrective:

> Around 82 per cent of the health budget goes to high-cost urban hospitals that serve a small number of people—those who can afford to pay for the services—while only 18 per cent is invested in basic health services. University students are subsidized with public funds at a level 18 times higher than that provided to students in the lower grades, despite the fact that only one per cent of university students come from the lowest income groups. Thus, the rich and powerful absorb the lion's share of social sector spending.[44]

Thus, hidden behind the encouraging numbers are—very much in a Marxist vein—power structures that ensure that the benefits of growth accrue to a disproportionate degree to the wealthier classes. The evidence collected here makes a compelling case that, in the absence of enlightened state intervention, either income growth has little benefit for the poor or, in cases where growth increases social sector spending, the benefits are distributed disproportionately to the urban middle- and upper-income sectors of the population. And, foreshadowing our discussion in the following chapter, the linchpin of the problem seems to revolve around the state, a state that either intervenes in favor of the poor or ignores their plight.

The World Bank

> Our dream is a world free of poverty.
>
> World Bank Mission Statement

Even if the hopes vested in job creation and the trickledown theory now appear, at best, naive, and, at worse, immoral, it would be facile to set up an antagonistic polarity between a free-market apathy and left-wing compassion. It would be facile because, since the Second World War, a number of institutions have emerged to allocate financial resources and expertise to the problem of poverty in the developing world. Although there are many such institutions, the World Bank dwarfs all of them in terms of its financial resources ($28 billion lent to developing countries in 1998 alone, compared to $4.5 billion, the entire budget of the UN for social and economic problems).[45]

Founded in 1944 as an institution to foster reconstruction in war-ravaged Europe, the World Bank has since broadened its scope to the whole developing world under a specific mandate to "fight poverty with passion and professionalism for lasting results."[46] While, during the Cold War, it was often seen as a capitalist vehicle of conscience, particularly American, waging a propaganda war with the Soviet Union for the hearts and souls of the Third World oppressed, recently it claims to have adopted a more independent position. Now, less dogmatic in its thinking, more prone to an inclusive approach, and armed with a cadre of sociologists, anthropologists, and social sector experts, it actively seeks to be the prime mover in poverty reduction throughout the globe.

The World Bank is still in no hurry to forego its ideological affection for the free market. But it, along with many major players in the aid community, has come to recognize that money alone, whether in the form of loans or investment, has done little to alleviate the structural causes of poverty in less developed countries.[47] Instead, the process, they acknowledge, has amounted to the transfer of capital into leaky containers, that is, into corrupt or incompetent institutional environments that have squandered and

abused the funds received. Now, under such rubrics as "good governance"—
the promotion of transparent and disinterested institutional structures—and
"conditionality"—making the disbursement of loans dependent on institutional and policy reform—the World Bank is trying to adjust its policies to
better accommodate the poor. Microcredit programs—lending to small
entrepreneurs who lack the financial strength or collateral to secure funds
from conventional banks—have applied free-market principles to empower
the poor while at the same time fostering financial discipline and self-
esteem, two character traits which welfare benefits cannot provide. And in
response to widespread mismanagement of natural resource revenue by
African governments (Nigeria and its squandered petrodollars is the most
notorious example) the World Bank, in a pipeline project in Chad, has
recently pioneered the innovative use of escrow accounts (accounts held and
managed by a third party to ensure compliance with certain contractual
obligations) in order to guarantee that government royalties are targeted to
social sector spending, not private pockets.

However, despite these recent efforts, there are a number of reasons why
the World Bank's efforts to alleviate poverty have not had very promising
results. These range from an in-house incentive and promotion culture
dictated more by the need to disburse loans than to create an effective
project, poor oversight and follow-up on projects, and, despite its image of
cosmopolitanism diversity, an ideologically homogenous staff of mainly US-
educated economists still heavily under the sway of mainstream economics.
Lords of Poverty, Graham Hancock's highly critical study of aid and development agencies, provides many examples of the problematic culture of the
World Bank. In 1986, when then World Bank President Barber Conable
wanted to streamline operations and lay off 700 executives, it cost the bank
$175 million or enough to pay for the elementary school education of over
60,000 poor children. What is more, irrespective of the high cost of sever-
ance pay, it is notoriously difficult to fire anyone at the bank, most of all the
so-called "dead wood" of ineffective middle managers. There is no real culture of reprimanding beyond removing incompetent staff from line positions
and sending them further up the ladder, or into consultancy limbo. As for
general incompetence, here the bank's own self-critical assessment is damning enough. According to an internal audit carried out in 1987, out of a
representative sample of 189 projects worldwide, 106 or almost 60 per cent
were either "complete failures," or had "serious shortcomings".[48] Further
facts speak for themselves. Although it has lent a quarter of a trillion dollars
to developing countries since its inception in 1944, there are still one billion
people living in desperate poverty. Even worse, such lending has done little
to reduce income inequalities between richer and poorer nations which have,
in fact, doubled over the last thirty years.[49]

Despite these shortcomings, while both the World Bank and its chief
critics (at least on the left of the political spectrum) have poverty alleviation

as their main objective, the former can claim the higher ground in at least one respect. It is under routine pressure to make significant cross-the-board policy prescriptions which have high media visibility, and are highly sensitive to social and political repercussions. At times, these prescriptions betray the neoliberal faith in the benefits of economic growth, or a preference for reducing public expenditure rather than raising taxes. However, these criticisms notwithstanding, radical critics who employ emotionally charged rhetoric about exploitation and abuses of power, often without awareness of the local realities, expose themselves to the countercharge of naiveté and amateurism.[50] Although now both the World Bank and IMF are routinely subjected to grassroots demonstrations, during the April 2000 protests in Washington many of the activists interviewed by this author could only draw a primitive cartoon of the bank: a puppet in the hands of US imperialism and American transnational corporations. Many could not tell the difference between the IMF and the World Bank, had no awareness of the World Bank's extensive research into poverty in the developing world, nor an understanding of the considerable leverage which sovereign loan recipients have in how their money is spent.[51] This may have been a failure of the activist leadership, or its deliberate strategy (it is much simpler to generate hostility toward a foe with the use of caricatures). But given the level of ignorance, it is no wonder that, despite all their idealism and success in generating media attention, the extent of their disruption was primarily limited to blocking the commuter traffic around the World Bank and IMF buildings.

Uninformed radicalism faces an uphill battle to seriously challenge the bank, but informed radicalism *has* challenged the forward motion of policies that have a negative impact on the poor. A case in point is the structural adjustment programs (SAPs) which many developing countries embarked on in the late 1970s and early 1980s, under heavy pressure from the World Bank and IMF. In order to contain inflation and stabilize their economies, governments were encouraged to reduce social spending such as health, sanitation, and education programs, reductions that disproportionately affected the poor. And policies to develop cash crops for export to increase foreign exchange not only had a negative impact on the environment, they also displaced peasants in favor of capital-intensive plantations.[52] If, as the bank claims, poverty alleviation is its main objective, then the SAPs were a disastrous bungle of the highest order. The litany of damages, according to one expert referring particularly to Africa, was as follows:

> First, restraints on government expenditure were associated with a curtailment of public investment and therefore deteriorating infrastructure. Secondly, tight monetary policy, foreign exchange shortages, depressed expectations and deficient infrastructure led to reduced private investment . . . Thirdly, cuts in public expenditure per capita on education further weakened the human resource base.[53]

The World Bank itself glosses over this dark period by simply noting that, "in the early 1980s, policy-based adjustment lending overshadowed the bank's poverty reduction objectives," and then, goes on to note, "but eventually enabled the Bank to address more effectively the relationship between poverty and the policy environment."[54] Given that it encouraged the reduction of social safety net spending, it is not clear exactly what better understanding it gained of the policy environment appropriate for poverty alleviation. As we have noted above, the bank has now gone beyond simplistic linkage between economic growth and poverty reduction. Its understanding of development has evolved toward a more sensitive appreciation of the social costs of unfettered capitalism, and it has made strides together with their sovereign borrowers, to address these concerns. But on the whole, it remains ideologically hostile toward aggressive state intervention in favor of the poor, and often uses deceptive information to defend *laissez-faire* policies.

Because the World Bank has now positioned itself as an ally of the poor, and because it has orchestrated a consistent campaign to convince its critics that its free-market dogma is a stigma of its past, this is a serious charge and bears closer examination. To give just one example, in a recent study of labor issues around the globe[55] the World Bank argued against the minimum wage ostensibly to support the interests of the poor. Following mainstream textbook wisdom, it claimed that: 1) the minimum wage priced low-skilled labor out of the market, or forced employer and employee to bargain separately outside of the formal labor market; 2) that such measures have little bearing on the rural poor (the highest segment of poor), who operate in informal markets unprotected by the minimum wage; and 3) that it raised production costs thereby reducing employment. Each of these arguments can be proved or disproved depending on various country case studies, the only interesting aspect for our purposes, is the extent to which the bank operates from a flawed starting point. Instead of determining the basic wage necessary for subsistence and then fostering policies to achieve it, it constantly steers the argument toward the market distortions the minimum wage creates, or its macro-economic outcome. Its starting point is macro not micro, the broader investment climate, not the needs of the worker.

Consistent with mainstream economics, the bank argued that increases in the minimum wage negatively affect productivity, force lay-offs, and deprive workers of employment opportunities, workers who are, for whatever reason, willing to work at any price. In short, it argued that increases in the minimum wage, and minimum wages in general, are opposed to economic expansion and job creation. But recent research shows that there is "an increasingly weak link between the minimum wage and low-wage employment opportunities." Using models which expand the cost structure of wages to include intangibles such as recruiting, training, and motivating low-wage workers, a recent study by Jared Bernstein and John Schmitt has found that, while only marginally affecting employment opportunities, minimum wages in the United States have been an effective instrument to raise earnings of low-wage workers.[56] What this suggests is that in many cases profits supply a sufficient buffer for the employer to absorb marginal wage increases. It also suggests that, for low-skilled labor, wages are less related to the profits they generate than to the market price they command. They are, as Marx discovered, determined by the cost required to sustain the laboring power, but little else beyond.

Nonetheless, however much the World Bank remains loyal to the supposed iron laws of mainstream economics, it is safe to say that ideological constraints are now less obstructive to its work than political and administrative issues. The fact of the matter is, World Bank lending programs are generally the outcome of complex political negotiations between the bank and sovereign borrowers. In this climate, often clouded by a local culture of corruption, or by unproductive political wrangling within the bank itself, both bank and borrower often lose sight of poverty-reduction objectives. Furthermore, the bank is crippled by overlap and duplication of effort, a messy chain of command, resistance to reform, and member country "mafias" that promote their own regardless of competence. The bank is no longer a pawn of American imperialism, as many of its critics contend. But given these shortcomings, reform seems unlikely anytime soon. Given the bank's often legitimate criticism of its critics, i.e., that they do not understand its internal workings, perhaps it is best to conclude with a recent internal document, subsequently leaked to the press. In direct and undiplomatic language rarely heard at the institution, the bank staff summarize their woes better than any critic ever could:

> We are overburdened with growing, uncoordinated and un- or underfunded mandates that are given to us all the time. We are disheartened by the lack of any clear direction. And we are concerned that the management rhetoric of teamwork, culture, ethics, accountability, is the mantra adopted by senior management but which we see practiced far too rarely . . . Bank staff today are more demoralized than ever. This does not make for a productive environment in which staff can be challenged to work towards the important goal of a "world without poverty."[57]

Philanthropy

We have discovered that the mainstream paradigm of job creation and income growth has done little to alleviate poverty other than to keep the poor at or below the subsistence level. And even in cases where poor countries profited in aggregate from per capita income growth, the benefits both in terms of personal income and increased public subsidies were unevenly distributed. We have also seen that the World Bank, however sincere its anti-poverty commitment may be, has not sufficiently resolved its ideological and administrative problems to implement its poverty-reduction mandate effectively. If such paradigms or institutions have had mixed results, and if the non-Marxist is ideologically opposed to the reappropriation of surplus either by allocating a greater share of profits to the worker, or, more typically, via redistributive taxation, then appeals are often made for philanthropy to fill the gap. Philanthropy, or charity, is consistent with free-market ideology in that it invests the wealthy individual with the freedom and right to decide on whether and how he wishes his surplus income to be distributed. In contrast to taxation, which die-hard free-market advocates and many wealthy individuals see as a punitive charge for working hard, philanthropy is the main channel by which they *willingly* allocate their surplus to the worst-off.

In the most neutral terms, one's position toward philanthropy depends on: 1) one's faith in government to allocate surplus in the form of tax revenue toward the public good; 2) one's attitude toward both the right *and* competence of private individuals to disburse their surplus wealth among charitable causes effectively. These two points fundamentally conflict because, due to the tax incentives that foster philanthropy, any private allocation of surplus wealth automatically deprives the government of tax revenue. Thus, the real question is not whether wealth is available to alleviate poverty—it most certainly is—but whether private endowments do a better job than governments.

This is the fundamental question. One could catalogue at length the individual acts of goodness by the rich, and all the individuals who profited from them, but what interests us most are the structural and systemic benefits of this philanthropy. The fact is that despite the retinue of advisers who vet proposals and are supposed to prevent overlap, in reality the outcome of philanthropic giving is often eclectic, piecemeal and utilitaristic. There is a good deal of vanity mixed in with the altruism, a trend reflected in often disproportionate donations to elite universities (often the alma maters of the philanthropist), projects which offer commercial tie-ins or enhance the profile of the giver's corporation, or whimsical pet projects based on the personal interests of the donor. In the latter case, this means not only that the new breed of philanthropists wants its personal stamp on its choice of projects, but it also wants the gratification of power, of seeing a clear and simple link between their donation and its return. And even when the giving is relatively selfless, such as the tradition of church charity, the effects are generally stop-gap and temporary. Some charities will feed, others will clothe, others will feed and clothe, but provide little shelter, and all do so only at certain times and places. There is no contract, no legal or constitutional obligation, no system in place that would guarantee the provision of these goods over a long-term period and at a consistent rate. Instead, such measures are for the most part designed as a temporary reprieve from misery:

Christmas gift collection, the schoolchildren's canned food drive, the summer camp for ghetto children. All such efforts are not to be mocked. But they are at best a temporary balm.

The degree of philanthropy in a given country is often a direct function of the efficiency of the government redistribution of income and its commitment to social services. Europeans are quite rightly baffled by the emphasis Americans proudly place on voluntarism and philanthropy for the simple reason that these are normally duties charged to the state. Welfare states have naturally fewer philanthropic institutions than more *laissez-faire* countries because they tax surplus wealth more heavily. But precisely because such states have done a better job at alleviating widespread poverty, the burden of proof that philanthropy is an effective surrogate to redistributive taxation lies with those countries, such as the United States, that heavily rely on and incentivate it (through tax deductions). Ultimately, the problem is not only one of vanity, but also co-ordination and competence. For philanthropy, as a poverty alleviator, to be an effective alternative to government intervention, it must not only distribute an equal or greater amount of surplus, it must do so in a more efficient and targeted manner.

And this is an impossible task. Only a centralized body, with its centralized data collection, staff of experts, and nationwide network, can determine and satisfy systemic social needs. Even while acknowledging some of the shortcomings of the bureaucratic welfare state, there is still much to be said for the co-ordinated approach, one that harks back to the state socialism of Ferdinand Lassalle and Louis Blanc. In its untainted innocence, it expresses faith in the strength of collective wisdom, as reflected in this piece of Blanquist pamphleteering:

> Q: Why is it desirable for the Government to take the initiative in Social regeneration?
>
> A: Because it is too vast a work . . . to be easily accomplished by isolated individual attempts. It requires nothing less than the united energies of all, powerfully exercised by the most upright and intelligent. The Government undertaking to regenerate society is like the head consulting for the health of the body.[58]

After decades of massive state investment in poverty relief, our faith in the government as the sole locus of reform may be a little less absolute than Louis Blanc's, but there is a timeless validity to the notion that co-ordinated efforts of the best minds are more effective than the sporadic good wishes of volunteers. This central organ need not necessarily be the government, if wealthy individuals inherently distrust it, or feel that their wealth will be misallocated toward causes that they have no personal stake in. But then this is not a problem of government in general, but a question of the legitimacy of particular governments. For tax evasion and tax-free charitable giving will rise in proportion to the citizenry's mistrust of government to allocate their surplus wealth properly. But philanthropy is not the answer. It only reflects the inadequacy of the state and the vanity of the rich. In short, if the poor must be passive recipients of proactive benevolence, if hospitals and schools must appeal to a benefactor to receive medical equipment or textbooks, this represents less the good heart of fellow citizens than a failure of the state to distribute social goods equitably.

The common ground: the theory of human capital

The surest escape route from poverty—the poor's ability to accumulate human capital.

World Bank, *Poverty Reduction Handbook*[59]

As we have noted above, the Marxist view sees poverty in terms of systemic exploitation that deprives low-skilled workers of their rightful income. But the opposing view, that the poor are responsible for their condition and that in a market economy, hard work, discipline, and innovation will be rewarded, also has a certain credibility. Commonly then, the debate breaks down into a squabble about how to determine the boundaries of individual responsibility, and how to apportion blame. Wherever the Marxist sees a victim of economic injustice, the capitalist finds an autonomous agent who chooses not to work hard enough to improve his station in life. Wherever Marx blames institutional forces for the fate of the poor, the capitalist traditionally sees poverty as a natural fact of life, but one whose barriers are not insurmountable, given particularly the number of highly successful merchants and businessmen who have risen from the most humble conditions. These two views, the one monolithic, the other more individualistic, are at such loggerheads that the only way to find some common ground is to examine the issue abstracted from ideological prejudice.

One promising area of common ground seems to lie in what economists call human capital theory, the inquiry into the relation between a worker's income and the investment in his self-development, i.e., his human capital. Its origins go back as far as Adam Smith who noted that, "a man educated at the expense of much labor or time . . . must be expected to earn over and above the usual wages . . . the whole expenses of his education, with at least the ordinary profits of an equally valuable capital,"[60] and more recently gained a rigorous analytical foundation in the pioneering work of Gary Becker in the 1960s.[61] Human capital theory is, in one sense, ideology free. It simply states that in a free-market commodity prices are determined by relative scarcity, and the relative scarcity of skilled labor is higher than that of unskilled. Therefore, to improve one's wages, it makes sense to invest in education and training to acquire new skills. Underlying all of this is a meritocratic assumption: skills are not innate but acquired.

For Marx, self-development and self-realization lie at the heart of his philosophy, not so much in terms of achieving higher material reward, but in the more abstract sense of achieving satisfaction through labor. But the historical conditions in which he wrote led him to assume a rather static view toward unskilled labor. In the mid-nineteenth century, the proletariat was, in terms of its skill level, frozen in place. It had no access to education nor the means to pay for it. Therefore, the idea of human capital theory in terms of providing access to opportunity—although in a certain sense it has close kinship to Marxist ideals—was unrealistic under those historical conditions. Barred from any hope of self-development, the poor were driven to seek more radical solutions.

In the modern era of mass education, such opportunities are theoretically open to the poor. However, because poverty and inequality persist despite these opportunities, any hopes vested in them must be qualified by the numerous obstacles that bar access to their full enjoyment. Although we can make allowances for inequalities of beauty, health, intellect, discipline, etc., we can still conclude that access to opportunity depends on a number of factors that are class-dependent. For example, the US education system is often cited as an example of a meritocratic system, one which raises skill levels and therefore wages, and is available to all those willing to work hard, independent of their material wealth. Some have even argued that higher education, open to all irrespective of their background, has replaced income as "the arbiter of class position."[62] All this is true and yet, upon closer inspection, a number of material considerations do come into play when considering the relative access to such opportunity. When the poor go to college they defer entry onto the labor market. This means not only that they cannot contribute to the family's subsistence, but also that they must burden the family's financial resources. In addition, as part of their financial aid package, a stipulation of almost all but the wealthiest colleges is that one also works on campus. This cuts into study time and socializing, both of which are fundamental to the college experience. Furthermore, with the increasingly competitive entry to US elite universities, middle- and upper-income families now regularly employ private tutors to boost test scores for their children, a luxury few poor families can afford. Thus, there are a number of invisible barriers which create an uneven playing field. One can theoretically assume that investments in self-development will be rewarded through higher wages, but in practice these investments require a set of environmental and familial conditions independent of the factor of hard work, the rather prosaic determinant of wealth and poverty favored in the conservative perspective on poverty.

To gain the necessary skills and move into a higher paying position requires not only that such surplus generators as credit and education are available, but that the worker is able to forego wage payments during his or her retraining time. But many poor whose wages support a family cannot afford the luxury of not working. The point then is not that low wages are unfair (though if they are below subsistence level they most certainly are) but rather that the opportunities—through education and training—to move to a higher wage are not evenly distributed. One needs both time, understood as unpaid wages, *plus* the resources and/or the state-subsidized opportunities to advance that self-development. "Time," as Marx states

> is the room of human development. A man who has no free time to dispose of, whose whole lifetime, apart from the mere physical interruptions by sleep, meals and so forth, is absorbed by his labor for the capitalist, is less than a beast of burden. He is a mere machine for producing Foreign Wealth, broken in body and brutalized in mind. Yet the whole history of modern industry shows that capital, if not checked, will recklessly and ruthlessly work to cast down the whole working class to this utmost state of degradation.[63]

Despite its polemical tone, this is an uncontroversial statement. Time, either in the form of extra leisure, or in the ability to defer wages during a period of self-development, is necessary to accumulate surplus. Though they would not necessarily posit it in terms of an antagonistic relation between capital and wage, proponents of market-led poverty alleviation such as the World Bank make a similar point. Wage differentials depend on skill levels which in turn depend on education. Furthermore, access to education and the ability to pursue it depend on freedom from basic wants. Thus, we could say that below the primary good of education—the major benefit of surplus time and money as well as the major vehicle of self-development—lie a host of secondary basic infrastructure needs such as sewage, roads, health care whose existence does not necessarily enhance education, but whose absence certainly hampers it.

Finally, we should allow ourselves one utopian conceit. The enticements of capitalist consumer culture distort the working class's vision of its own potential, a potential hidden not in money but in time. It is time that allows the worker to nourish the familial bond, to interact with friends and acquaintances and, ultimately, through education and training to make something more of himself than he already is. But the poor are more likely to forego surplus time in favor of extra income. Though their wages may be low, they will often work longer hours and more days to compensate. In doing so, they may approximate the living standard of the middle class, and wear its accoutrements with barely disguised pride. Yet not many of the working poor will work fewer hours to attend night school and acquire a degree that will allow them to earn more money for a shorter working week. It is a rare case of will power that will forego immediate gratification in favor of future reward. No amount of structural reform can disburden the individual from that responsibility. Politically dictating a living wage, or the efficient redistribution of surplus, will not, in and of itself, refocus the individually determined priorities of the poor. Thus, the hope must remain that the poor are not only offered the opportunity to improve their human capital, but that they also understand the value of improving it.

Conclusion

Both Marxists and mainstream economists would concur that the individual's exit strategy from poverty depends on accumulating surplus, which in turn, depends on equitable access to social services. Where Marx distinguishes himself is in his skepticism about the ability of capitalism to reform itself *willingly*, and about the commitment of the state, dictated as it is by the interests of the middle- and upper-income sectors, to distribute surplus wealth equitably. Marx is uninterested in the effects of capitalist exploitation, he wants to go to the root causes which he finds in the wage system. Because the profit incentive conspires to keep wages for unskilled labor down, because wages are connected to the subsistence level basket of good rather than the value of the commodity produced, because that subsistence has a minimum toward which all wages drive whereas profits have no maximum, and finally, because no increase in wages or decrease in labor time will change the fundamental antagonism between capitalist and worker, he advocates the abolition of the wage system altogether. By this he does not mean to abolish remuneration, but rather a system where labor is a commodity in a marketplace that conspires "to sink the average standard of wages, or to push the value of labor more or less to its minimum limit."[64]

Although Marx saw the reappropriation of surplus value as the key escape channel from poverty, he held out little hope that this could be done through incremental measures, and least of all, if it were a negotiation process between capital and labor. Instead, radical political action would have to lead the way. Such political action would direct itself toward the kind of poverty for which there were answers. Thus, it would exclude the absolute poor, those who cannot work, nor make ends meet, and concentrate instead on poverty born of the theft of labor power. Once popular revolt had brought about the requisite changes, then the state would no longer be in collusion with ruling-class interests. It would either wither away or, through some form of central control, become a neutral arbiter administering public goods. The equitable access to these goods would allow for self-development and ultimately a style of life as envisioned in Marx's communist utopia.

In the following chapter on corruption, we will examine why the modern state often fails to redistribute surplus. If poverty represents the failure of the market to distribute goods equitably, corruption represents the inability of the state to compensate for that failure. It is therefore the logical next theme in our investigation. The baton now passes from *economic* to *political* science. In the capitalist system, the odds are so stacked against the working poor that there is frankly no economic solution. To reallocate surplus which the capitalist system generates, an enlightened state and political culture are required.

4

CORRUPTION

Politics is the only alliance by which contemporary philosophy can come true.[1]

K. Marx

In the previous chapter, all our arguments coalesced around the idea of social surplus and its redistribution. If it is unappealing to either expropriate property (because it is unlawful and dishonest), or return to the worker his personal surplus value (because it is so difficult to determine), then we are left with the more abstract scenario of social surplus. Along these lines, the surplus that the worker under capitalism generates but that, for whatever reason, cannot be returned to the worker directly (through better wages and benefits), can be reallocated by an enlightened state. A state, through the revenue it generates from taxation (a form of social surplus), can allocate funds to alleviate poverty and social strife. It can make public goods more accessible to the poor, and it can provide the poor with the tools to enhance their human capital and thereby their value on a free and open labor market. So why does this not happen? Why do we have democratic states grounded in principles of "life, liberty, and justice for all," that provide little if any means for the poor to better their lives? In the following chapter, we wish to address this dilemma in terms of the concept of corruption.

If poverty is the ugly face of unregulated capitalism, corruption is the ugly face of unfinished democracy. Unfinished because, though the liberal tradition has often viewed democracy as a set of *freedoms from* (most recently in the events of 1989—freedom from tyranny and the restriction of individual rights), the postcommunist experience has also exposed democracy as a work in progress, a set of *freedoms toward*, a process of building institutions that would ensure a more equitable access to the social surplus. This experience has presented compelling testimony that democratic principles—whether parliamentary representation, universal suffrage, or the sanctity of private property—are absolutely meaningless when superimposed on a nation without the proper institutions to enforce them or the proper culture to respect them.[2] What has emerged instead is a culture of cronyism, bribery, and abuses of power that operate under a covering mantle of democratic ideals —strongly proclaimed, and weakly enforced—a culture that not only delegitimates the state and public office in the eyes of its citizens, but also

95

hampers economic growth and the distribution of surplus wealth. This, the culture of corruption, is the specter haunting the global polity.

Just as poverty, in the previous chapter, served as a leitmotif to explore Marx's critique of capitalism, here corruption serves a similar function in terms of Marx's critique of democracy and the economic power structures that underlie it. Although corruption is commonly understood as the perversion of some ideal, as Hegel pointed out, corruption can actually appear in two forms: 1) the "abuse" of a system whose foundation is good (the common understanding); 2) a "great and general corruption" which infects the underlying foundation to its very core (the broader conception we will apply in our inquiry).[3] Hegel cited the Catholic Church at the time of the Reformation as an example of the latter case. Because it saw itself as the sensuous embodiment of God, Hegel argued, the Church had no incentive to seek a "higher spirit" outside of its own institutions. Instead, it sought it only in its rituals. "The Church, in its devolution to mere ceremonial observances, supposes itself to be engaged with the Spiritual, while it is really occupied with the sensuous."[4] From a Marxist standpoint, democracy in the service of capitalism has equally degenerated to a "grand and general corruption." While paying lip-service to the ideals of equality and justice, the liberal democratic ideologues fail to acknowledge that democracy has become but a capitalist veiling strategy for the embrace of its outer sensuous form, the liberty of autonomous agents to pursue their own self-interest. Working only within a narrow conception of freedom, they have abandoned the broader conception, the egalitarian ideals that lie at democracy's core.

In the history of political thought, it was arguably Marx who first provided a compelling case for a broad rather than narrow definition of freedom and democracy. He raised the issue of whether rights once declared and encoded in a liberal democratic constitution are also rights that are granted. And if they are not granted, then they must be historically achieved. "Liberation," Marx states in the *The German Ideology*, "is a historical and not a mental act."[5] The preconditions of freedom cannot be abstractly posited, they can only be formed in the *real* world by *real* means. There is no freedom, justice, or equality until people have adequate clothing, food, shelter, health care, and enough surplus to better their lives. Thus, not only does Marx rely on politics to reform where capitalism cannot reform itself—to, so to speak, realize philosophy by civilizing an alienated mankind—he also broadly questions the underlying premises of liberal democratic thought. Along these lines, a thought directed primarily at securing private liberties of the autonomous agent against an autocratic state, can only poorly accommodate the broader conception of liberty which has economics at its core. For Marx, the vested interests of capitalism that restrict, and benefit from the restriction of, economic emancipation of the working poor are such that only a radical transformation of society, through parliamentary or extra-parliamentary means, can wrest them from the powers that be. In a way, Marx's political thought speaks of little else. It is sketchy on what criteria dictate the choice of means, on how the proletariat will rule (or administer social goods), and ultimately, given the difficulties of distributing goods by way of a top-down command structure, on the role of central planning under communism.

But where it is quite explicit is in seeing socialism not as the opposite of democracy but as its fulfillment. Marx's political thought considered that the ideal of socialism equaled true democracy of which the liberal variant was only an intermediate stage. Indeed, even in countries with weak socialist traditions, such as the United States, the main objective of their socialist parties and progressive press has been to hold democratic institutions accountable to the ideals they professed. Their attacks on the establishment were motivated less by dreams of utopian communes, than by the ideals of "honest government," particularly faced with corrupt municipalities and a mainstream press beholden to corporate sponsors.[6] Similarly, we can eschew utopian schemes and still argue that democratic government should represent the higher ideals it claims to profess. In Marx's framework, this implies allying oneself with the fundamental tenet that the state, rather than serving monied interests, should serve the greatest number to secure the greatest freedom for all. While making allowances for the wide degree of interpretations on the role of the state, this tenet offers considerable latitude for the role of institutions in the distribution of socially determined goods. Or, to phrase this in even more neutral terms, we could say that the key question about democracy is not how to overthrow it but, following the political theorist Claus Offe, "to what extent market outcomes must be accepted (in the name of efficiency) or corrected (in the name of equity and justice)."[7] If the Marxian ideal of democracy is based on correcting market outcomes in the name of equity and justice, then corruption of that ideal would involve all those forces that impede achieving this objective. Intriguingly however, the reigning neoliberal orthodoxy takes exactly the opposite view. Within its narrow view of corruption, it assumes that the democratic ideal is hampered most when the private abuse of public power distorts market efficiencies. Thus, to protect these efficiencies, it argues that state must be withdrawn to the greatest extent possible from the market.[8]

Admittedly, after a century of turbulent swings between pro-market and pro-state visions of economic development (see box below) we are much more reticent about allocating any disproportionate power to either the state or the market. In terms of humanity's collective wisdom, we have passed beyond the bloated welfare state, beyond the fiscal and monetary instability of huge public debt, and beyond the repressive social engineering associated with the Soviet bloc and Asian communism. Yet, to remove the state from the market—to subordinate equity to efficiency—fundamentally undermines the ideals of democracy.

The weak state–strong state pendulum

In the history of twentieth-century political thought, there have been countless variations on the tension between freedom from and freedom towards. These have included Isaiah Berlin's distinction between negative and positive liberty, Hayek's distinction between freedom from coercion and freedom from necessity, Gramsci's distinction between the nightwatchman state and the Hegelian ethical state,[i] and, finally, more generic distinctions between *laissez-faire* and interventionist states. In all cases, they reflect two, usually opposing, views on the role of the state in ensuring that the social surplus be equitably distributed. Whereas the classical liberal position sees the state primarily as a neutral arbiter protecting individual rights to property, its alternative, which would include a wide range of authoritarian, predatory, state socialist, or developmental statist models, sees the state as a transcendent or collaborating authority regulating civil society on behalf of a self-interested elite, or the broader citizenry.

Of course, these two distinct positions are not as diametrically opposed as is often imagined. In times of war or national crisis, a nightwatchman state often adopts several characteristics of the ethical state in order to centralize decision-making better, and mobilize the general population. At other times in history, pro-capitalist states have adopted pro-labor interventionist policies to pre-empt social unrest (Gramsci refers in particular to the socially progressive legislation of the Bismarck and Disraeli regimes).[ii] In general, however, contemporary history seems marked by swings, often radical and violent, between statist and liberal visions of the political order. For example, in the aftermath of the First World War, decrepit monarchical regimes and their entrenched bureaucracies gave way to chaotic liberal democracies which in turn proved fertile breeding ground for the rise of fascist state capitalism. The end of the Second World War brought back liberal democracies with safeguards, particularly in former axis powers, against the resurgence of extremist elements, and introduced the added complement of supranational authorities such as the United Nations, World Bank, and IMF, designed to assure stability in an increasingly complex global environment. The 1960s and 1970s witnessed a revival of the activist state in developing countries as an instrument of modernization and in the United States and Europe as a social safety net, which in both cases led to a rapid growth in deficit-led public spending. This crisis then gave way to the Reagan and Thatcherite eras of privatization, low taxes, and weak government. Finally, in the 1990s, these two visions clashed inconclusively. On the one hand, the recognized social costs of neoliberal economic policies and the fiscal costs of lavish social spending gave way to the so-called Third Way ideology of Clinton and Blair, that melded traditional progressive concern for the have-nots with hybrids of both market-led and state-led experiments in governance. On the other hand, the so-called Washington Consensus—the trilogy of price liberalization, privatization, and currency stabilization pursued by the World Bank and the IMF (which had some success in Latin America in the 1980s)—had controversial results when applied to the biggest project of all, postcommunist Russia. Foisted on impressionable Western-minded reformers, it led to a criminal pilfering of state assets by insiders, widespread impoverishment as pensions and wages could not keep pace, with liberalized prices, harmful and volatile speculation and pyramid schemes, and a massive decline in industrial output. But the greatest irony of this whole episode is that the Washington Consensus, which claimed to represent the collective wisdom of capitalism, ignored one of the most understated ingredients of Western development over the past century, that the state by way of credit subsidies, direct support, and stimulus packages had played a critical role.[iii]

i I. Berlin, *Four Essays on Liberty*, F. Hayek, *The Road to Serfdom*, Chicago, University of Chicago Press, 1994, pp. 29–30, A. Gramsci, Selections from the *Prison Notebooks*, edited and translated by Q. Hoare and G. Smith, New York, International Publisher, 1991, p. 262.

ii A. Gramsci, Selections from the *Prison Notebooks*, p. 262.

iii For an informed critique of the Washington Consensus, see Ute Pieper and Lance Taylor, "The Revival of the Liberal Creed: The IMF, the World Bank and Inequality in a Globalized Economy," New School University, *CEPA Working Paper*, 4, January 1998. For classic treatments on the state's role in fueling economic growth, see Karl Polyanyi, *The Great Transformation*, Boston, Beacon, 1957, and A. Gerschenkron, *Economic Backwardness in Historical Perspective*, Cambridge, MA, Harvard University Press, 1962.

We can illustrate this briefly by developing further Hegel's distinction between the narrow and broad conception of corruption. In the narrow sense, corruption refers to the public abuse of power for private gain. Under corrupt conditions, elites benefit from and exploit their monopoly access to bureaucratic levers—e.g., export/import licenses, building or drilling permits, health, safety and environmental code inspections—to promote their own welfare or that of their clients of patronage. Bribes, kick-backs, and pay-offs circulate up or down a whole chain of authority. Whatever benevolent purpose a piece of regulatory legislation may have had originally is soon lost in a matrix of arbitrary decisions based on financial negotiations between the agent who seeks a permit or license, and the bureaucrat who grants it. And the criteria for judging proposals, projects, or license applications have less to do with their merit, than their hidden or unspoken price tag. It is not difficult to see the damage which systemic corruption does, not just to the legitimacy of the state, but also to all the social sectors that the state regulates. In the granting of licenses and permits, a byzantine dialogue ensues between impossible laws and either bribes to circumvent them, or falsified documents to comply with them. In the recruitment of personnel, often the most qualified or law-abiding individuals avoid state agencies by fleeing to the private sector or overseas.

The narrow definition of corruption adequately describes the diverse ways in which public power is abused for private gain. But, as an expression of the failure of democracy in general, it is far too narrow. It cannot accommodate the complex interdependence of political power and economic interests that lies at the heart of Marx's political thought. Currently, the reigning orthodoxy on corruption is motivated by a narrow conception, a package of Washington Consensus-style policies designed to remove the state from the economy. The mantra of the neoliberal advisers of the late 1980s and early 1990s, the Washington Consensus was coined in a seminal article[9] that, in the aftermath of the Latin American debt crisis, proposed a set of policies which the Washington establishment and its international financial institutions considered integral to policy reform. These included, broadly, enacting fiscal discipline, securing property rights, encouraging the privatization of state-owned enterprises, and the deregulation of economic activity. Divesting the state from public investment projects and privatizing state-owned enterprises, the neoliberals argued, would restrict inefficiencies and reduce the temptation for bribery by private firms seeking government contracts.[10] However, various ways of state reform, transparency building, and election monitoring notwithstanding, these limited measures will do little to ensure that the state adequately upholds the public good. Instead, advocates of this view end up endorsing an overly optimistic view of the market's ability to provide efficiency, and an overly cynical view of the state's ability to provide equity. Since they reduce all political behavior to rent-seeking, they have difficulty attributing any function to the state other than as a source of private revenue for self-interested parties.[11]

A broader formulation of corruption, on the other hand, would still uphold the state as the main vehicle for the equitable distribution of access to the social surplus. It presumes that there is a common good that society can strive for, and that removing the state from the process of achieving it will not increase, but lessen the chance of it being achieved. Along these lines, we define corruption not simply as the self-interested act of rent-seeking in the political arena, but more broadly as the failure of the liberal democratic state to uphold adequately the ideals it claims to profess.[12] Thus, our broad definition of corruption refers more generally to the vulnerability of states to market forces, to the power of capital, to the influence of wealthy voters and interest groups. In short, following Hegel, it refers to "a great and general corruption" in which the democratic polity has lost touch with its higher aim.

The public good

If we accept this broad definition of corruption, then we also need to define the nature of this higher aim, i.e., the public good. For if we do not define the public good, then it is unlikely we will be able to determine deviations from it. For our purposes, we will use the following definition, one which not only preserves the state's emancipatory potential, but also the individual liberties of civil society: the public good is the equitable distribution of access to social surplus. Given that there are so many different ways to define the public good, one could rightly ask why one definition, that is, the distribution of social resources for the benefit of the majority, should be preferred. There are two answers to this. Firstly, with the exception of maintaining a standing army and defending the national interest, the purpose of the modern state is nothing other than to redistribute wealth in kind to the greatest number. By in kind we mean the whole set of public services—schools, police, libraries, parks, roads, etc.—which are redistributed to the populace from their tax contributions. The criteria for allocating these resources, though often obscured in the process of parliamentary give-and-take, are generally populist in nature, in the sense that they are designed to provide the maximum benefit to the greatest number of people. And, in a rather matter-of-fact way, they are biased toward the poor. This is so because though the wealthy individual might pay more in taxes, he can afford private schools, private security, perhaps even a private oak-paneled library in his home. In fact, except for public roads, he may actually benefit very little from the considerable sums he donates to the state coffers. Nonetheless, in a modern civilized state, he accepts this burden and pays it willingly. Or, even if he does not pay it willingly, the mechanisms for enforcing collection are developed enough to make tax evasion more trouble than it is worth.

The second reason why the public good should be defined as equitable access to social surplus is that it is a function of the state's civilizing tendency. Following Marx, society's movement from alienation to humanization implies an increasingly complex understanding of what constitutes the basic human needs, needs which in the twenty-first century could be satisfied by a more equitably distributed social surplus. Through the nineteenth and twentieth centuries, democracy, step by step, responded to this sliding scale of increasingly complex needs. The increased political potency of organized labor and mass strikes, and the ability of marginalized citizens to speak effectively with their vote did much to squeeze concessions from the powers that be. Ironically, the era that earned Prussia the moniker of the first modern welfare state took place after not before Bismarck passed the 1878 anti-socialist laws. The consummate pragmatist striving to appease a restless underclass—and to take wind out of the socialist sails—Bismarck passed in the subsequent 12 years laws on sickness and accident insurance, and old age and disability measures. In short, the public good as answering to the needs of the majority is the appropriate definition precisely because it has defined the way in which the modern state has evolved. Even though the motivation may have been more about ensuring social stability than promoting the cause of the worse-off, as previously disenfranchised sectors of the population gained a political voice, the modern state responded and expanded.

Within that expansion, straying at times all the way to totalitarianism, critics have raised a number of concerns related to this broader mandate of the state. Hayek, working from an understanding of such a mandate, one in which the values of the community are placed above those of the individual, argues that this necessarily leads to compulsion to comply with the community's ends even when they contradict those of the individual.[13] Kolakowski argues that freedom is not about desire—that is, to have things which one might not otherwise possess—it is rather about individual choices which were denied citizens in those societies, overtly communist ones, that claimed to act according to the broader understanding of freedom.[14] But it is still possible to construct a more limited definition of that broader freedom, one that ensures equitable access to the social surplus, but does not impinge on individual choice. As the legal theorist Ronald Dworkin has formulated in a recent work, a complete democracy, one which makes equality an indispensable virtue of democratic sovereignty, can provide for equality through the initial outlay of resources, with citizens accepting responsibility for subsequent, freely made choices. What this implies is that although citizens should have equitable access to the social surplus, the state cannot provide for nor determine how they choose, or not, to take advantage of it.[15] The state, for example, can provide for a quality education to underprivileged minorities, but it cannot ensure that individuals of this group take proper advantage of it. It can provide for libraries and cultural centers in underprivileged areas, but it cannot force individuals to make use of them. Arguably then, within this narrower definition of a broad understanding of freedom there are not only safeguards against distorted attempts to level natural differences in talents and work ethics, there are also sufficient degrees of opportunity presented that any individual could properly take advantage of them.

If what is being described here appears like a form of enlightened paternalism, then that is the intent. Between the opposite poles of maternal coddling (of the full-fledged welfare state) and orphanhood (of the neoliberal ideal), lies an area in which the state recognizes its duty to provide an adequate environment for individuals to empower themselves. But simply choosing the mean between two extremes is often an overly convenient solution. After all, Western society has traveled down the road of paternalism before, often with disastrous consequences. Therefore, we need now to return to the Hegelian origins of the modern state, a time in early nineteenth-century Prussia when the ideal of an interventionist bureaucracy was seen as a panacea for a fragmented society. It was a time when, for the reform-minded Prussian elite, the state was nothing less than a *Kulturstaat*, a vehicle that would "embody the most progressive, most enlightened cultural values and would through its 'philosopher bureaucrats' educate the nation for higher purposes."[16] Indeed, although Hegel's idealized state was based on the limited experience of early nineteenth-century Prussia, his political thought presents a model for understanding the state in general. Amidst the lingering euphoria of the victory over Napoleon, at a time when Schinkel's neo-classical city planning gave Berlin some claim to call itself "the Athens on the Spree," a case can be made to call Hegel's Prussia, "the classical country of the modern bureaucracy."[17] Yet, subsequently, through the eyes of Marx, we need to also explore why this ideal state turned corrupt, why it transformed itself from a mediating institution between the public good and civil society into a self-perpetuating power in its own right. Only then can we establish some basic principles to ensure that the modern state remains accountable to civil society while upholding its mandate to serve for the public good.

Marx's political thought

The disinterested bureaucracy: Hegel's Prussian model

There are many ways to review Marx's engagement with Hegel's political thought, but for our purposes we will only concentrate on one of them, namely the category of universality, or more specifically, disinterestedness as it relates to the bureaucracy. A disinterested bureaucracy, one where self-interest does not impinge on public service, is essential to realizing the state's responsibility to work for the public good. Disinterestedness also lay at the heart of Hegel's statism in so far as the state could only claim, as Hegel himself did, to transcend civil society, if it had no ulterior motives (or self-interested pursuits) in the exercise of its authority.

As is by now familiar, Hegel's political thought revolves around a tension between civil society and the state. While civil society, as the realm of private property and economic exchange, forges a type of freedom for the abstract individual by means of the social roles he assumes therein, it is limited by the extent to which these roles are guided by particular ends. Instead, it is in the state—made up of the universal class, the bureaucrats, and the monarch, the state's subjective representative—where the citizen finds freedom as opposed to necessity, self-realization as opposed to self-satisfaction. Hegel's state is not only a neutral arbiter among self-interested agents. It is an active instrument of progress. It is the absolute and highest vehicle of historical progress. It is, as he famously said, the "Divine Idea as it exists on earth." Recalling our discussion in Chapter 1, the state is Hegel's God surrogate, an endpoint in history that embodies the higher aims of reason in a collective context. In more practical terms, this Hegelian notion translates into a statist political philosophy grounded in an elite and rational decision-making body which actively intervenes in civil society. One may or may not take issue with this position. But what is important for our purposes is that the universal, if not mystical, claims that Hegel attributed to the bureaucracy are derived from a particular historical reality, namely restoration-era Prussia of the first half of the nineteenth century. Thus, if we are to look for a model, however nostalgic, of a successful interventionist state that was relatively corruption-free, we need look no further than the Prussian period known as "bureaucratic absolutism."

The idea that Prussia could represent some kind of archetype of the Good State might strike Anglo-American readers as odd given the popular militaristic images of spiked helmets and stiff military officers who would, most notoriously in the Second World War, subordinate individual conscience to the demands of duty and obedience. Although the militaristic image of Prussia lingers, and may never be fully erased, the true picture is something slightly different. In fact, Prussia's influence on Germany, particularly as a forerunner to the modern welfare state, was more pronounced in the realm of bureaucratic efficiency than in military exploits. Yes, Prussia established itself in Central Europe through military expansion most notably in the eighteenth century under the stewardship of Frederick the Great. But, in the nineteenth century, and particularly between the so-called Reform Era immediately following the Napoleonic Wars and the 1840s when Marx and the Young Hegelians turned critical of the state, Prussia underwent a period of domestic consolidation and rapid economic growth. This era, which combined bureaucratic absolutism and protectionist measures to stimulate economic growth, is the historical context from which Hegel derived his idealization of the bureaucracy. Thus, at the time when Hegel spoke of the Prussian bureaucracy as the "universal class," when he placed the state at the pinnacle of his system, there were some grounds for such a lofty endorsement. "Between the Reform Era and the 1840s," notes one historian of Prussia, "the bureaucracy occupied a position comparable to that of Plato's guardian class . . . Officials saw themselves as Hegel described them, as 'the class in which the consciousness of right and the developed intelligence of the mass of people is found.'"[18]

The bureaucracy's claim faithfully to represent the public good derived from a number of conditions that during the early and mid-nineteenth century coalesced to create something close to an ideal state, one that enjoyed a wide degree of patriotic support, and cultivated a disinterested and meritocratic bureaucracy. The first condition that is often absent in corrupt countries but was prevalent in heavy doses in Prussia was a strong sense of national identity and patriotism among the civil servants. The War of Liberation against Napoleon, wherein the underdog Prussia defeated a superior French occupying army, particularly with the help of an inspired general mobilization, revealed to some extent the authenticity of that patriotism. It was reinforced, ironically, by the very artifice of the Prussian state. Patriotism was based less on a strong sense of ethnic self-awareness, like Bavaria or Saxony, than on a belief in the rationality and efficiency of the state as such. Prussia, we must remember, emerged on the Central European plain, not as an organic growth, but as a set of institutions constructed by the human will and imagination—in fact, by a charismatic series of Emperor Fredericks working through an efficient bureaucracy. As a result, the patriotism that undergirded this model bureaucracy was based not on tribal loyalties, but on a belief in rationality as the basis for enlightened rule.

Rationalistic patriotism was connected to two other conditions, namely the presence of a disinterested elite, and the cultivation of technocratic competence based on a meritocratic system of education rather than heredity. The disinterested status of the bureaucracy was encoded in the Prussian constitution of 1794, the General Law. It was considered in that system unique to Prussia as yet another *Stand*, or estate, but not an ordinary one. Civil servants did not have to pay taxes but—in order to avoid conflicts of interest—also could not participate in municipal or provincial self-government. Furthermore, unlike in England, Prussian aristocrats, who made up the bulk of the civil service, were not allowed to work in the private sector. Their professional life, outside their family agricultural holdings, was given over to state service, either in the military or the bureaucracy. Thus, safeguards were in place to foster a disinterested elite, firstly by generally restricting entrance to those with means enough not to be tempted by illicit gain; secondly by creating incentives—tax exemptions, a system of military-style rankings, awards, pins, and medals, and other ornaments that could appeal to the soldier-boy-within; and thirdly by the fact that the very absence of a parliament and political parties, that is, of democratic organs in general, allowed the bureaucracy to make and implement decisions independent of the often conflicting priorities of special interest groups in a democracy. Instead, entrance and advancement were based on technocratic competence. "The objective factor in their appointment," Hegel wrote of the bureaucrat, "is knowledge and proof of ability. Such proof guarantees that the state gets what it requires, and since it is the sole condition of appointment, it also guarantees to every citizen the opportunity to devote himself to the general estate."[19] In other words, the meritocratic emphasis in recruitment reinforced the harmony between civil society and the state. By attracting the most qualified citizens, the bureaucracy monopolized the decision-making apparatus of the polity.

According to Prussia's technocratic creed, politics was not a matter of winning a battle among competing ideologies, but simply rationally administering the affairs of the state. Without such a unifying ethos, as is lacking in modern corrupt polities, the state becomes a mere extension of civil society, albeit a particularly fruitful extension. It becomes the arena where the most powerful group or tribe can enrich itself. It becomes a breeding ground for kleptocracy and nepotism. In Prussia, on the other hand, the civil servants came from aristocratic families who entered public service for its prestige, or out of a sense of national duty, but rarely for reasons of economic self-interest. Such an example can be broadened to consider the positive role which elites potentially play in fostering a climate of disinterestedness. Not only are they financially secure, their status as the leading class confers also prestige and a sense of responsibility to safeguard the national interest. Because their authority and social position rests on the traditions and laws that also undergird the state, there is less of a conflict between their private interests and public obligations. In the Hegelian ideal, they are one and the same. But the modern element in Hegel rests in the fact that that unity was grounded not only in a synergy between noble birth and public responsibility, but between the meritocracy of education and the rule of reason. "Hegel," writes one expert on the Prussian bureaucracy, "was to give philosophic expression to this ideology of an official intelligentsia whose claim to right and recognition rested on its education and culture which promoted its own status characteristics as the very essence of the state."[20]

If all these conditions made the Prussian bureaucracy to a large extent adequate to its idealization in Hegel's system, why did Marx develop such a virulent anti-statist position in his critique of Hegel and especially if the bureaucracy had harmonized the interests of civil society and state? But according to Marx, not only did no such harmony any longer apply in his day, it had been in fact totally reversed. The state, rather than an objective embodiment of the public good, had become but one of many agents of the particular interests of civil society. And its self-anointed universalism obscured or "mystified" the fact that it was only a particular articulation of the interests of a particular class. In that sense, Marx's early demands for greater transparency and more democratic decision-making, which we will address in what follows next, are consistent with the typical agenda of the bourgeois reformer. Initially, his main concern was not social justice for the worse off, but the narrower goal of eradicating press censorship and democratizing political decision-making.

The public sphere and press freedom

Until Marx theorized radical means to make the state more responsive to the working class, he considered the main obstacle to disinterestedness in the Prussian bureaucracy to be its lack of transparency and accountability. A free, critical press was integral to ensuring that accountability. Indeed, in terms of his lifetime output, Marx was not only as much a journalist as a philosopher/economist, but his main contributions to political thought co-incided with a period of intense journalistic engagement as editor of the liberal daily *Die Rheinische Zeitung*. His articles from that period in the early 1840s dealt with legislative topics as discussed in the Rhineland Diet, such as its repression of the customary right of local peasants to collect wood for fuel on landed estates and, on the national level, issues of press freedom and censorship in the Prussian state. Above all, it was an attack on behalf of, not the proletariat, but the new breed of middle-class intellectuals who were outside the civil service and did not enjoy being lorded over by the bureau-cracy nor having their freedom of expression restricted. Marx's advocacy of a free press corresponded, at least in the German context, to the nascent stages of a *public sphere*, the coffee houses, newspapers, guilds, student organizations, and clubs that provided fertile ground for critical opposition to the state. Within this arena, and from his editor's pulpit, Marx challenged the bureau-cracy's control over information and knowledge, its attempt to insulate the decision-making process from open debate.

In an article from the *Rheinische Zeitung*, Marx elevated the press to a mediating institution between the general will of the state and particular interests of individuals. The press was the "head and heart" of the citizenry, the arena in which "rulers and ruled alike have an opportunity of criticizing their principles and demands, and no longer in a relation of subordination, but on terms of equality as citizens of the state; no longer as individuals, but as intellectual forces, as exponents of reason."[21] The press ideally mediates between the bureaucracy and the people because it allows the latter to voice their opinion from a position of equality. Rather than top-down decision-making, the press advocates consensus via debate, letting all sides air their views so that the bureaucracy can make an informed decision.

Thus, Marx's earliest political writings challenged less the undue influ-ence of economic self-interest among agents of the state than their dispro-portionate decision-making power. Appeals to delegate to the press and, more generally, the sphere of public criticism a mediating role between general and particular interests were a function of democratic yearnings among the educated middle class marginalized from the bureaucratic elite. Though such appeals seem conventional in modern terms, ironically this emphasis on the public sphere and its non-militant critical discourse has resonated longer and louder among twentieth-century Marxist or quasi-Marxist philosophers, notably Jürgen Habermas and Terry Eagleton, than his better known insurrectionary rhetoric. Even by utopian socialists of his day, such as Marx's later employer, the *New York Daily Tribune* founder, Horace Greeley, the press was seen as a vehicle to "mainstream" socialist ideas by creating mass awareness, and undermining the establishment's monopoly on information. Likewise, in Marx's advocacy of a free press, he was to attack the Prussian elite not for wielding the bureaucratic apparatus as an instrument of economic interest, but primarily for disguising its agenda behind a veil of universality and disinterestedness. When Marx speaks of Hegel's mystification, of the bureaucracy's attempt to "protect the imaginary generality of the particular interest,"[22] that interest is not of an economic kind, but of power in general. And that power manifested itself primarily as a petty form of careerism. As he argues in the *Critique of Hegel's Philosophy of Right*, "in the case of the individual bureaucrat, the state objective turns into his private objective, into a chasing after higher posts, the making of a career . . . the state only continues to exist as various fixed bureaucratic minds, bound together in subordination and passive obedience."[23] And even when, in the preceding sentence, he refers to the bureaucrat's materialism, he has in mind a particular kind of non-economic self-interest. "Within the bureaucracy itself, however, spiritualism becomes crass materialism, the materialism of passive obedience, of faith in authority, of the mechanism of fixed and formalistic behavior, and of fixed principles, views and traditions."

Political versus human emancipation

When Marx finally comes to consider the more abstract dimensions of political life, he continues to operate through a tension between civil society and the state, and human and political emancipation, a tension developed primarily in his early essay, "On the Jewish Question." Although the essay formally concerns proposed changes in the legal status of Jews, it expands to tackle a broader range of issues concerning the relation between state and civil society and between the rights of man as an individual and as a communal being. "None of the so-called rights of man go beyond egoistic man, beyond man as a member of civil society, that is, an individual withdrawn into himself, into the confines of his private interests and private caprice, and separated from the community."[24] As we saw in Chapter 1, within this schema the Jews are transformed from a particular ethnic group with a particular political agenda, to an antithesis of Christian and communal values. They are identified with egoism and materialism and a host of negative capitalist traits which can only be overcome by communism. "What is the secular basis of Judaism? Practical need, self-interest. What is the worldly religion of the Jew? Huckstering. What is his worldly God? Money. Very well then! Emancipation from huckstering and money, consequently from practical, real Judaism, would be the self-emancipation of our time."[25] While one could easily pause here to consider Marx's anti-Semitic tone, he is really operating in a matrix inherited from Feuerbach and the Young Hegelian tradition. In that tradition, the philosophical reading of Christianity implied seeking out its secular referents, its underlying moral code which could withstand rational scrutiny. Since, in a very dialectical sense, Christianity did not emerge in a vacuum but in and through its tension with an opposite, Judaism, this implied that Judaism also required a secular referent.

Likewise, it was impossible to simply expose the illusion of Christianity without salvaging its valid anthropological correlate. One had to salvage the residue, the alienated substance, which in the case of Christianity was the Incarnate God. Its human secular referent then became love, or intersubjectivity, or some sense of preconceived communality. "The so-called Christian state needs the Christian religion in order to complete itself as a state. The democratic state, the real state, does not need religion for its political completion. On the contrary, it can disregard religion because it is the human basis of religion realized in a secular manner."[26]

The real state of secularized Christianity must transcend the metaphorical state of secularized Judaism—the pursuit of mammon and practical need, the state dictated by the petty concerns of civil society. But if the empirical essence of Judaism, as Marx claimed, was huckstering and the pursuit of profit, and if the "practical Jewish spirit has become the practical spirit of Christian nations," that is, the world which must be transcended has been Judaified, then what would be the empirical essence of Christianity shorn of its mythic, alienating substance? From this essay, one can only surmise that the real state of Christianity would simply be everything that the Judaified world was not. It implies a society free of private property, of the social antagonism caused by the individual pursuit of gain, and a rather wooly Feuerbachian unity that would emerge once the rift between "man's individual-sensuous essence and his species-existence has been abolished." As the closing words of the Marx's essay declare: "the social emancipation of the Jew is the emancipation of the society from Judaism."[27]

The radical proposal to abolish egoism is based, in this early form, not on careful economic analysis but rather on philosophical concepts inherited from Hegel and Feuerbach. As we argued in Chapter 1, the introduction of economics into Marx's political theory takes place in terms of speculative theological constructs which, because they are so absolutist and vague—e.g., man must overcome egoism and unite with his species-being—ultimately lend themselves to radical political interpretations. It may well be that he never overcame the temptation of this secularized religious vision: de-alienating Christianity meant building heaven on earth which in turn implied overcoming its secularized earthly opposite, Judaism, understood as the pursuit of mammon. It meant that one could simply posit abolition of property as the answer to man's ills because this was the neat and formal negation of a Judaified society. The real Christian state could then be nothing but a state without property. In Marx's scheme, the ideal democratic state, the "real state," is one which communes with higher ideals that underlie the Christian religion, a religion which, under optimal political conditions, would no longer be required. The existing democratic state, on the other hand, was simply an ideological veil covering the egoistic pursuit of economic gain. In this distinction between the ideal and the real democracy, the distinction between human and political emancipation comes fully to light.

The new disinterested class: the proletariat

For all his lack of a unified system, Marx's political thought can still be divided into two very distinct phases. The first, outlined above, would encompass his critique of Hegel, his ardent advocacy for a free press, and his broad critique on the limits of political as opposed to human emancipation. The second would encompass the proletariat, its education toward self-awareness of its plight, its formation into a cohesive political force, and the means and tactics by which to seize power from the bourgeoisie. The essays of the early 1840s "On the Jewish Question," and "The Critique of Hegel's Philosophy of Right," arguably straddled these two phases for it is here that Marx introduces the proletariat as the universal agent of reform, one not yet rooted in economic science but rather in Hegelian speculative constructs.

The universality of the proletariat, as Marx argues in the "Critique of Hegel's Philosophy of Right", demands that its propertyless status should become the norm for society as a whole. "By demanding the negation of private property, the proletariat raises to the rank of a principle of society, what society has made the principle of the proletariat, what, without its own co-operation, is already incorporated in it as the negative result of society."[28] The demand to abolish property emerges from the propertyless status of the proletariat, its universal common ground. Property divides and feeds off the proletariat. Property has created the class which will destroy it. In short, property has created its opposite, an opposite that represents a total emancipation of the human being. Finally, this leads to talk of revolution. There can be no middle ground, not due to historical but purely philosophical, reasons.

> The thorough Germany cannot make a revolution without making a thoroughgoing revolution. The emancipation of the German is the emancipation of the human being. The head of this emancipation is philosophy, its heart is the proletariat. Philosophy cannot be made a reality without the abolition of the proletariat, the proletariat cannot be abolished without philosophy being made a reality.[29]

Although Marx's proletariat would become the principal agent in his theory of revolution, these closing remarks to "The Critique of Hegel's Philosophy of Right" contain little if any human, historical content. Philosophy has simply determined that the proletariat is the universal class, that it has replaced the bureaucracy as this class, and that its universality is dictated by the fact that it suffers the most, exists in the greatest number, and has the least amount of property. With its agent, the proletariat, in place, philosophy can realize itself. Its main objective is human emancipation which implies the self-negation of the proletariat. The proletariat, along these lines, ceases to exist, because the conditions that gave rise to it—capitalism, property, the bourgeoisie, etc.—have disappeared.

But how could this universality be shaped into a cohesive political force? Would it reform the state from within through a critical press and the ballot box? Or would it reform from without through barricades and mass protest? Marx seemed to adopt different views depending on the national context. In England, the United States and Holland, for example, the workers could potentially achieve their goals in a democratic political system. In more backward states with entrenched landed gentry, and a repressive autocratic regime, more radical responses were called for. As a late industrializing nation with an increasingly vocal working class, Germany provided something of an in-between scenario. It was here that Marx held out the most hope for "a dictatorship for the proletariat." "Between capitalist and communist society," he wrote in "The Critique of the Gotha Program," "lies the period of the revolutionary transformation of one into the other. There corresponds to this also a political transition period in which the state can be nothing but the revolutionary dictatorship of the proletariat."[30] For all the alarmist imagery that this term has conjured up over the past century, particularly under Lenin when it took on an explicitly tactical dimension in his political theory, we must not forget that in Marx the proletariat, as a universal agent of revolution, originates as a simple conceptual substitution for Hegel's bureaucracy. In fact, Marx's criteria of propertylessness as a sign of the self-less proletariat eerily echoes remarks by Hegel's contemporary and theoretician of the bureaucracy, Freiherr von Stein, "[the bureaucrats] are allied with none of the classes of citizens that constitute the state, they are a caste in their own right, the caste of clerks, without property, and therefore unaffected by its fluctuations."[31] Not that Marx's theoretical substitution did not have historical consequences. The philosophical grandeur of the German demanding human, not just political, emancipation implied concretely targeting the human basis of unfreedom that lay in an unjust economic system. To abstractly declare a new set of constitutional rights would not suffice. Only the radical sweep of a revolution by which the proletariat seized control of, and universalized, the state could ensure full human emancipation.

And yet the term "dictatorship of the proletariat," has a much more marginal role in the Marxian corpus than commonly assumed. Although Lenin called it—perhaps in a self-serving vein—"the very essence of Marx's teaching," it is anything but. In the 40 or so volumes of Marx's collected works, the phrase, "dictatorship of the proletariat," is used only eleven times. And, as revisionist Marxologists have for some time now exhaustively explained, the origins of the term dictatorship have little in common with its twentieth-century meaning, a meaning filtered through the legacies of totalitarian regimes. Instead, as the revisionists have argued, the dictatorship referred to by Marx derives from the Roman concept of *dictatura*, the extralegal and provisional government in a time of national crisis.[32] Unlike Lenin's elaboration, the definition did not rely on the oligarchical rule of a small elite, but instead presumed, however naively, that the prior mass education of the proletariat would make it, when the time came, fit to rule by means of an extended grassroots network of local councils. In short, the dictatorship of the proletariat was understood as the interregnum government between capitalism and socialism. Its extralegal character was a logical outcome of any postrevolutionary political culture when the old laws and institutions no longer applied and new ones had not yet formed. In those instances when it was used in reference to particular historical events, such as the revolution of 1848 and the Paris Commune of 1871, it conforms to precisely that description, a short-lived and extralegal form of government.

Now, it is true that the French Revolution, upon which Marx modeled much of his theory, had altered the Roman sense of *dictatura* in one crucial respect. Namely, whereas in the Roman republic interregnum rule was intended to safeguard the status quo, the Jacobins applied their dictatorial rule to shore up the gains of the revolution and install new institutions. The forward-looking nature of the new form of dictatorship implied the eradication of the status quo and its institutions. It implied a fresh start. Since it cannot be denied that such radicalism is implicit in Marx's original use of the term "dictatorship," the question then remains what is the meaning of "eradication" and "fresh start"? What levels of violence do they conceal? The answer to this question is, in many ways, contingent upon national historical contexts. But what remains clear is that the use of terror is in the Marxian lexicon something quite independent of the dictatorship of proletariat and, in any case, not central to that dictatorship, as Marx defined it. As for the violence associated with it, where it does appear in the writings of Marx and Engels, it almost always does so as a direct response to atrocities carried out by organs of the state. It was always Red Terror retaliating against White Terror. Even during the Paris Commune—which Engels famously singled out as the one true precedent of a dictatorship of the proletariat (dictatorship because it was temporary and extralegal) the reign of terror, culminating in the execution of the Archbishop of Paris and several other priests, was in response to atrocities carried out by government troops. The executions of the priests, however tragic, desperate, and pointless, pale next to the 30,000 Parisian protesters who were killed, not during the street-fighting, but during the mass executions that followed. In short, the violence either implicit in, or later appended to, the term "dictatorship of the proletariat," is in all cases couched in terms of a retaliation or response to violence perpetrated by the powers that be. Without apologizing for the ambiguity with which Marx coated the phrase "dictatorship of the proletariat," such a formulation allows us to distance it from the Bolshevik and Stalinist applications of the term. The Soviet state, as one bastard form of that dictatorship, betrayed the original Marxian definition.

Nonetheless, although the "dictatorship of the proletariat" may not imply the totalitarianism that vulgar critics assume, it rather naively does not contend with the possibility of serious opposition by elites to worker control over the organs of the state. If Marx and Engels were not necessarily advocates of violent revolution, they also do not explain how exactly the minority ruling elite would cede power to a majority even if this transition were legitimated through democratic elections. Their, at least early, cynicism about formal democracy in general, and universal suffrage in particular, is such that emancipation is only possible through radical socio-economic reform. But they did not explain how or why the educated and economic elite would democratize access to power. This lack of clarity leads one to believe that Marx and Engels not only assumed that these elites would not cede power willingly, but that they would naturally use all forms of violence under their control to resist challenges to it. And the response of the French police during the days of the Paris Commune only confirmed this view in their eyes. At best, one can say that the extralegality of that dictatorship was legitimated on the grounds that the whole notion of what was or was not legal was considered liquid in times of radical transition. More importantly, it was legitimated by the in-built determinism of their logic which granted the proletariat a natural, but as yet unrealized, right to rule. Injustices that oppressed a majority would be rectified by a majority made conscious of its oppression. Once conscious, they would enact change and, until new institutions were in place, by means considered extralegal by the ruling elites.

The withering away of the state

But if the workers took over the bourgeois state and its repressive military apparatus, what form of political organization would take its place? Would it be, for all intents and purposes, still a state, yet called by another name? The role Marx envisioned for the state, particularly as a vehicle of socialist transformation, is still highly disputed among his sympathizers.[33] Even those authors who detected a strong anti-authoritarian and anti-bureaucratic bias in Marx's view of the state were, during the Cold War, counterbalancing the legacy of Stalinism and prevalent facile notions of the "dictatorship of the proletariat."[34] Nonetheless, Marx's own formulation of the state gave wide latitude for conflicting interpretations.

The formulation is contradictory in many ways, partly due to Marx's lack of a systematic theory, to the variety of existing states from which he developed general theories (whether Prussia of the 1840s, or France of the 1871 Paris Commune), and to the evolving influence of workers' parties on the political establishment which affected his skepticism about the state's self-transformative capacity in general. All these ambiguities make Marx's anti-statist concept of the "withering away of the state" one of the most over rated and opaque in the corpus, over-rated because it was articulated vaguely at best in two places, briefly in *The Communist Manifesto*, and more explicitly, in the following paragraph from *The Poverty of Philosophy*:

> The working class, in the course of its development, will substitute
> for the old civil society an association which will exclude classes
> and their antagonisms, and there will be no more political power
> property so-called, since political power is precisely the official
> expression of antagonism in civil society.[35]

It is opaque because, whatever the withering away of the state may imply,
Marx constantly emphasizes the tension between man as a self-interested
individual in civil society and as a member of some superior sphere, the
sphere of community and common purpose. Thus, even if the antagonisms
of civil society disappeared, the resulting social structure would still be some
form of a state-surrogate, a political representation of unity, both transcendent and immanent within the citizenry. Yet, he never articulated what this
form would look like or why, most confusingly, it would have to be called
something other than a "good" or "better" state.[36] At best, we can say that
what was envisioned was not the abolition of a transcending authority, but
rather the abolition of an authority representative of the powerful classes
rather than society as a whole.

To create that better state was, however, a task that fell not to Marx but
to Ferdinand Lassalle. Lassalle, who founded the first German socialist party
in 1863, the General German Worker's Association (the forerunner to the
German Social Democratic Party) did exact concessions from the government, did effectively introduce a third voice into German political life alongside the liberal bourgeoisie and the aristocrats, one that by 1914 represented
a third of the German parliament, and ultimately, introduced many of the
principles embodied in the modern German welfare state. While Marx took
a principled stand against Lassalle's desire for compromise with the Prussian
state, given his general endorsement of socialist party activity in Germany,
one could surmise that his opposition was more a function of professional
jealousy (i.e., that while Marx remained a *persona non grata* in Germany,
Lassalle had usurped his place as a leader of the socialist movement) and a
personal hostility toward, specifically, the Prussian state. If we can presume
that Marx would have approved of the state's concessions to worker parties,
then the projected "withering away of the state" would simply represent a
point at which the antagonism between the state and the needs of the
worker has been reconciled. In the absence of class antagonisms, the divisiveness and partisanship of political life would wither away and, with a
consensus formed, the state would merely administer needs rather than impose an alien law.

Until not too long ago, such a concept would have seemed unfathomable.
But it now has modern resonance in our postcommunist era of moderation
and Third Ways, a time when we are beginning to question the endurance
of political parties as the once radically opposing classes these parties represented gradually merge toward a technocratic center.[37] And yet, optimism

may be premature. The 2000 US presidential election was, in many senses, a test of the state's ability to reconcile class antagonisms effectively. The barely victorious Republican party campaigned on an anti-Big Government platform which tried to paint the state as an intrusive bureaucratic behemoth that impinges on fundamental liberties, but particularly the liberty to spend one's personal income freely. However, as the Democratic party countered, and unlike the nineteenth-century state which Marx attacked, the twenty-first-century state far better represents the interests of the poor than the conservative free-market or anti-statist policies that proffer a mix of charity, voluntarism, and self-empowerment rhetoric to address the needs of the poor. This dramatic *volte face* in the perception of the state's role has not been a sudden event. Over the past 150 years, the regimes of Bismarck, Disraeli, and Theodore and Franklin Roosevelt, to name a few, have gradually realigned the priorities of the state toward a more inclusive mandate. What this implies is that, in a classical Marxist vein, the state does represent an era of class antagonism, but one in which it is ideally aligned not with the monied interests but with the poor and disenfranchised. For, as the 2000 elections remind us, and as the new Bush administration might reveal, if the state were to really wither away, to cease regulating, enforcing, and taxing to counter the abuses and social fall-out of capitalism, then the poor would lose their only ally.

Corruption in modern democracy

As we just noted, Marx did not envisage a state responsive to the needs of the working class. But history did not refute him entirely. Some states were responsive, others were not. It is for this reason, perhaps, that his model of proletarian leadership branches off into two quite distinct legacies, one, an elite-led proletarian insurrection which led to the Bolshevik revolution, Third World insurgencies, and leftist mass actions in the West, and secondly, socially progressive legislation within the confines of a parliamentary democracy which led to the European welfare state. Of course, although both strategies were tailored to existing historical conditions, neither seems to have accommodated the possibility that self-interest might perpetuate itself among the working class, either in the demagoguery of its leaders, the chronic exploitation *of* the state by individual welfare recipients, or the corrupt entrenchment of labor unions in the political process. These charges, popular among conservatives, have some merit, not least because they reflect the potential for corruption at all social strata, and, in many ways, the self-interested nature of our participation in the political process.

But this should not deflect from the overall concern, namely to transform the democratic state from a transparent vehicle of monied interests into one that equitably distributes social surplus for the benefit of the poor. Along these lines, Marx's relevance to the modern problem of corruption can best be explained by configuring contemporary polities as incomplete, unfulfilled or perverted democracies which fail to provide that equitable distribution. Marx, who saw true democracy or communism as a harmonization of self-interest and the public good addresses this problem not only through an economic critique, but also by reflecting on the means which the disenfranchised citizenry can apply to foster a more immediate link between their objectives and those of the state.

In what follows, we will examine briefly how Marx's critique of liberal democracy can be applied to three modern categories of corruption, categories, so to speak, that hamper the completion of democracy: 1) the arrogance of power; 2) the manipulation of subsidies; and 3) the manipulation of the electoral process. The arrogance of power is an outgrowth of Marx's critique of the Hegelian state, a state which, despite its best intentions, can often not remain disinterested from the temptations offered particularly given its access to the public trough. This category, though shades of it regularly surface in advanced democracies, is most prevalent in underdeveloped countries which seem to be particularly marked by systems of patronage and rent-seeking. The manipulation of subsidies and the electoral process is an outgrowth of Marx's emphasis on the class-based nature of the political decision-making. These reveal the susceptibility of the state to powerful class interests, irrespective of whatever democratic ideals may be encoded in its constitution.

Once we have sketched out these modern categories of corruption, we will then, in a subsequent section, propose and discuss some of the possible antidotes. Two of these, the realist and the de-monopolist position, both associated with the narrow neoliberal view of corruption, are distinctly non-Marxist in their approach. The realist, who assumes that politics is simply the pursuit of self-interest by other means, adopts a cynical perspective toward the efficacy of collectivist ideals in public life. The de-monopolist tends to find the root of all corruption in an overly zealous state and its bribery-prone bureaucrats. Therefore, they argue, the state, through privatization and de-monopolization, must be removed from the economy. Other antidotes draw heavily from certain key features of Marx's political thought: the critical role of the press and the public sphere to foster transparency and ethical state decision-making, and the openness to violence as a transformative vehicle of the oppressed, particularly when the oppressor has control over state-sanctioned forms of violence. And, finally, there is one antidote that, though very critical for the stability of the global polity, was neither mentioned nor foreseen in Marx's work. This is the supranational authorities that, in the name of broad principles of social justice, can and should impinge on national sovereignty when democratic ideals have been abused. They offer one of the best prospects to mitigate not only corruption but also the endemic abuses of capitalism.

The arrogance of power

As we saw in Marx's critique of Hegel, the state often hides its self-interested agenda behind a legitimating veil of universality and disinterestedness. To be sure, a unifying ethos can, under the proper conditions, guarantee disinterestedness; but, just as easily, it can be manipulated as a legitimating ideology for the powers that be. For example, in the postcolonial democracies of the developing world, many military coups legitimated themselves on the perception that civilian leadership, unlike the military, lacked the Hegelian sense of a national ethos and disinterestedness necessary for honest government. However, as many cases demonstrate, the military's anticorruption rhetoric in opposition is often blatantly contradicted once it assumes the reigns of power.

> As appealing and as simple as the military's answer to corruption may appear to be [notes one Africa observer] several decades of military rule in Nigeria, Ghana, Zaire, Sierra Leone, Uganda, Sudan, Somalia and many other African countries have conclusively shown that the military neither has genuine intentions, nor the capacity to stamp out corruption and other forms of official malfeasance. If anything, military officers have shown themselves to be more adept and more brazen in their corrupt practices.[38]

Indeed, particularly without the unifying force of an external threat, the military becomes just another self-interested and parasitical class that enriches itself from the public trough. In such cases, it not only abuses public trust, it also blatantly violates its own self-professed norms of honesty and duty to the state. While paying lip-service to these norms, the arrogance of power and the potential for private gain in most cases outweigh the pious and patriotic rhetoric.

The manipulation of subsidies

A more subtle form of corruption involves the manipulation of subsidies in favor of the politically most powerful classes, what we might call the class distribution bias. Here, the state is not necessarily in the hands of the wealthiest group, but in the service of the professional and middle class. We could say that this form of corruption occurs when wealth *legitimately* transforms itself into political power. In this category, we would place two related phenomena.

1   The widespread tendency for social spending in developing countries to favor urban areas and the middle class. Subsidies on transport, health, education, and public works become a commodity on a market of political

favors and rewards granted to the most powerful or vocal constituents. These constituents may not be corrupt themselves. In fact, they might even feel that they are acting in the national interest. In a developing country, a new modern hospital in the capital will be seen as a sign of prestige, and will provide care for urbanites, but it will be built at the expense of 100 rural clinics. In such examples, the wills of the politicians and their constituents coalesce in a seemingly legitimate manner.

2   The tendency for government subsidies to fall into the hands of the local ruling class, urban or otherwise. This can happen even when the government's intentions are socialist in character. For example, when the Vietnamese government established a subsidized lending program targeted toward rural peasants, it was the wealthier landowners—better informed, possessing more financial collateral and local political influence—who ultimately benefited. They would apply for and receive loans from the government which they would then relend to the poorer peasants at a higher rate.[39] Likewise, in India, the World Bank has reported that agricultural input subsidies, such as fertilizer, irrigation, fuel, etc., "have gone overwhelmingly to wealthier and agriculturally advanced regions and to larger farmers. They have therefore not been an effective anti-poverty instrument."[40] Such misallocations are not only a function of the higher volume and productivity yields of larger economic entities but also of their geographic placement and political clout. In terms of public investment in irrigation, villages closest to the water source benefit the most, and these tend also to be wealthier and more fertile regions. Likewise, large landowners often orchestrate the construction of publicly funded wells on their property. The case of India is not unique. But in all examples, the ruling class agents are not engaging in any form of illegal behavior. They are merely manipulating the state, the subsidy granting machine, to secure their self-interest.

The manipulation of the electoral process

Representative democracy relies not only on a bond of trust between the elected official and his constituents, but also on trust in the mechanism by which such officials secure power. But in the United States, the country most vocal in exporting democracy to the developing world, and most dogmatically defensive of the efficiency of its own system at home, the electorate currently expresses widespread cynicism and apathy, if not disgust, with the overbearing influence of high-income individuals, special interests, and corporate lobbies on the electoral process. According to a 1993 poll, 57 per cent of Americans thought that Washington was controlled by lobbyists and special interests. Another poll from the same year found that 33 per cent of those sampled thought that the offices of Congress could just as well be auctioned off to the highest bidder.[41] Indeed, the soaring costs of political campaigns due to the increased role of advertising, polling, and the new cadre of elections specialists, consultants, strategists, lawyers, press liaison officers, and issues advisers, has made election impossible without the financial backing of wealthy interests.

To be sure, not all wealthy individuals seek to impose free-market policies —tax breaks, welfare cuts, corporate incentives—on the electoral process. In fact, if the 1960s pitted poor activists against the wealthy establishment, the 1990s has witnessed the ascent of financially influential groups with often socially progressive leanings, such as the Hollywood film community, or the Silicon Valley hi-tech sectors. The problem, of course, is that irrespective of the shared ideological values that might be broadcast loudly at fundraisers, there are unspoken compromises, or at least perceptions thereof, which handicap the optimal impartiality of politicians. Implicit commitments are built into these networks of relationships that, no matter how pious the rhetoric, reflect the simple fact that donations usually come with strings attached. Thus, an ethnic lobby which might share a candidate's liberal or socially progressive attitudes toward education will reassess its support if that candidate adopts a less friendly foreign policy toward the lobby's mother country. Importantly, the issue here is not the inherent complexity of politics. Any successful mainstream candidate must harmonize a disparate range of constituencies to stay in office. The real problem is that, more and more, the decision as to which constituencies to alienate depends very much on their financial contribution to the campaign war chest, rather than their support in the ballot box. Along these lines, the Democratic Party which, up until the 1990s, had built its reputation on championing the causes of the poor and marginalized, and on the ability of government to address them, has been, perhaps irretrievably, stigmatized by its collusion with Big Money interests. By gravitating toward a nondescript political center, by opportunistically embracing whatever cause might secure the best short-term financial benefit, it has revealed the fragility of its commitment to the poor. This is not just a question of its hypocrisy, but rather of its over riding need to secure and sustain power. That, in turn, implies juggling a host of competing interests and preferences not just with blocks of voters but also within individual voters. The unemployed Kentucky miner who would support government funding for a local adult education center, may also be against gun control or same-sex marriages. The ex-'60s radical turned Hollywood mogul who would support the legalization of marijuana or a more lenient immigration policy, might also lobby hard to widen global distribution of American commercial cinema. Even "noble" special interests such as the National Education Association, the teacher's union, might use their leverage for self-preservation, for example, by lobbying against stricter and more frequent testing of teacher competence. Certainly, all these truisms of political life militate against any black and white solutions to the corruption of the electoral process. As Daniel Bell remarks, "What is left, what is right, what is liberal and what is conservative have all become jumbled as different political candidates rapidly shift ground, especially when, looking at public opinion polls, they claim to be responsible to the volatile expression of the voters."[42]

On the whole, however, capitalist interests stand to gain the most from influencing the political process in their favor. For they need to seize the power of the state to ensure that its power is not applied. Although they attack Big Government for its overly-interventionist policies, they need to take control over that same government—by either corrupt or legitimate means—to ensure that it does not intervene to correct market outcomes in the name of equity (such as raising the minimum wage, or improving safety and environmental laws). Unlike in Marx's day, the democratic state is no longer intrinsically opposed to the working classes. But its Achilles heel is its vulnerability to monied interests to shape and define its agenda. What Marcuse remarked in the 1960s still holds true today.

> The Left has no equal voice, no equal access to the mass media and their public facilities not because a conspiracy excludes it, but because, in good old capitalist fashion, it does not have the required purchasing power. And the Left does not have the purchasing power because it is the Left.[43]

In the capitalist democratic process money may just be an objective indicator of influence, but as long as that influence is unevenly distributed, the majority of voters will remain cynical and disenfranchised.

Antidotes to corruption

The realist perspective

> A political system in which the "people" expresses its "will" (supposing it to have one which is arguable) without cliques, intrigues, lobbies and factions, exists only as the pious wish of theorists. It is not observable in the West or anywhere else.[44]
>
> Vilfredo Pareto

The bargaining intrinsic to the political process leads us right away to a discussion of one of the prime antidotes to corruption, a simple denial that it exists at all. This perspective has a long and distinguished pedigree in the annals of political thought. From Sir Thomas More, Machiavelli, and James Harrington, through to the Italian Elitist school of Mosca and Pareto, and finally in modern public choice theory of James Buchanan and Gordon

Tullock, a powerful counterbalance to the foregoing Marxist account of corruption quite frankly accepts that politics is about power and power is about self-preservation. Along these lines, bureaucrats and politicians, in the economic parlance of the public choice theorists, are merely self-interested utility maximizers.

For those who adopt the realist perspective, Marx's contention that the state only serves narrow economic interests is far too limited. Social theorists like Max Weber and Vilfredo Pareto have argued that the influences that guide the behavior of the state cannot be reduced to economics or class interests alone. If anything, they are more about power structures and the interests of groups, many of whose allegiances cut across class lines. In the case of Weber, the bureaucracy cannot be classified as simply an instrument of the ruling class, but rather an autonomous structure of domination. In the case of Pareto, the complexity of elite behavior made an exclusive focus on class untenable. As he wrote in *Les Systèmes Socialistes*:

> The class struggle, to which Marx has specially drawn attention, is a real factor, the tokens of which are found on every page of history. But the struggle is not confined only to two classes: the proletariat and the capitalist; it occurs between an infinite number of groups with different interests, and above all between the elites contending for power. The existence of these groups may vary in duration, they may be based on permanent or more or less temporary characteristics . . . The shipowners combine to get shipping bounties; the retailers act in concert to crush the big shops by taxes; fixed stallholders cabal to prevent or hamper itinerant streetsellers; business men in one region unite to do down those of another region; "organised" workers to deprive "non-organised" workers of jobs; the workers of one country to exclude from the "national market" the workers of another country.[45]

It has been a staple of Marxist thinking to denigrate both Weber and Pareto as bourgeois apologists who deflected attention from the control of capital over the state by reformulating the notion of elites in terms of a complex rather than monolithic theory of class. Yet, there are countless historical examples that support Pareto—most famously, perhaps, the patriotism of German workers during the First World War that helped undermine the communist pacifist movement, or equally, the patriotism of the average blue-collar American during the Cold War. Marx certainly underestimated the range of sentiments—nationalism, ethnic and regional pride, etc.—that compete with class consciousness as a motive for certain types of action. More importantly, he seems to lack a theory of generic structures of power, structures which account for a large variety of non-economic forms of conflict, of gender, race, tribe, and creed, structures whose chemistry defies easy explanation partly because they are grounded in certain irrational and historically deep-seated emotions.

This is a legitimate challenge to Marx's political thought. Nonetheless, the realist perspective that accepts corruption as a natural fact of political life can accommodate neither any normative dimension to politics—that politics should serve the public good—nor the economic basis of its power. It does not hold the state and the political arena to something higher than it appears to be. Nor can it accommodate the possibility that public officials may have interests beyond their own self-interest and self-preservation. Admittedly, more recent variants of realism such as public choice theory emerged in the 1960s in response to overly romantic notions of what Big Government could achieve. But today many industrialized countries, and particularly the US, are living in an era of budgetary surplus where the mantra of fiscal austerity need not apply to, or at least, interfere with the state's ability to finance necessary public goods. If one abandons any hope that the state and public-office holders embody a higher purpose, then one is left with a realist's *laissez-faire* fatalism that delegates to the market the distribution of public goods, a service which it cannot equitably provide.

De-monopolization

Admittedly, the realist's argument is fortified by all the high-level officials who funnel the nation's oil revenues to secret bank accounts, who squander national resources on vanity white elephant projects or military toys, who dole out construction projects that are never completed, who award import and distribution licenses to family and friends. And they all do so because they have monopolized access to state resources, whether these are diamonds for Sierra Leone rebels, petroleum royalties for the Nigerian leaders, amphetamines and heroin for the Myanmar junta, or cocaine for Colombia's leftist insurgents. Just as capitalism has no in-built incentive to reform itself, neither does the weak or undemocratic state, particularly when monopolized access to wealth generation provides so many benefits to the few in power. If poverty alleviation requires an enlightened state to temper market forces, how can this be achieved if the agents of the state are equally susceptible to the temptations of profit? Are we attributing too much rationality to a mechanism that after all may simply be made up of self-interested human agents? And, if so, what can be done to restrict the range of self-interested choices by public servants who, whatever their real motives may be, profess an interest in alleviating poverty?

In the previous chapter, we concluded that only an enlightened state redistributing surplus in the interests of the poor could mitigate those ills which capitalism cannot or will not correct by itself. This conclusion vested much faith in the ability of the state to act as an arbiter of fiscal resources biased toward the worse-off. But such faith runs counter to the notion expressed by many theorists of corruption, particularly on the economic side, that the larger the state, the larger the potential for abuse of the public good.[46] As formulated by Mosca:

> The state control over the means of production would leave the administrators of the state—who are sure to be a minority—in a position where they should be able to combine all economic and political power in their hands and to appropriate the largest share in such a manner as would advance the career of their sons and proteges.[47]

Furthermore, studies by the IMF have regularly linked high levels of corruption to high levels of government intervention in the economy. The more discretion government officials have in private-sector transactions, such studies argued, the more temptations there will be for abuses of power.[48] An IMF study carried out in 1996 and based on interviews with 165 elite public and private sector leaders in 63 developing countries, found that over 80 per cent of the respondents favored deregulation and liberalization of the economy as a means to curb corruption.[49] Such results have been conveniently summarized under a formula provided by the leading corruption expert, Robert Klitgaard. It holds that Corruption equals Monopoly plus Discretion minus Accountability or $C = M + D - A$. Monopoly provides opportunities for state agents to enrich themselves, Discretion is the abuse of the monopoly for private gain, and the lack of Accountability refers to the absence of adequate oversight and monitoring either by the media or higher authorities.

Along these lines, mainstream or narrow anticorruption strategies are often linked to de-monopolization, a reduction of state intervention in the economy. But even when bureaucratic tasks offer so many avenues for enrichment—whether they be the granting of crude oil concessions and import licenses, or customs control—blocking these avenues may not necessarily restrict corruption. The problem may lie deeper, in a lack of loyalty to the state, low salaries for bureaucrats, laws that are so irrational and contradictory that they are easy to break with a good conscience, and finally, in a cynicism even among state workers that the state represents nothing but the cronyistic objectives of a particular elite. In short, restricting the state's role in the economy offers few guarantees that the needs of the public will be better administered. On the contrary, the majority of people, who would not normally be able to afford the goods that the state subsidizes, would be, and have been, disenfranchised once the management of these goods is delegated to the private sector and its profit-orientated definition of value.[50]

Such has been one of the lessons of privatization, i.e., the sale and delegation of state-owned enterprises to the private sector. Along these lines, while privatizing former state-owned companies can lead to greater efficiencies, just as often it can lead to chaos when applied to such public goods as transport, power, and sewage, that benefit from a strong coordinating and regulatory body. The privatization of British Rail into some 80-odd private companies led to highly publicized delays and accidents; the privatization of the Soviet airline Aeroflot in the 1990s ruptured the supply lifeline of many remote cities which, in market terms, were no longer profitable destinations. And, on a more general level, the true legacy of privatization in Russia will not be the new efficiencies promised by the foreign advisers, but rather the fact that two-thirds of the shares of the 16,000 firms sold in voucher auctions went to enterprise insiders.[51] Finally, when critical goods such as electricity or sewage have been privatized in the developing world, the market pressures on the foreign companies who are awarded these contracts often take precedent over any sense of responsibility to local poor who had previously benefited from subsidized rates. Then the shift from state to market is simply a shift from the maximization of bureaucratic self-interest to the maximization of profit.[52]

This is not to belittle the argument for efficiency, nor caricature the de-monopolist position. Greater transparency, accountability, and more effective systems of incentives and disincentives are all required to ensure that the state lives up to its responsibility. Furthermore, some economists who embrace the de-monopolist position still see a need for the state to regulate or even partially subsidize even when it is no longer a direct service provider.[53] But to deprive the state of its subsidy-granting power and hope somehow that other private parties will assume it, or to argue that access to public goods should be based on individual purchasing power, only opens the door to anarchy and sporadic pockets of comfort in an otherwise underserviced social sector.

The strong state

Acknowledging that a corrupt state and its agents cannot be a neutral arbiter does not mean that shifting responsibility to the private sector will improve the situation. Instead, the task at hand must be, first, to assume that the state is the only authority that transcends the profit-driven incentives of the private sector, and then try to establish means to control and foster that neutrality. In other words, the problem with the state is not its monopoly on services that should otherwise be delegated to the market, but rather how a state can legitimately uphold its natural and monopolistic mandate without turning corrupt.

As mentioned above, such faith in the state to harmonize and give direction to a fractured society runs counter to the widespread notion that minimizing the intervention of the state in the economy mitigates the potential for corruption. But a number of historical examples suggest that a strong state can transcend the divisiveness of civil society and promote the general social welfare, and in some cases do so without impinging on the rights of property or the fluency of free trade. The Prussian Customs Union of 1817, which dismantled a host of confusing and obstructive tariff barriers among the various principalities, was a product of an interventionist yet disinterested state. Likewise, Mussolini's government, though blackened by political repression and its unholy alliance with Nazi Germany, brought some efficiency to a corrupt and chaotic society, and did so, in the early stages, with the backing of a citizenry who had become disillusioned with an unsuccessful parliamentary democracy. An authoritarian state with a charismatic leader, a ruthlessly efficient mechanism of punishment and reward, and a clear hierarchy was seen as a disinterested transcendent polity as opposed to the messy arena of liberal democracy where, at least in Italy, the opportunities for corruption had been heightened not lessened by the multiplicity of decision-makers. Fascism was not the correct response to Italy's failure of democracy. But, by the same token, Italy in the postwar period seemed to learn few lessons from the fascist experience. In its wake, Italy reintroduced the weak state. Its Constituent Assembly, fearful of any one branch of government arrogating to itself too much power, made each equally weak, leading to a fractured coalition government which, through a system of party-political quotas divided up the opportunities offered by the management of government agencies. Instead of one authority acting in the name of the public interest, government became a set of clientelist and profit-seeking oligarchies.[54]

Tax evasion and the weak state

Given that the state's mandate is based on allocating social surplus for the public good, its failure to collect and efficiently redistribute tax revenue is a failure of the state as such. Under optimal conditions, the state raises revenue from the people it claims to represent and then distributes it according to priorities set by a consensus among the state's decision-making bodies. Though the people cannot track how each tax dollar is spent, there is a tacit expectation of a return in terms of public goods on the individual citizen's contribution to the state coffers. Once that return is no longer apparent, then the legitimacy of the state is undermined. As such, the level of tax compliance in a given country is a fairly good indicator of both the quality of a country's government and the legitimacy it holds in the eyes of its citizens. High levels of systemic corruption lead to low levels of government revenue, thereby undermining the purpose and efficiency of the state.[i] Why then does the state often fail to appropriate the social surplus adequately? The failure may lie in the mechanism of collection and enforcement, public perception of state competence, or simply, an indifference by the populace, particularly its wealthier members, toward public services in general. Weak states with often unequal income distribution suffer from all three factors. When, for example, in 1998 some 70 billion dollars of Russian money was transferred to the Pacific island of Nauru,[ii] one suspects that not only did the state fail to stem tax evasion, but also that those who made their money, either legally or illegally, in the era of wild capitalism, had no respect for either the state or the marginalized citizens, e.g., the workers on the state payroll awaiting long overdue paychecks, who might benefit from public tax revenue. Furthermore, because this class of tax-evading citizens is financially secure, they have sought private (and better) alternatives to public services. As a result, as the tax base eroded—the Russian government managed to collect only 50 per cent of its targeted tax income in 1997[iii]—public services fell into deeper disrepair. This example is not only a symptom of a weak state, but also of a sick and atomized society, one where there is no interest in public good, only private gain. We may or may not want to put the blame for this condition on an excessively *laissez-faire* market system. The point here is only that the *raison d'être* of the state rests on its redistributive capacity and is particularly favored to those who cannot access the same public services by private means.

i See, Vito Tanzi and Hamid Davoodi, "Roads to Nowhere: How Corruption in Public Investment Hurts Growth," *Economic Issues*, vol. 12, Washington, DC, International Monetary Fund, 1998.
ii "Tiny Island of Nauru Reinvents Itself," *International Herald Tribune*, 29 October 1999.
iii Valeria Korchagina, "Tax Man Pits Children Against Parents," *Moscow Times*, 2 September 1998.

In yet another example, the widespread notion that minimizing state intervention minimizes corruption could not be more false when applied to Russia. In hindsight, it seemed the ideal cure. The logic read: The Soviet Union imploded from its own bloated and corrupt *nomenklatura*. State ownership of industry had not only hampered the natural incentives for innovation and enterprise built into the free market, it had served primarily as a feeding trough for a new elite.[55] Thus, following the fall of communism, an aggressive policy of privatization was pursued. Unfortunately, rather than being an unbridled success for the free market, the case of Russia has illustrated how corruption and inequalities flourish in weak, non-interventionist states. As Stephen Holmes noted in a recent article on Russia,

An insolvent state, in the pertinent sense, is one that cannot extract, in a way that is widely deemed to be fair, a modest share of social wealth and then channel the resources extracted into the creation and delivery of public services, rather than into pockets of incumbents and cronies.[56]

If a state cannot collect taxes, guarantee property rights, enforce antitrust laws, and punish wrong-doing, in short, if it cannot provide basic services, civil society fractures into a myriad of competing power structures and private service providers who cater to the needs of the wealthy. And if there is no state to care for the worse-off and mitigate income disparities, then, as we have seen in Russia, the introduction of capitalism only benefits the pre-existing power structures. Since 1991, the rise in consumer prices has far outpaced the small gains in wages and pensions, leading to a situation where 80 per cent of the population has no savings whatsoever. The result: an estimated 45 million Russians have fallen below the poverty line while those who have benefited from the reforms, some 4 to 7 million people, have an average monthly income ranging from $500 to $100,000.[57] The blame for this social disaster cannot and should not be placed solely at the feet of the free-market reforms—but it can be placed squarely at the feet of those reformers and their foreign advisers who naively expected that the free market could alleviate poverty *without* the support of a strong state.[58]

In such cases of social instability, it is no surprise that the citizenry then waxes nostalgic for authoritarian leaders. Not just in Russia, where Putin, an ex-KGB operative, has revived retrograde structures after years of rampant anarcho-capitalism and the moral drift of the Yeltsin era, but also in mid-'90s Latin America where populist strongmen have re-emerged after faltering democratic experiments. In Bolivia, in 1997, voters brought back the former dictator, General Hugo Banzer Suarez. That same year, a poll taken in Paraguay found only 16 per cent of the population content with democracy in the wake of the dictatorship of General Stroessner.[59] In Peru, President Fujimori (since deposed) abolished Congress, and clamped down on guerrilla insurgents while still implementing free-market programs. And in Venezuela, a country that has squandered much of its oil reserves, the left-leaning former paratrooper, Hugo Chavez has taken power on a mandate to weed out corruption and help the poor.

The advent of such throwback regimes at the beginning of the twenty-first century raises a troubling internal conflict at the heart of democratic thinking, one that pits universal suffrage and majority rule against freedom of property and the press, and vibrant parliamentary opposition. In that sense, it reinvigorates the Marxian dichotomy between political and human emancipation. For such strong-man regimes reflect the fact that the poor are willing to forego abstract democratic rights (political emancipation) in the hope of concrete economic benefits such as land and housing reform and a more equitable distribution of public goods (human or economic emancipation). They vest their hopes in charismatic leadership that promises to stamp out corruption and regulate the oligarchical networks of power that operate freely in a weak democracy. One might easily counter that this is not the voice of reason but of desperation, the desperation of the impoverished and ignorant to whom the savvy autocrat can peddle unrealistic dreams. Yet, one could easily respond that, faced with a concrete failure of supposedly democratic organs to answer to their needs, the poor in such cases act in an entirely rational manner.

Violence

Whether rational or not, critics have used the appeal to violence or the extra-parliamentary authority of the strong state as a testimony of Marx's anti-democratic tendencies. "The difference between Marxist and democrat," wrote one such critic, "is that the latter believes it is possible to achieve economic change by peaceful political means, but that nothing short of revolution will satisfy the Marxist."[60] While allowing for ambiguities in the Marxist position on violence, this categorical contrast between Marxism and democracy could not be more patently false. It principally ignores the fact that Marx himself made no such categorical statements. Instead, he argued that both peaceful and revolutionary means could be applied to achieve socialist objectives depending on the socio-economic conditions in a given country. While he believed, for example, that reform through the ballot box could achieve these in advanced capitalist countries like Great Britain and the United States, in backward agrarian states under autocratic rule, he felt that violent revolution was a more apt solution.

As noted in Chapter 2, Marx's defense of violence rested on two main arguments. Firstly, in cases where the state, in order to secure its power, used violent repression, the masses were equally entitled to respond in kind. This premise has undergirded left-wing revolutionary theory from Lenin through the anti-colonialist ideology of Franz Fanon, to the more radical European terrorist groups of the 1970s, such as the Baader Meinhof gang and the Red Brigade. These historical examples are far too complex to address in full here. At best, we should only note that the legitimacy of their claims had generally less to do with formal legal arguments (when is state-sanctioned violence legitimate? When is violence against the state legitimate?) but rather with the degree of public support which these movements garnered. And the degree of support depended to a large extent on the graphic visibility of the crimes of their adversary, whether they were those of generic Western imperialism or of a national regime. Thus, violent opposition to the brutality of apartheid was easier to justify than the more dubious theoretical arguments used by European terrorists to justify their assassinations and kidnappings of corporate CEOs. The Marxist guerrillas of Colombia have gained some public sympathy from the extralegal acts carried out by right-wing paramilitaries, whereas the Islamic terrorists who bomb civilian airliners have had a more difficult case to make. Whatever moral credit their cause may have had is soon eroded by their indiscriminate killing of innocent civilians.

When we observe the Marxist tradition in broad historical terms, something similar has occurred. While violent rebellion was originally seen as a legitimate response to oppressive autocratic regimes who had the military at their disposal, and briefly gained even a kind of lyrical nobility during the Paris Commune, the subsequent Bolshevik and Stalinist abuses of state power in the name of socialist objectives forced a reassessment. To a certain extent, the Stalinist terror dwarfed to such a large degree whatever abuses were carried out by the state in capitalist countries, that the first argument for revolutionary violence lost all credibility, at least among social progressives in the West.

The second argument for violence against corrupt states could be called the "revolutionary outlet" argument. In cases where the masses are marginalized, because the legislative branch is either ineffective or infected by nepotism and kleptocratic links to its ruler, there is no outlet for reform other than revolution. But Marx did not really anticipate that the West European bourgeoisie would eventually grant a series of basic rights to the working poor, i.e., the rise of the social welfare state. In cases where reform seemed like an unviable option, Marx encouraged revolution not as spontaneous uprisings, but as movements orchestrated by a preparatory political organization. Such organizations would not impose their agenda on an uncooperative society, but rather harness historical momentum in their favor. Corrupt states would not simply collapse due to pressure from below, rather their own internal contradictions would give rise to conditions ripe for a revolutionary seizure of power. And, to this day, when resignation, anger and cynicism among the populace collide with the stubborn, if not smug, entrenchment among the elites, revolutionary uprisings ensue. The Cuban revolt against Batista in the late 1950s, Romanian revolt against Ceausescu in the late 1980s, and the Indonesian revolt against Suharto in the late 1990s, though each representing a different chemistry between the government and the governed, were all carried out in the name of direct democracy, the people's wakening to the illegitimacy of their state.

Watchdogs and direct democracy

Those wary of violence and anticorruption coups vest their hopes in strengthening civil society and providing teeth to the traditional watchdogs of the state, i.e., the media, advocacy groups, and public opinion polls of the citizenry.[61] As we have noted, Marx's ideal of direct democracy rested not only on the expansion of rights discourse to include economic freedom, but also on an active and educated citizenry debating common ends in the public sphere. Until recently, the aim of direct democracy has seemed elusive if not utopian. But the last decade, in particular, has brought about an impressive professionalization of grassroots movements and watchdog groups. While pursuing their original mission, organizations such as Amnesty International or Greenpeace have also efficiently "played the market" to recruit talented writers, lawyers, and researchers who are at home in the establishment while often ideologically opposed to it. Along these lines, mass movements in the form of mainstream non-governmental organizations have become, very much like the role Marx assigned to a free press, a powerful mediator between the marginalized and the decision-makers.

Likewise, the increasing sensitivity of decision-making to polling data, and the instantaneous barometer of public opinion provided by on-line surveys, also provide avenues for more direct forms of democracy. A case in point here is the hotly contested debate over taxation in the United States. In a recent CNN/*Time* poll, 74 per cent of the Americans sampled voted to allocate the surplus toward social security, rather than have the tax money returned; and in a related NBC/*Wall Street Journal* poll, 55 per cent of the public preferred using the surplus for "unmet needs" such as education, health care, and national defense, whereas only 34 per cent preferred a tax cut.[62] Assuming the government has some legitimacy, this preference has a majoritarian logic. Because the majority earns little income, they have more to gain from an improvement in public goods than they would from nominal personal tax relief. As a percentage of income, the lion's share would anyway go to the wealthiest class. The results of such polls may or may not impact on Congress's decision, but increasingly they represent a barometer of the public will that cannot be ignored. Furthermore, such polling data can gauge the public position on important issues more quickly and more frequently than can the two-, four- or six-year election cycle of the legislative and executive branch. Finally, polls circumvent entrenched structures of power to which congressional representatives are beholden and make an unmediated determination of social values. This type of direct democracy, even though it has yet to be institutionalized, is an intimate cousin of Marxian thinking. The state, assuming that it has credibility in the public eye, determines values on the basis of unmediated public opinion, and accordingly apportions resources to benefit the public good. This mediation of the public will through the empirical reality of polling data is a form of democratic state planning with few of its totalitarian implications.

Supranational authorities

Finally, to expose corruption in a given country is meaningless if the perpetrators cannot be prosecuted and punished. This implies a need to strengthen supranational authorities which can actively collaborate with the local watch-dogs and press. The United Nations, the World Bank, the IMF, the OECD, and powerful industrialized nations can all play a significant role in restrict-ing the private exploitation of public wealth. How is it, for example, that it took the Philippine government twelve years to secure the return of illegal Marcos funds, over $500 million, stored in Swiss bank accounts? How could the former dictator of Nigeria, Sani Abacha, store $654 million in 140 different accounts spread over 11 Swiss banks?[63] How is it that nearly half the total of Russian money stored in Swiss banks, close to $20 billion, was illegally obtained?[64] Even if we allow for the fact that drug cartels and organized crime will always find safe havens for their illicit profits, there is no excuse on the part of the West to allow states, and particularly poor ones, to be deprived of much needed revenue due to the greed of their leaders. Nor is it ethical to allow poorer states to suffer the mass depletion of fiscal revenues through tax evasion simply because they are not able to prevent it. Through supranational intervention and international co-operation, more vigilance could also be exercised to cut off illicit funding, either in the form of drugs or precious metals, for illegitimate insurgencies, those which, either on the basis of referenda or some other means, have been determined to have little or popular support. Since this implies not only the imposition of sanctions and boycotts, but also their efficient enforcement, there needs to be greater will among the wealthiest countries, particularly the United States, to relinquish fiscal sovereignty to supranational institutions that can execute this mandate divorced from partisan foreign policy interests.

Of course, to demand more vigilance on the part of supranational author-ities raises complex issues of national sovereignty. But even if the ideal of uniformly efficient institutions and governments around the globe is many years away, the first step is surely to prevent the complicity between West-ern banking institutions that legitimate illegal funds and the corrupt for-eign leaders who become their clients. However paternalistic and neocolonialist it may sound, sovereignty in that respect is a privilege not a right. Those countries that cannot trust their leaders with honestly managing public revenue, must have it managed for them. There should be little tolerance for puerile African leaders who, upon losing an election, take to the jungle and create further atrocities and instability in their raw quest for power. This is the sad truth of leadership in the developing world. Decades of Third World antipathy toward First World paternalism, whether in the military, com-mercial, or cultural sphere, have done little to generate efficient govern-ments that earn the trust of their citizenry. Decades of instability and immiseration, greed and arrogance, disrespect for law and equity in its policies and leadership, have irreparably compromised any moral credit the local elites had at the dawn of the postcolonial era. It is to that extent baffling that critics of globalization rarely include local elites and ruling officials as targets of their invective, for such elites share much of the blame for their squandered opportunities and the corruption that has befallen their nations. For this reason alone, the divisive North–South paradigm of leftist development theory is today obsolete in the field of politics. While it still holds true for the exploitation of unskilled wage labor, in terms of mitigating corruption, Western and supranational entities appear, in fact, to be the only hope of reining in corruption in states that cannot rule themselves.

Finally, supranational entities can regulate the abuses of transnational corporations which operate across liquid boundaries and often wield more economic and political leverage than the poor countries that host their factories. If it was once hoped that states could regulate capitalism by means of their domestic laws, now it is clear that only co-ordinated action on the part of supranational entities can encourage, if not force, these transnationals to comply with universally applicable labor and environmental standards. At this stage, most of such efforts—either under the auspices of the UN or the OECD—have only resulted in non-binding gentlemen's agreements. To arm these agreements with an enforcement capability would require not so much a change of will, as a change of mandate. This implies giving international organizations the authority not only to propose policy suggestions but also to police them. This is the major problematic shaping the new world order, a moment of hesitation and tension as nation-states deliberate how and whether to relinquish their sovereignty to supranational authorities in the name of universal ideals.

Conclusion

Just as capitalism does not reform itself voluntarily, neither does the state that serves its interests. Capitalism does not reform itself voluntarily because to raise wages, improve benefits, improve environmental standards, or make philanthropic donations, either diminishes profits or raises the retail price of goods or services. This erodes competitiveness and eventually leads to a firm's demise. Thus, capitalist firms adopt socially progressive measures only under the pressure of state regulation, primarily because such regulation is universally binding, i.e., does not demand unilateral self-corrections by any one firm in a competitive market. Equally, the liberal democratic state will not broaden its definition of freedom to include basic economic goods such as universal health care, will not weed out corruption and self-interest among governmental institutions that are supposedly serving the public good, unless the electorate demands it. Or, if the government is deaf to the demands of the electorate, then it will respond only if the people take to the streets and overwhelm the military. These basic principles stand as valid now as they did in Marx's times. They emerge from a realistic penetration into the power structures disguised behind the optimistic rhetoric of liberal democracy. As one contemporary observer remarks,

Marxism captures the real ontology of capitalism in all its various potentially transformational moments like no other system. In this regard, any realist appreciation of capitalism must bend toward Marxian insights, almost involuntarily. Marxism at its best, therefore, is Realism, and the good Marxist is one who keeps reality in focus as the determining factor of theory, rather than the texts of Marx, which can easily be turned into the pseudo-ontology of the Word.[65]

Following this definition, one might conclude that all too often, the most committed Marxists were not good Marxists. For good realism, honestly applied, would have to expose firstly the flaws of capitalism based not on sentimental gestures and protests, as many grassroots activists are prone to do, but on a thorough analytical understanding of their adversary. Yes, there is a moral component to any anti-capitalist protest. But, as Marx's disciple Kautsky declared, very much in the spirit of Marx's antipathy to sentimentalism, "With ethos alone, without a deeper economic and historical perception, one cannot get very far."[66] This implies that anti-globalization activists, especially the young anarchists who, at times, seem to possess more enthusiasm than education, must grasp not only the complexities of the institutions they criticize, but also the legitimate mandate of these institutions to stimulate investment, entrepreneurship, and fiscal responsibility, all essential properties of a robust society. Secondly, good realism would have to expose not only the vacuity of political emancipation in an impoverished, corrupt, or negligent democracy, but also how historically the Marxist goal of human emancipation has gone drastically awry. That goal provided communist leaders with a convenient mandate to trample on individual liberties in the name of an abstract and elusive New Society, one which never had nor could have a definitive shape, one which was always arbitrarily defined by the leaders and the party. In short, in the aftermath of the living communist experiment, no amount of revisionism can erase the tremendous human cost of these failed utopias.

Nonetheless, even if the goal of human emancipation is not entirely workable as a political objective, certain aspects of Marx's political thought can mitigate the crippling effect of corruption on the efficiency and legitimacy of the democratic state. The state as an instrument of monied interest can be transformed into an agent of the public good. And the institutions of civil society—the press and pundits, the watchdog groups, organized protests—can hold public office-holders accountable to the noble purpose they claim to serve. Finally, Marx professed the hope, however naive, that the citizenry would one day become educated enough to rule itself. Admittedly, in a complex modern society, there will always be a need to delegate the administration of the public good to a group of elected leaders. This perhaps explains why, with the exception of the Paris Commune (a model with limited modern application) Marx was never able to articulate the shape of a truly direct democracy, one without recourse to mediating institutions such as the state. But if a vibrant civil society holds them in check, these mediating institutions, of which the state is the most important, need not take on a life of their own. When held accountable, they can administer the public good, one defined, first and foremost, as attending to the needs of the poor.

5

BANALITY

When all economic misery and pain has vanished, laboring
humanity has not yet reached its goal: it has only created the
possibility of beginning to move toward its goals with renewed vigor. Now, culture is the form of the idea of man's
humanness.[1]

G. Lukács

If the masses are no longer poor, and their states are no longer corrupt, what
are the remaining barriers to freedom? What is freedom if you live a middle-
class life in an efficient polity? One might argue that it then becomes an
entirely personal issue, a task of setting and achieving goals, of finding
satisfaction in one's chosen vocation, of deriving pleasure from friends and
loved ones, and, ultimately, of realizing one's full potential. These problems,
a cynic could argue, became central to Marxism, its Western variety, only
when there were no others left to criticize. Indeed, as we learned in Chapter
2, when the most egregious abuses of capitalism had been reined in, when
states began to regulate and enforce, the Marxists began to look for more
insidious signs, the commodification of culture, the manipulation of desire
through advertising, the peddling of a false ideology that seeks status, self-
esteem, and personal worth in material goods. The cynic is right in the sense
that these questions only come to the fore when the more serious ones have
either already been addressed, or have been addressed enough not to arouse
mass protest. But that does not make them any less poignant. For Marxism
is not about negativity for negativity's sake, i.e., an uncompromising intel-
lectualism that can only criticize and find fault, it is about liberating the
creative potential of the human being through his or her labor. Yet, here
new obstacles arise. In the modern era, as greater productivity and medical
advances expand our lives beyond work, we are burdened with a new kind of
freedom: how to spend our leisure time. In turn, however, our scope to shape
this leisure sphere and find therein space for autonomous and creative
expression is perpetually inhibited by capitalist influences on the production
of culture.

Banality, which we turn to next, is the sum total of these influences, and
the most open-ended and elusive of our three themes. In its most common
usage, banality is synonymous with the trivial, the trite' and the unoriginal.

In fact, the banal is not just unoriginal it is tedious and off-putting in its unoriginality. At its most basic level, it refers to all subject matter that fails to transcend the ordinary, such as conversations on the weather, the daily commute, or personal computing. The banal also refers to the inauthenticity that derives from replication and simulation. Not all forms of replication are banal. Mass production has brought extraordinary benefits to the common man, but what is banal are those replications of cultural products that devalue and dumb-down our understanding of their original context and meanings, e.g., the impressionist reprints on dormroom walls, or the fake Greek columns on ranch-style homes. Finally, at the deepest level, the banal refers to all forms of de-spiritualized and impersonal human interaction. When Hannah Arendt coined "the banality of evil"—in a work of the same title on Eichmann and his role in the Holocaust—she was referring to the utter failure to engage humans as human beings in their sacred and immutable individuality. In its capitalist context, this tendency manifests itself in all forms of human interaction where the individuality of the human agent is replaced by the generic fact of his or her purchasing power; where, in terms expressed by the early Marx, Being is replaced by Having; when the human value of the agent is replaced by his or her dollar value as consumer. Collated, all these various definitions of banality add up to the condition of culture under capitalism.

Under capitalism, banality is to culture what poverty is to economics and what corruption is to politics. All these negative terms, or obstacles to freedom as I refer to them, play off their opposite. In the case of banality, it plays off a concept of an ideal culture, a culture untainted by dollar-determined value and de-humanizing forms of leisure. As we reviewed in Chapter 2, the Marxist tradition of cultural criticism, as a corollary to the tradition of romantic anti-capitalism, was built on the contrast between culture and technology, reverie and rationalism, on essentially an ideal of culture besieged by the fragmenting and de-humanizing effects of industrialization. Among early twentieth-century Viennese intellectuals such as Lukács and Weininger and the members of the Frankfurt School, it emerged as a high culture response to capitalist mass production, and the corruption by science and technology of the arts. They pitted the pettiness of functionalism against the grandeur of creative thinking, specialization against the generalist knowledge of the cultivated individual, in short, the Philistine against the Renaissance man. Today, much like *fin-de-siècle* Vienna, we are similarly living in an era of unprecedented technological dominance, one that, besides the medical and scientific benefits it has offered us, is obsessed with time-saving gadgetry, hyperconvenience, and consumption. It is, as the philosopher Weininger wrote of early twentieth-century Vienna, a "time without originality and yet with the most foolish craving for originality."[2]

In the postmodern era, we may be more aware that the world of capitalist culture has turned liquid, transient, and ephemeral, that borders have melted between high and low culture, that savvy corporations rapidly co-opt and reproduce the countercultural, and that the lifespan of consumer tastes and fads has shortened dramatically. Worthy critics have documented this phenomenon with the appropriate sarcasm and panache. But ultimately, it is a dead-end street if we do not have some understanding of what should be happening, if we do not take a step back and consider what purpose, if any, an ideal of culture should serve. Without a hierarchy of aesthetic values and a hierarchy of leisure structures in which to appreciate them, in short, without criteria to judge between good and bad culture, any notion of an ideal culture (understood as one relatively free of banality) is meaningless. This essentialist vision does not mean that culture should be repoliticized; only that it should recuperate its utopian, even elitist, dimensions which postmodern discourse has tried so hard to eradicate.

In order to restore some meaning to the concept of culture, we might then be well served to begin with some basic distinctions. For Lukács, in many ways the founder of the Marxian variant of romantic anti-capitalism, culture was simply "the ensemble of valuable products and abilities which are dispensable in relation to the immediate maintenance of life."[3] While some might find the broadness of this definition limiting, it has two advantages. Firstly, it places the discussion in terms of a simple dichotomy between basic and surplus needs. Thus, whatever else we might say about the concept of culture, this distinction rather aptly captures the sense in which culture is that realm of surplus needs which not only separates humans from animals, but also, in broadest terms, encompasses all those extra dimensions that make our life worth living beyond basic survival (entertainment, friendship, family, love, etc.). For Marx, this realm of culture as surplus time is the end-goal of his theory of emancipation. "A man who has no free time to dispose of," he noted in *Value, Price and Profit*, "whose whole lifetime, apart from the mere physical interruptions by sleep, meals, and so forth, is absorbed by his labor for the capitalist, is less than a beast of burden. He is a mere machine for producing Foreign Wealth, broken in body and brutalized in the mind."[4]

Secondly, this broad definition of culture incorporates an already modernized form of Marxism, one that transcends class distinctions to embrace the oppressive lifestyles of not only the marginalized poor, but also the majority, working middle-class. As the American media perennially uncovers during an election year, the dual-income couple's greatest concerns are not relations with China, space exploration, or agricultural subsidies but simply how to get more sleep and spend more time together. In that sense, the plight of the urban poor is tragic, but that of the suburban working couple is sad in a different way, given that the life they lead—deprived of leisure time, sensuality and ecstatic moments—upsets the middle-class logic of deferred gratification. That logic promises rewards that never materialize. In preparation for their adult life, they studied hard, got the right degrees, yet ultimately ended up with a soulless life full of a kind of routinized hectic energy—commuting, petty chores, interspersed with rigidly scheduled "quality time"—in order to sustain the relationship. These everyday life questions elude political solutions but they are clearly a function of our capitalist society, one where, contrary to the adage, time is not just equal to money, it is worth far more. For money cannot ennoble the spirit, develop a personality, or enhance our understanding of the world around us. Only time can provide for this. And however much the working man of any class strives toward that day when he can retire to his hobbies or passions, that day remains entirely elusive or comes too late. Culture, as the realm of surplus needs, clearly then depends on a certain amount of time in which to enjoy it. Conversely, deprivation of time impedes not only our satisfaction of surplus needs, but also the self-development required to explore higher forms of culture. With this basic definition in place, we can proceed to define what constitutes good and bad culture, and how this distinction is, to a large extent, determined by capitalist logic.

Again, we might say here, by way of preliminaries, that some consider that postmodernism has rendered obsolete the distinction between authentic and inauthentic culture. It is true that, whatever its other faults, the postmodern sensibility was a helpful antidote to the cultural elitism of the early generation of critical theorists such as Adorno and Horkheimer. To write off mass culture and the culture industry in conspiratorial tones, in terms of dichotomies of manipulators and manipulated, of a profit-seeking elite force-feeding cultural goods to stupefied masses, is far too simplistic. It not only ignores many of the good things in popular culture or, for that matter, many of the bad in high culture, but it also discounts the autonomy of individuals to make consumption choices about their cultural goods. Nonetheless, postmodernism may have gone too far in the other direction, advocating an aesthetic free-for-all, and over-relativizing the criteria used to judge cultural forms. Admittedly, while it is easy to mock the sterility of pseudo-italianate suburban villas, or "revived" historic districts, the eclecticism of the postmodern, particularly urban environment, demands that each experience of that environment be inherently subjective. But this is not to say that we should fully adopt the postmodern viewpoint and simply delegate judgment to the experiencing subject. However much the postmodernist may want to disagree, there *is* a hierarchy to experiencing subjects and the quality of their aesthetic appreciation. And it has an indisputable empirical basis: the quality of one's perspective on culture and its goods is a direct function of one's experience and education, all, in turn, a function of how one exploits one's leisure time.

Marx's culture theory

If culture is the sum of things that ennoble man beyond the satisfaction of his basic needs, the question then becomes: what kind of culture ennobles man? Because Marx left no systematic work on culture or aesthetics, and since he provided few clues to the leisure structures of the postcapitalist world, the answer to this question is quite short. Marx's view of the liberated man enjoying his surplus is dilettantish and individualistic. It is *against* specialization and *for* the well-rounded individual. In communist society, there would be no painters, just people who, among other things, paint. In the absence of a profit-incentive, man would work toward developing his creative faculties, pursuing interests that enrich his life and provide extra dimensions to his personality. Human relations would be free from the corrupting influence of money.

But beyond this simple hope, a number of themes and concepts are imbedded in the Marxian corpus that later lent themselves to a variety of cultural theories. Although Marx left behind no systematic treatise on art, two separate traditions of Marxist culture theory evolved, in the Soviet bloc and the West, respectively. The two traditions are radically different and can best be distinguished by their contrasting agendas, one optimistic the other pessimistic. The cruder of the two is the optimistic form for the simple reason that, as it evolved in the Soviet Union under the rubric of Socialist Realism, it undermined both the critical and the individual dimension of art in favor of uplifting and transparently propagandistic narratives that furthered state interests. Alexandr Zhdanov, Stalin's commissar for culture, spelled out the objectives of Socialist Realism quite clearly:

> to help the state to rear our young people correctly, to answer their need and questions, to bring up the young generation in a spirit of optimism and faith in its cause, to make it unafraid of obstacles and ready to overcome all obstacles.[5]

Socialist Realism traces its legacy back to nineteenth-century realist portraits of the common man, and a certain critical fatigue with the self-indulgence and pessimism of literary modernism, but in its Soviet form it became but a caricature of art. To this day, even with the benefit of hindsight and the more sober assessment it allows, there is little good that can be said of the pompous, oversized celebrations of the common man, the tedious unidimensional dramas praising pipelines and tractor factories, the crude mythologies to socialist sacrifice which characterized this tradition at its height. As a result of this legacy, even in the West, a critical aesthetic which bemoans, perhaps correctly, the continued cynicism, self-indulgence, and over-use of irony of contemporary art has not yet been able to proffer a viable *optimistic* counterbalance. Not only is the tainted legacy of Stalinist socialist realism still so overbearing, among the cultural consumer there is an ingrained wariness of politicized art forms, those that wear their righteousness too openly on their sleeve.

Instead, the more vibrant dimension of Marxist cultural theory is, and has always been, its negative form. In the twentieth century, theorists drew their inspiration from two main sources: 1) the early Marx's Feuerbach-influenced theory of alienation; 2) the theory of commodity fetishism as developed in *Das Kapital*.

The theory of alienation

Marx's theory of alienation, as described in the *Economic and Philosophical Manuscripts*, was outlined in some detail in Chapter 1. Here, suffice it to say that Marx's theory evolves from a critique of Hegel, and particularly his notion of alienated self-consciousness. Consistent with his objective of liberating man from the opiate of religious mysticism, Marx roots self-consciousness in a sensuous, nature-bound relation to labor. Though conceding that Hegel also acknowledges that labor is the source of man's self-creating, Marx claims that, "labor as Hegel understands and recognizes it is abstract mental labor."[6] In Marx's view, however, this is extremely limiting. Because most people are not philosophers, but rather workers locked into a struggle for survival, really the only alienation worth speaking of is the alienation of man from his own labor. If one has no control over the product of one's labor, as is the case of the unskilled wage laborer, then one is rightly alienated from one's power of creation or, to say the same thing, from oneself. Thus, the transcendence of alienation would imply a blurring of the distinction between work and play, a world given over to leisurely pursuits as part of one's aesthetic education. If one were to remove the economic dimension, that is, the revolutionary task of transforming capitalism into something more benign, then one would be left with a vision of labor similar to the romantic Schillerian ideal. Modeled on ancient Greece, that ideal posits a vision of the free individual who is fully formed, who does not work, and has the leisure and the means to cultivate all his latent capabilities to their full extent.[7]

We might agree that this vision of the monied aesthete is a sensible and appealing notion of the good life. And we can find this appealing even while recognizing that it depends on a considerable aesthetic education, one which gives the subject the motivation and discipline to pursue his or her interests without distraction from other more easily digested leisure goods. It is a vision wherein each person is a producer not a consumer, active rather than passive. The point here is that, although Marx correlates the transcendence of alienation to an economic and political process—the revolutionary transformation of capitalism—in fact the vision he paints of the restored man could not possibly be fulfilled in economic terms alone. As a result, once the concept of alienation is extended beyond the workplace, there is a danger that it loses its explanatory value. For then, what of all the other forms of alienation, the fact that we suffer, struggle, and die, that we often yearn for things, people, or talents we can never possess? Or what about the views of non-Marxian sociologists such as Mannheim or Weber who relativized economic alienation in the context of a host of general negative symptoms of modernization? In their view, technology and modern forms of power all work to separate the individual from control over his labor. In this broad schema, the soldier is alienated from his weapons, the jet-bomber pilot from his victim, the civil servant from the instruments of his rule. We can readily see that defining alienation as simply a mediated and obstructed relation between a subject and object quickly becomes a rather unwieldy concept, a generic catchall to define the predicament of man in general. As Daniel Bell rightly pointed out as early as the 1950s, the greater the scope which Marxist sympathizers attributed to the alienation defined in the early *Economic and Philosophical Manuscripts*, the less distinct it became.

> The themes of alienation, anomie, bureaucratization, depersonalization, privatization have been common coin in the sociological literature for more than a decade and a half. In the light of all of this, the recent attempts to proclaim the theme of alienation in the early Marx as a great new theoretical advantage in the understanding of contemporary society is indeed strange.[8]

However, to his credit, Marx's focus on alienation has slightly more limited parameters than simply a broad indictment of the de-humanizing effects of technological progress. Nor, on the other hand, is it entirely limited to the alienation of the proletarian worker under capitalism.[9] It is, as outlined in the *Economic and Philosophical Manuscripts*, primarily directed at the corrosive impact of money, as the mediating bridge between man and his needs. Money is the "alienated ability of mankind" in so far as it affords man objects that he might not otherwise be able to obtain on the basis of his innate human qualities. As such, money alienates the human being from his essential properties and powers.

> He who can buy bravery is brave, though he be a coward. As money is not exchanged for any specific quality, for any one specific thing, or for any particular human essential power, but for the entire objective world of man and nature, from the standpoint of its possessor it therefore serves to exchange every quality for every other, even contradictory, quality and object: it is the fraternization of impossibilities. It makes contradictions embrace.[10]

The ugly rich man with his gorgeous trophy bride is only the most glaring of contradiction which money creates and makes possible. Money essentially distorts the communication and exchange of authentic qualities that correspond to the ideal of de-alienated human interaction. The difference between authentic and inauthentic living is thus the difference between Being and Having. Love should only be exchanged for love, art can only commune with a cultivated mind, influence over others can only be achieved through charisma. One cannot buy love or loyalty, nor can one buy into sophistication.

Commodity fetishism

While these may be timeless maxims not out of place in the Christian canon, early twentieth-century romantic anti-capitalism, or other moral positions that frown upon the temptations of earthly goods, what Marx and the Western Marxists challenge is the transformational quality of money. They condemn its ability to create the illusion of authenticity and freedom, and its tendency, in capitalist culture, to conflate quantitative with qualitative measures of value. In the Marxian opus, this dual character of money was spelled out most clearly in the section on commodity fetishism in *Das Kapital*.[11] These remarks enabled later Marxists to broaden their frame of reference away from the worker's struggle to the more general role of money in culture, harnessing Feuerbachian notions of mystification and projection along the way. It allowed them to speak not only about the alienation of the worker, but the alienation of the capitalist and the bourgeois cultural consumer as well. Whereas money might appear as a condition of freedom for the capitalist, in the fetish theory, this condition proves illusory, an insatiable source of material goods that distract from the real source of his woes. Lukács, who made Marx's fetish theory central to his analysis, provides here a simple description:

> The man of the fetishized world, who can cure his disgust only in intoxication, seeks, like the morphine addict to find a way out by heightening the intensity of the intoxicant rather than by a way of life that has no need of intoxication.[12]

The section on fetishism in *Das Kapital* draws upon Feuerbach's theory of religious projection accenting the other-wordly character of commodities, abounding with the imagery of mystification, of transposing illusory values onto lifeless things. In its neo-Marxist variant, we find the religious imagery sustained in the form of Guy Debord's definition of the spectacle: "a technological version of the exiling of human powers in a world beyond" and "the spectacle is the material construction of the religious illusion."[13] The fetishized commodity appropriates ethereal qualities and symbolic meaning—freedom, power, the erotic—that transcend its basic utility. Not surprisingly, critics have focused on advertising (the "illusion industry" as Wolfgang Haug called it) as one of the chief mediators of fetishism, i.e., of commodities amplified and packaged to represent something they are not. "In these images," Haug wrote in *Critique of Commodity Aesthetics*, an important work in this genre, "people are continually shown the unfulfilled aspects of existence. The illusion ingratiates itself, promising satisfaction . . . it reads desires in one's eyes, and brings them to the surface of the commodity."[14]

The structure of banality

The theories of alienation and commodity fetishism form the raw ingredients of Marxian culture theory. Together, they condemn the infiltration of capitalist structures into man's cherished and potentially emancipating zone of leisure and surplus time. On this foundation, we can now inspect more closely how these two interlocking theories contribute to our understanding of inauthentic, or banal, culture. We will structure this analysis primarily with reference to the state of American culture at the beginning of the second millennium, not only because its culture dominates the globe, but also because it does so through such unadulterated capitalist methods of distribution. Indeed, as early as the 1930s, for European leftist critics—the liberating effects of jazz aside—America has been used as a "shorthand for all that was undesirable or disturbing about Western life."[15] We need not endorse the words of one French critic, "It is solidly organized egoism, it is evil made systematic and regular, in a word it is the materialism of human destiny,"[16] to recognize that, as the most consumerist society in the world, the United States presents ample material for any study on the links between culture and money. Building on the two pillars of Marx's culture theory, we will review below three of their classic applications in Western, particularly American, society. These three applications, which we will label the perversion of value, the manipulation of desire, and the simulation of reality, together form the basic structure of banality.

The perversion of value

As originally formulated by Lukács, the perversion of value is the symptom of a trend by which economic relations replace social relations, and the intrinsic value of goods is replaced by their external commodity value. Under capitalism, "Everything ceases to be valuable for itself or by virtue of its inner (e.g., artistic, ethical) value; a thing has value only as a ware bought and sold on the market."[17] It is the placing of a price-tag on things which earlier defied commodification. It puts up "for sale" items that should not or, under ideal conditions, would not be placed on the market. It is that phenomenon which lends itself easily to the language of prostitution and debasement because the violated value of the woman, her inner sanctum, is a powerful image of the debasement of value in general. "The money economy will increasingly gloss over the fact," Lukács' mentor Simmel wrote a hundred years ago, "that the money value of things does not fully replace what we ourselves possess in them, that they have qualities that cannot be expressed in money."[18]

We recognize this debasement when a favorite actor or sports hero, now past his prime, promotes hair weaves, holiday homes, or weather-proofed siding on late night television. Though his voice remains clear, and his gaze as strong and sincere as always, his dignity is hopelessly compromised by the product he peddles. He prostitutes himself for the sake of an endorsement fee. We recognize it when a sports stadium which used to carry the name of its city or local hero renames itself after a dot.com corporation often ending in the letter x, a letter whose sanitized, technical aura could not be less compatible with nostalgia, loyalty, and sense of place. On Broadway, the famous Selwyn Theatre is being renamed the American Airlines Theatre, the Winter Garden Theatre may soon be renamed after the luxury car, Cadillac, and Boston city council has even considered selling the naming rights of subway stations to the highest corporate bidder. The point here, as we have mentioned in other chapters, is not that these acts, however desperate, do not follow the logic of capitalism. They invariably do. As Mandel pointed out in *Late Capitalism*, it is in the expansive nature of capitalism in this particular late phase to turn "services into commodities," to replace "service capital with productive capital," and, in general, commoditize the public goods which were originally paid for with taxpayers' money.[19] To commoditize what one can commoditize, to sell what can sell, these are the hallmarks of the system. But the perversion of value is de-humanizing in the most literal sense of the term. As in the case of the sale of stadium naming rights, the human dimension—the local heroes, philanthropists, or politicians who were identified with a distinct sense of place, and who gave distinction and identity to that place by way of their name has been erased by the need to generate extra income. The significance of names as organic markers of local identity and tradition is conveniently ignored.

The perversion of value also extends to human interaction. Americans complain about the gruff professionalism of waiters in Europe, as much as Europeans are bemused by the cloying friendliness of waiters in America. The difference lies in the tip. In Europe, it is included in the bill so the only reason for the waiter to transgress the border between client and service provider is because of a genuine chemistry between the two parties, a sentiment ulterior to the financial incentive. In America, that chemistry is manufactured from the get-go—the smile, the fake curiosity, the engaging conversation. But watch the smile turn to bitterness and spite if a tip below the smallest 15 per cent is offered. It may well be that working for the tip provides an extra incentive but it also injects an element of artifice into normal human interactions.

Still, while it is easy to pronounce oneself piously in favor of real value, as opposed to market-driven value, it is at times difficult, in an economy so fully commoditized as America's, to separate the two. In publishing, we know that all good literature does not sell poorly, nor does all commercialized pulp sell well. The fickle nature of the consumer should not be underrated. There is, in fact, a hidden authentic value behind the dollar value of a consumer choice. And, assuming one is not the most die-hard avant-gardist, that hidden value could be said to lie at the heart of the very nature and function of art, that it must find an audience. A work that does not find an audience may genuinely be too advanced or controversial for conventional tastes. But other times, it may simply be bad art masquerading as high culture, too pompous to care whether it has an audience or not. As an example, we might cite the dramatic increase in independent film-making over the last decade. These films are often labors of love made by talented individuals who made a conscious choice to avoid the Hollywood system and set out on their own. Some are good, but others—as the film critics, once their greatest champions, are starting to realize—are, if not downright amateurish, then intellectually pretentious, unappealingly self-indulgent, or gratuitously rebellious, fractured, and confusing. The Western Marxist contrast between the commodity value of a cultural product and its inner value may then not always be as clear-cut and convenient as it promises. It may reflect a rather simplistic understanding of how financial decisions are made in the cultural industry. Whether a given film or book will sell is only an outer reflection of a deeper measurement of the film's or book's appeal to a good number of people. The criteria behind judging that appeal may vary from the intuitive hunch of a studio or publishing executive to elaborate polling of trial audiences. What critics of the culture industry fail to realize is that works which are deliberately crafted to suit a particular audience or particular trend rarely convince those who have the power to bring them to a larger audience. In fact, there is probably a greater synergy between conventional aesthetic criteria and the marketplace than most progressive culture critics wish to acknowledge.

Nonetheless, the "perversion of value" remains a compelling indictment of cultural production under capitalism. Its greatest strength as a critical perspective lies perhaps in its absolutism, that value should be judged by aesthetic criteria outside the market domain. Although it allows for the possibility that the market may at times reward authentic cultural production, it also raises healthy suspicions that cultural goods which cater to the lowest common denominator only do so to optimize financial gain.

The manipulation of desire

The manipulation of consumer desire is an outgrowth of Marx's idea of "secondary exploitation," the idea that no matter how much the worker is exploited as a producer, there might always be some surplus left over to be exploited as a consumer. Not just his basics—rent, or food—but all the products that, to however small a degree, could add something to his quality of life. To stimulate demand, to create new markets for its excess capacity, corporations must constantly fabricate new desires and peddle new dreams. There is nothing particularly original about this observation. It goes back to the earliest writings of the Frankfurt School and, outside the Marxist camp, to Christopher Lasch's classic, *The Culture of Narcissism*, published in the late 1970s. There he wrote,

> [Advertisement] plays seductively on the malaise of industrial civilization. Is your job boring and meaningless? Does it leave you with feelings of futility and fatigue? Is your life empty? Consumption promises to fill the aching void; hence the attempt to surround commodities with an aura of romance, with allusions to exotic places and vivid experiences.[20]

What has changed is that advertising is now confronted by a world-weary, ironic consumer who has become more elliptical and abstruse in his preferences. Advertising must, therefore, to an ever increasing degree, stimulate interest by subtly distancing the narrative and imagery of the commercial from the commodity it advertises. By way of association, it often peddles an illusion of freedom while making no direct allusions to the brand advertised. This is, in turn, reinforced by the state-of-the-art visual style, fragmented and fractured, multi-layered and distorted. Commercial producers, familiar with the iconic vocabulary of the audience, speak in terms of meta-narratives, parodies, and sampled riffs from pop culture. By doing so they not only flatter the individual buyer's cunning, they are able to simulate a grander and more dramatic context for their product beyond its limited use-value. At times, high culture references are employed to give a sophisticated allure to the product. Cue Bach . . . a prominent stage actor recites Shakespeare on the virtues of fidelity and trust . . . now cue logo: Union Bank of Switzerland. Or, cue Mozart . . . a blurry vehicle navigating tricky curves against a stunning alpine backdrop . . . Cue logo: *There is an Art to Living High. Jaguar*. Other times, the product acts as a catalyst for daily life's significant moments or, more depressingly, as a tease for what might be or might have been in a better world. A brand of coffee when poured hot and shared at a bay window becomes a symbol of reconciliation for the cute, estranged couple. The sport shoes pounding the inner-city basketball court become a symbol of excellence, camaraderie, and belonging. The utility vehicle perched on a mountain top symbolizes escape and a masculine longing for the free wilderness. Or, as in one recent McDonald's ad, a shy young couple on their first date by chance order the same toppings on their hamburgers, not only confirming McDonald's convenient flexibility, but also the promising "common ground" which binds this new couple together. By seamlessly integrating commodities into everyday life, and not just everyday life but its milestones—the first kiss, the son's first home run, the daughter going off to

146

college—commercials proffer the illusion that the commodity advertised is not simply something to be consumed but a symbolic arena for life's precious moments. Though the goal remains as crass as ever—to sell more goods—the veiling effort could not be more sophisticated. "Capital . . . in its esoteric interests," as Haug deftly summarized it, "adopts the lofty illusion that it is the highest creator of the human spirit, and not profit, which is its determining aim."[21]

Even if these points have been made over and over again, the fact of the matter is the deception is getting subtler, more sophisticated, and more endearing to the viewer. And in many ways more sinister. One recent advertisement features a pair of toddlers lecturing their parents on the benefits of digital video technology. Reciting complex technical jargon as if it were entirely natural and spontaneous to them, the baby actors are meant to reinforce the notion that power will soon lie in the hands of a younger generation who consume the most up-to-date technology product. And, yet, the whole message is packaged in a terms of a harmonious family environment or, at least, Madison Avenue's idea of it. Parents look on lovingly, flattered by their offspring's intellect, not realizing that they are, in fact, the butt of the joke.

This kind of vacuous escapism may be bad, social status may be falsely determined by the kind of mark you have on your shoes, but if the fetishized meaning attached to banal objects were to be taken away, would we be any better off? What would people do when deprived of their illusions, of their escapes, no matter how artificial and short-lived? Some years ago, a lobbying group for advertisers launched one such appeal in an attempt to show that a world without advertising would be drab and dreary indeed. Between static shots of a city denuded of billboards and neon, it spliced darkly comical images of Romanian state television during the Ceausescu era: grey newscasters speaking stiffly against a white background as folk dancers twirled aimlessly in the background. Their message was two-fold. Not only does advertising add color to our universe, it provides the funds that allow for a greater variety and sophistication in our entertainment. But beyond the tension the ad campaign raised between the manipulation of desire through advertising and the lack thereof lies a deeper tension between a life stimulated by manipulated forms of escape and a life without. We defer again to the remark of Lukács.

> The man of the fetishized world, who can cure his disgust with the world only in intoxication, seeks, like the morphine addict to find a way out by heightening the intensity of the intoxicant rather than by a way of life that has no need for intoxication.[22]

We might readily agree that a rampant consumerist addiction reflects an empty life: that parents who accommodate every material whim of their children to compensate for not spending enough time with them, are not harmonized with their natural parental duty, or, even, that couples who go shopping together to avoid conversation during their free time and then make purchases which, like newborn babies, refortify the relationship, are somehow alienated from true love. But what exactly is a life free of intoxication? What kind of life has no need for sporadic escapes into a heightened experience whether through movies, pulp fiction, or personal experiences. In this respect, Lukács' comment that intoxication, or the need thereof, reflects a "disgust with the world," rings awkwardly pious. Through the avenues of entertainment, sports, drugs, sex, or alcohol we may be only exercising a natural right to heightened experience, to access worlds and vistas greater than our own, heroes, ecstasy, self-validation, or any number of experiences that transcend the normality of our daily lives. If these are all symptoms of alienation, then there is certainly nothing wrong with it.

Thus, we must tread carefully when considering, as Marxist culture critics had the tendency to do, the corporate world's manipulation of desire as a one-sided and purely self-interested act of emotional exploitation for the sake of profit. Prey it might on the lonely people who live grey dismal lives, the ghetto poor or "social unoriginals" who moronically seek status through brand-name items or shirts emblazoned with the logos of prestigious schools they did not attend. There are, indeed, fetishes at work here, and false projections of consciousness, and many other symptoms that can be traced back to Feuerbach's pioneering work in the field of religion. And now, one step beyond Feuerbach, not only do people project onto these fetishes, as in organized religion, qualities which they find lacking in themselves, there is a whole industry that does it for them, that creates and continuously updates this hip and sexy vision of a better world. But for all their awareness of the insidious nature of the culture industry, critics may be powerless to deny people the autonomy to choose their spice in life. For the issue is not only how the naive are financially exploited, but also how the leisure and culture industries nourishes the contrast between work and play, reality and unreality, between the routine and the fest, all those ecstatic moments in which we become incredibly aware of the preciousness of life. Anyone is free to forego alcohol, popular culture, junk food, or trash art. Anyone is free to forego intoxication and escape. But, except for a few satisfied ascetics who live on bread and water alone, most people would prefer to have goods and services that add color to their lives. Given the need for escape, blanket condemnations of mass culture have little redeeming value. For the alternative assumes a rare and almost unattainable ideal: the highly educated esoteric with an active internal dialogue, so active, so driven by a love for learning and creative expression, that he neither seeks nor requires any external stimulants. If this is what those who condemned the capitalist culture industry aspired to then it was a fairly narcissistic campaign indeed. It modeled itself on a vision of themselves, highly educated upper-middle-class European bourgeois, as ideal antidotes to the onslaught of mass culture.

Nonetheless, there was a grain of truth in their narcissism. The more educated we are, the more we are exposed to a diverse set of sub-cultures and sensual experiences. The more complex our identity, the better equipped we are to manipulate the manipulators. By becoming creators rather than consumers, by sifting through the grab-bag of cultural goods that present themselves to us, and building from it our own personal mental universe, the more able we are to affirm our own identity. In that respect alone, education is the best weapon against the patronizing cynicism of the advertising industry, one that assumes that its target audience can only expand its personal identity by association with consumer products. That aspect of Marxist culture theory is still relevant. Beneath the critique of mystification lies the fact that the advertising industry and the corporate consumer culture bestow on the consumer a false sense of individuality. Thus, though we might find the elitism of the Marxist culture industry school misguided (particularly because their education did not extend to youth culture and the street), their intentions are sound. They rest on the hope that man can and will develop himself enough to create his own world, and that by gaining an authentic voice he will not need to hide behind transparently false and commodified extensions of his identity.

The simulation of reality

The contrast between authentic and inauthentic forms of leisure is also reflected in the third application of Marxist culture theory, the ideas of reproduction and simulation. In its various guises, whether Debord's society of "the economic realm developing for itself," or Baudrillard's simulacra, the idea of simulation relates to the tendency of capitalist society to distort, reproduce, or repackage reality in ways that can be made more accessible to its market. It goes beyond the contrast between Being and Having, to one between Having and Appearing to Have. Simulation waters down and distorts, it is shameless in its pretensions, and vulgar in its tastes. Under the democratic pretext of making authentic culture accessible to the masses, it recreates the original model, disembodied from any meaningful context. It shapes and prunes to fit the needs of the market, not the substance of the original.

Behind the airport Irish theme bars with their fake weathered wood, Las Vegas's corny recreations of Paris or Venice, ethno-chic trends in fashion (*intifada* scarves, or Rastafarian dreadlocks), cuisine and music; and the retro-trend in design—new products based on old designs that appeal to consumer nostalgia—we can easily recognize the hallmarks of postmodernism. Simulation is that aesthetic sensibility of mix and match, of irony and pastiche, of melted borders between high and low culture and among all the genres in between. It is the playful juxtaposition of the old, new, and the renewed or new-old, that has been identified as the cultural logic of late capitalism. That logic, it was thought not too long ago, expressed a kind of end-station of aesthetic and cultural maturity. Once there were no longer any fixed patterns of taste, once the whole historical arsenal of cultural reference points can be interchangeably pilfered, and, finally, once there is no longer any orthodoxy to revolt against, then one can only assume that what lies ahead will be, at least in the short- to medium-term, more a multiplication of reference points than any fundamental qualitative shift. If now there seems to be a Thai restaurant on every corner, in a few years, customers will be able to choose Isaan Thai (north-east), which is spicier, or southern Thai, which uses more coconut. On the near horizon, we can envision a continuous breaking down of cultural archetypes into small and smaller units, a kind of hyper-defined reality based on the proliferation of options.

But at a deeper and more sinister level, the creativity of capitalist simulation is now such that it co-opts aesthetic paradigms and cultural forms that previously resisted co-option, that were, so to speak, unpackageable. In fact, today more than ever before, corporate marketing strategy masquerades behind iconography that is deliberately anti-corporate, anti-convention, and anti-uniformity. It celebrates rebellion and trendbucking all to flatter the underdeveloped individualism of the passive consumer. The lounge cafés with their artful scattering of new "used" sofas and reggae soundtracks are nods to bohemian culture that can be reproduced without any authentic bohemians. And sterile French "brasseries" open up in American cities with yellowing, pre-nicotined stained walls, nodding again to the intellectuals' smoking culture without any need for smokers. This kind of stylized scruffiness borrowed from the counterculture betrays a popular longing for cozy, familiar, and non-mass-produced environments, and capitalism has responded precisely by mass-producing such environments. As the competition intensifies, the life-span of counterculture novelty narrows. The lag-time between an original and a simulation, between a new counterculture fad and its co-option by the corporate mainstream is getting shorter and shorter. No matter that when these fads are co-opted they lose much of their original meaning, their social context, and their intrinsic value. Whether it's the baggy pants of ghetto hoods repackaged with better cloth and marketing in the suburbs, the cutting-edge artschool graphics internalized in mainstream pop videos, or indie rock anthems spliced into segments on the evening news, always just enough original meaning can be salvaged to give standard fare an added cachet.

The critic facing this scenario can only speculate when the limits will be reached. When the competition for novelty (stolen or borrowed from outside the mainstream), when all the attempts at shock, revulsion, hyperactive cameras, and frenetic bombardment of imagery will reach a saturation point. Already, in the world of fashion and glamour magazines, particularly those that consider themselves cutting edge like *Interview* or *I-D*, all one finds is a one-note song, a variation on the gratuitously obscene. There are playful and knowing images of mutilated mannequins, coon-eyed heroin junkies, sluttiness, suffering, sadism, and pedophilia, and umpteen tiresome takes on sexual ambiguity. Modern art is often little better, with celebrated young artists engaging in irritating forms of sacrilege for the sake of sacrilege. One could well say that there is nothing wrong with preserving animals in formaldehyde or displaying animal feces on a portrait of the Virgin Mary, or a crucifix soaked in urine, or a live female nude wrapped in sausage links (all recent works by prominent artists). What is disturbing is that these acts are presented as worthy aesthetic statements about the present day. If that is so, then all we can say is that the present is marked by decadence not in the loose sense of the term, but rather in the sense that art as critical opposition to a given status quo no longer has any meaning. Its own paper tiger dynamic—overemphasizing, for example, the repressive nature of conventional norms, e.g., religion, in order to satirize them—is already an outdated sensibility. And the showy use of grotesque imagery as code language for rebellion, novelty, and transcendence—however much accompanied by high culture textual exposition—hardly extends beyond the clever graphics of modern advertising. To be sure, as the English art critic Stallabrass has pointed out, the shock-values employed by modern artists are, in themselves, a defense mechanism against the possibility of rapid co-option.[23] But such a defense is increasingly fragile simply because the language of shock and satire has already been mainstreamed to the point that the capitalist culture industry can manipulate it as an effective marketing tool.

Perhaps, the only redeeming value of this decadence is that it has a limited life-span. The past teaches us that it will reach a point of exhaustion, that culture is, in fact, not a static vision of beauty but a pendulum swinging between the tingle of rebellious outrage and the comfort of the familiar. Indeed, art did not end with the black on black boxes of the 1960s or the sophomoric taboo-shattering of the 1990s, nor will fashion sink irreparably into heroin chic. Realism in art is eternally recurring, plaid skirts and khakis will make a come-back, and all will be well again. What this implies is that the critic must respect the corrective mechanism imbedded in consumer culture. The only note of sadness that can be accentuated is that, despite the critic's rhetorical flourishes and pulsating ideals, the art consumer's corrective mechanism is the only one that seems to count.

The new technological era

Banality is the outcome of the perversion of value, the commercial manipulation of desire, and the simulation of reality under capitalism. It infects the hallowed ground of leisure, and seduces the weak to project themselves falsely onto material goods. It is not only bad or derivative taste, it is vulgarity masquerading as freedom. All these things, subsumed under the Marxist critique of banality outlined above, still hold true in many cases today. But that critique has two major flaws. Firstly, it can only rail against, but cannot accommodate, the fact that masses will choose, and have always chosen, simple forms of escape. In the pre-television era of the nineteenth century, the zealots of socialist activism bemoaned the workingman's love of drink, the precious few hours of leisure squandered down at the local bar. So they formed workingmen's reading clubs, debating societies, discussion groups, and choirs. But ultimately, such well-intentioned efforts made little impact. The tedium of a day's labor demanded a stressless release, bawdy camaraderie, and bacchanalia, however brief and prosaic. This remains an iron fact. And the problem, if we could call it that, seems insurmountable. There is little that we can add other than to suggest, only half-ironically, that at least the institution of the corner bar provided an arena for conversation, joke-telling, and a playfully therapeutic processing of the day's events. It also established long-term friendships and, overall, reinforced a sense of local community. These days, suburbanization has killed the corner bar, giving way instead to atomistic forms of leisure: video outlets, net surfing, or cable sports networks.

The second flaw of the Marxist critique of banality is that it is locked in a rather archaic doomsaying about the oppressive dimensions of technology. This is a recent flaw in the sense that, up until a decade ago, mankind did seem at the cusp of all sorts of Brave New World scenarios. The cultural critic's response was to demonize the impersonal dimensions of technology. At that time, artists could still proffer video installations of black and white television static as profound aesthetic statements of anomie, and industrial rockers like Einsturzende Neubauten could legitimately grind away with chainsaws and pneumatic drills to declare the end of music. But all these efforts to denounce (while revelling in) Western technologically induced decline seem now quaint at best. It is no longer shocking to condemn advertising for seducing the young and feeble, to condemn television for its tried and tested formula of sex and violence, to condemn glamour magazines for feeding escapist visions of the good life to lonely people, to condemn group tours as an inauthentic experience of foreign cultures. For over a century now the denouncement of consumerism and technologically induced social atomism have been central to the platforms of a wide range of critics: neo-Luddites, Emersonian democrats and Deweyean socialists, the Frankfurt School, postmodern semioticians, and neo-Marxist sociologists. But all such pessimism, fueled often by nostalgic laments for some primordial community, is now being challenged by a new optimism about scientific progress and its benefits to the common man. The Frankensteinian vision of technology as man's creation run amok, an oppressive force that would either turn man into a cog in a mechanistic behemoth or simply obliterate him in a nuclear catastrophe, now seems more obsolete than ever before. Rapid advances in genetic science and medicine due to the ability of supercomputers to process data sequences rapidly, the democratization of information access due to the internet, and the harmonization of technology and art to create sensual and hyper-realistic fantasies are all positive dimensions of this new technological era.

The democratization of creative expression

Indeed, the democratization of expression that low-cost technologies and, particularly, the internet have fostered seems, on the surface, to be a positive development. It certainly challenges a number of the basic tenets of capitalism. Firstly, it circumvents all the constraints imposed on normal retail outlets such as economies of scale or limited shelf-space. Thus, the amount of available goods is multiplied far beyond conventional or vulgar tastes. Now, every imaginable taste or consumer good, no matter how rarefied, whether a 1940s comic book, Chinese herbal medicine, or alligator-skin boots, can be easily sated. Secondly, all the doomsayers who have condemned the growing standardization and uniformity of society, must now reflect on the millions of personal websites that empower individuals to express themselves to the outside world. And those doomsayers who condemned the anomie of the lonely suburban dweller must now reflect on the millions of chat groups that unite the like-minded. Finally, all the anti-capitalist doomsayers who forecast an ever-expanding corporate structure of hierarchies must now contend with the new economy's liquid power structures that are manipulated by those who best manipulate technology and ideas in rapidly changing work environments. It is the non-conformist innovators, not the loyal plodding clerks of the corporate system who will shape the economy of the future.

As postmodernism did to our understanding of culture, so cyberage has subverted many previously accepted truisms of anti-capitalist rhetoric. You don't want to be exploited? Fine, create your own company and pay your own salary. You don't want to work in a generic office space? Fine, work at home. You think that the masses are manipulated by oligarchies of the culture industry? Well, how can this be when there are 500 television channels catering to every whim? Where are the organs of control? Where are the subliminal messages forcing you to buy, secretly expropriating your hard-earned dollar? Are we then not moving toward that nirvana where everyman is in perpetual process of creation and reinvention, when the powers of his imagination are magnified and distributed through cyberspace, when skills which once took years to learn—whether to make a movie, or play the piano—can now be circumvented by simpling assembling pre-packaged creative products and calling them one's own?

On the other hand, at least in the field of art, technological democracy may turn out to be a mixed blessing. Its main significance seems to be in its simplification of once complex creative processes. In music, the modern eclecticism—where electropop sidles alongside 1970s' soul funk, latin fusion, or drum 'n' bass—results not only from the creator's increased exposure to these forms, but from the simplicity of recreating them. The electronic samples are pre-packaged, the loops and riffs are all ready to be stirred into the soup. The composer creators now compete with DJ recreators who have become celebrities in their own right (though the credits of their CD compilations modestly read "produced by" rather than "composed by." Or is the former activity now the higher badge of honor?) Likewise in film, the explosion of digital film-making and desktop-based video editing systems has enabled amateurs to make feature-quality films without passing through all the hurdles normally required to gain studio backing. One might think that this democratization of technology optimally satisfies Marx's vision of transforming consumers into creators. But the latest technology teases the impatient and may feed careless dreams. The evolution of the Sundance Film Festival is a case in point. Originally established as an independent showcase for low-budget films outside the Hollywood mainstream, it probably never assumed that films would become so cheap to make. The Hollywood mainstream was so small because few artists with an independent agenda or quirky sensibility could raise sufficient funds to cover the costs. Now over 60 per cent of the films submitted to Sundance are largely autobiographical video diaries.[24] There is nothing wrong with the memoir genre *per se*. But when not subject to the critical review that studio films undergo—based not on avant-garde cachet but on a story's narrative clarity and popular appeal—the democratization of film-making technology will hardly lead to better art. The fact that the story is now easier to tell does not necessarily make it more worthwhile telling.

Finally, new technology in the form of cyberspace has generated an arena in which the smallest ideas can acquire a *semblance* of realization. Every trivial innovation becomes the *raison d'être* for a new dot.com company. Have you ever found it difficult to find home-delivery for sparkling wine, a non-tacky wedding gift, thoughtful things to say to friends who have just lost a parent, or spare parts for your Citroën DS? As people abandon their 9 to 5 jobs to chase their entrepreneurial passion, however trivial it may be, one can only marvel at America's appetite for hyper-convenience, for the extra time or labor savings for which they are willing to pay a premium. Even those who seek only personal validation, cyberspace may provide but a semblance of self-esteem. Writers who cannot get published create their own webzine. The social dysfunctionals create their personal website. The knowledge that one's idea, prose, or photos are out in the "public eye" validates—with that special tingle of pride and self-satisfaction—one's existence in ways that the more conventional and complex arena of real-world accomplishment cannot. The difference, however, is that the freedom of cyberspace is unilateral, uncensored, unfiltered, and therefore delusional. Everyone becomes a hero in their own mind. Hits, no matter that they are the equivalent of a quick glance, a stroll by, a passing giggle, an overheard snippet of conversation, become the point of validation.

The multi-tasking viewer

Certainly, if we observe the contemporary pop-culture diet, it does seem designed for animals with an increasingly limited attention-span. But this is not necessarily because man is getting dumber. It may be just the opposite. In fact, pleasing a modern audience may be something like pleasing an impatient genius with conversation. It needs to be fed more layers of information, more visual clues and graphic messages, and at a far higher speed and rate of density. Subjects well-known need not be reviewed, only hinted at. Basic arguments need not be rehearsed, one can immediately turn to more subtle forms of analysis. Media saturation has meant that the facts of the story are out there almost immediately, clearing the way for ever deeper probing of all possible tangents and interpretations. Again, this may not be something to lament. It may be a function of our maturity. The mainstream press has adopted the characteristics of good academic scholarship. The basic facts are quickly told. What completes the picture are the detours and minor characters, the myriad of interpretive angles, in short, the meta-story. We can observe some of these changes more closely in televised sports commentary—normally viewed by cultural elitists with some distrust. Here, we witness not a decrease, but an increase in the depth of the play-by-play analysis. Tactics are reviewed, and statistics are cited with greater sophistication. In American football, for example, a division of labor has emerged in the commentators' booth, with defense and offense specialists at the ready with expert analysis, anecdotal insight, and cutting-edge graphics. And rather than being manipulative or invasive, this is, to the informed viewer, a richer entertainment experience. The consumer is not sitting still, frozen at a fixed mental age. Thus, prominent Marxist critics such as Fredric Jameson, who claim that technology has separated art from the ability of the viewer to appreciate it, may overstate the case.[25] The consumer is always only one or two steps behind. This cannot be otherwise. For the media always relies on a convergence of meaning between producer and consumer, a consumer who today is hungrier and savvier than ever before.

Sensual technology

Equally, the current state of pop music with its fractured beat, irregular pauses, multi-layered sounds, and jumble of sampled riffs corresponds to the way the consumer listens. Just by being able to download and create his own

CD—a little salsa, a little hard-core, some delta blues or ethno-fusion—he no longer wants to, or perhaps no longer can, appreciate a singular idiom in its full and authentic context. Because every form of music now floats outside its immediate historic context—the digitalization and re-issuing of many defunct records has reinforced this trend—it not only encourages eclectic comparisons and a broadening of tastes, but also re-evaluations and resurrections of previously derided artforms. While Adorno ridiculed muzak, his posture seems in retrospect quite static as we watch the saccharine, sweeping strings of Burt Bacharach cleverly and convincingly repackaged by everything from Tokyo pop to London dance music. Little did Adorno know that the soothing tones of muzak repackaged as *retro-lounge* might provide a welcome, if highly ironized, relief to a knowing crowd exhausted by mindless noise rock. Along the way, the Brave New World scenario of music has also fallen by the wayside. While the earliest electronic music such as *Kraftwerk* bought into a kind of misguided futurism—clinical, sanitized, and monotonous—modern groups such as *Air, Massive Attack* or *Morcheeba*, ply a sensual, eroticized sound of airy female vocals, hip hop rhythmic syncopation, and elaborate sampling to defy those culture critics who saw technology as driving a wedge between art and human emotions. In fact, such groups have humanized the electronic medium as a flexible and expressive backdrop for highly sensual creativity. They use technology not only to retain but also to amplify the erotic component essential to all good popular music.

Conclusion

In the newly interactive world, it is too early to tell whether the plethora of simulated realities provide Everyman with the next best thing to the original, or, instead, proffer a set of mentally damaging delusions. Will they widen horizons or foster a culture of atomized sociopaths? The fact of the matter is, the trajectory of the information revolution is still impossible to divine. The speculative madness that fueled information technology in the 1990s, one that envisioned a parallel online universe eventually subsuming the real world, has recently run up against sobering realities; namely, that web companies still need to make money the old-fashioned way by selling goods and services that people want to buy, that online publishing and music distribution may be the wave of the future but not until consumers, flooded with free information, have an incentive to pay, and that the much vaunted "emancipatory claims" for the knowledge economy may—given the stultifying narrow preoccupations of many so-called "knowledge workers" turn out to be very hollow indeed.[26]

One thing is clear. While the new technologies will democratize access to information, and provide various cultural benefits (e.g., digitalization of archival material) they will also accelerate media saturation, commodification, and counterculture co-option. Without alternative strategies, capitalism will simply harness the new tools to sell more products to more people. How are we then to fortify the individual to withstand the encroachment? In this study we have formulated two general principles that are Marxian in character but also applicable to the postcommunist age: a) to strive wherever possible to restrict market criteria in the determination of goods and services which have a social benefit. The Althusserian definition of communism, as "the absence of relations based on the market," serves as the utopian end-goal of that attempt; b) to enhance through political action, state-led or otherwise, the equitable distribution of access to the social surplus and thereby the individual capacity for self-development. Both these avenues have been explored in the present study and both offer possibilities to alleviate capitalism's tendency to perpetuate poverty and corruption. Banality is, for a variety of reasons, more resilient to institutional or political remedies. The choices individuals make regarding their leisure time, particularly whether to be entertained or educated, should remain free. And the dazzling diversity of cultural forms now available ensures that there is something available for every taste. Nonetheless, in terms of the capitalist encroachment on culture, i.e., its tendency to pervert value, manipulate desire, and simulate reality, there are two strategies that broadly follow the principles outlined above. Firstly, in terms of separating as much as possible the inherent value of cultural goods from their market value, one answer is to provide more public subsidies for cultural goods. In the United States, where government support for the arts is woefully underfunded,[27] there is a tremendous shortage of institutions that provide non-banal forms of leisure. This is particularly the case in rural areas, and even medium-sized cities in the provinces, where there are few alternatives to shopping and televised sports. There is a hostility in American society toward public support for the arts that is hard to explain but may relate to its hostility toward the artist in general. Some remnants of puritanical zeal contribute to a mind-set that considers artists parasitical lay-abouts. An extremist pragmatism concludes that those who cannot make money from their creative output must not be any good. And, on the political level, there is a sense that the whole art community is held hostage to leftist interest groups who have no other ambition than to mock and satirize sacred American values. The disbursement of taxpayer funds will always be a battle over conflicting priorities. But to ensure that cultural products are not banalized, there needs to be a greater political will to subsidize cultural institutions, creative artists, and intellectuals. A starting point may be state-sponsored funding in rural areas remote from galleries, theatres, and the like. Funding should be directed not necessarily toward the most modern or innovative artists, but those whose narrative voices could restore to disembodied, media-saturated communities a sense of place and cultural heritage: cowboy poets, quilt-makers, blue grass mandolinists, and all the writers and artists who draw their inspiration locally. The focus on tradition would assuage conservative critics of state funding for the arts particularly by demonstrating that the writer or artist is not simply a self-indulgent parasite of the taxpayer but a conduit for restoring community-based narratives.

Secondly, in terms of distributing social surplus to enhance self-development, the focus lies on education. The level of a consumer's education determines his vulnerability to banal forms of culture and leisure. Education not only allows the consumer to appreciate a greater number of cultural goods, it also provides us with the acumen to see through cynical attempts at manipulation by the culture producers. It heightens our aesthetic sensibility, making us immune to clichés, maudlin sentimentalism, gratuitous shock value, and any number of devices that are regularly employed by Hollywood and Madison Avenue. Finally, education allows us to create ourselves. Once this urge to create has been kindled, we no longer feel the need passively to absorb conveniently packaged sensual stimuli. The institutional remedy is not only to promote public investment in education. It is also to promote investment in forms of education that broaden the mind but do not automatically have a financial return. For the skills that promote creativity and self-expression are not necessarily those most valued in the marketplace. And yet, it is these skills that enable us to see the world in a fundamentally different way. They give us the courage to take that leap of faith toward some more fulfilling realm. These truisms are the staple of any motivational speaker but what Marx adds to it is the sense in which all these dreams remain empty without certain institutional remedies. This is not to disburden the individual of his responsibility. Ultimately, only he can take that leap of faith. But it is saying that no amount of self-respect and yearning for a more creative life can overcome the lack of institutional environments that will foster progress. This implies better resources for adult education, sabbatical programs, maternity/paternity leave—in short, resources which enhance the family environment and create space for self-realization.

Television and human capital development

Increased investment in human capital will largely be wasted if we cannot wean children away from passive forms of leisure like television. Critics of television at times over-zealously condemn its anti-intellectual bias—for today, we can easily surf away from soap operas to documentaries on Stalingrad or panda-mating rituals—but they are right to express alarm at its deleterious effect on the development of the young mind. Television cultivates a lazy intellect and short attention-spans, a dangerous function considering the amount of time that small children, particularly American, spend in front of it. According to US surveys, 7- to 17-year-olds average between 25 and 30 hours per week, while pre-school children, who make up the largest TV audience in the country, may be viewing up to 60 hours per week.[i] And according to the US National Assessment of Education Progress, a test which measures reading skills among fourth graders (roughly 9-year-olds), 34 per cent of the "low scores" (mostly male black and hispanics) watched more than six hours of television every day.[ii] While many academic studies have documented the detrimental effects of TV-viewing on child cognitive development, particularly in the language-sensitive period of infancy, the basic outcome can be expressed in a simple truism: it is *easier* to watch TV than to read, and it is easier to read than to write, yet only those children who can read and write well will excel in school and later life. As verbal, social, and communication skills suffer, as the inherent human capacity for complex thought is crippled, children increasingly prefer the entertaining sedation of television to the harder world outside. Television retards the development of the mind not so much by the material it communicates—after all, it simply allows the passive spectator to access richer and more diverse spectacles—but by the fact that it relegates the creative subject to a spectator role. In doing so, it consumes valuable leisure time, time which could better be spent elsewhere. In this respect, parents and other critics of the content of television programming miss the point. Instead of assuming that the television is a necessary reality in the life of the young and then seeking ways to improve it, they need to find ways, however radical this may sound, to stimulate mental growth independent of the television.

i "Summary of Research on the Effects of Television Viewing," *un-TV Guide*, online at http://www.sover.net/~gmws/untv/research.htm.
ii Kate Zernike, "Gap Between Best and Worst widens on US Reading Test," *New York Times*, 7 April 2001.

But perhaps most importantly, a significant social investment at the pre-school level would equip individuals for self-development early on. Before they enter the workforce, children have no other obligation than to learn and play and develop themselves. It is, for the most part, an idyllic age of leisure. Yet, leisure time squandered early on will relegate the child, and future generations of children, to permanent spectators. In an age saturated with information and visual stimuli, the winners will be those who can process and recreate the raw data in new and original forms, ones that reflect their personal imprint. In this age, the level of education will increasingly become the distinguishing marker among people. Since power will be based on the ability to create, access, and manipulate information quickly, it will lie in the hands of the superior intellects. The losers left behind will simply consume what others create.

The work of Marx and the Marxists remains one of the main stimuli to thinking critically about the de-humanizing impact of capitalist relations. Even if we abandon radical social engineering and its documented human costs, we can still aggressively pursue a more modest goal: to chip away at the self-legitimating normality of market forces. This we can only do if we have the education to understand the ultimate goal: to live in a world where we express our true selves through our labor, where the people are represented through the political process, and where our leisure time is immune to the manipulative designs of the capitalist culture industry. It may be banal in its own right to conclude, after all this, that one elixir lies in better education for pre-school children. But such a conclusion satisfies both conservative demands to focus more on family values and individual self-empowerment, and progressive demands that society provide equitable access to human capital development.[28] The difference between the two positions lies in the degree of willingness to allocate capitalism's surplus toward a goal that ultimately undermines its power.

NOTES

PREFACE

1 Slavoj Žižek, "Class Struggle or Postmodernism?" in Judith Butler, Ernesto Laclau and Slavoj Žižek, *Contingency, Hegemony, Universality: Contemporary Dialogues on the Left*, London, Verso, 2000, p. 127.

1 INTRODUCTION

1 H. Marcuse, "Some Social Implications of Modern Technology," in A. Arato and E. Gebhardt (eds), *The Essential Frankfurt School Reader*, New York, Continuum, 1982, p. 161.
2 See U. Beck, *The Brave New World of Work*, trans. P. Camiller, Cambridge, Polity Press, 2000, and J. Rifkin, *The End of Work*, New York, G. P. Putnam's Sons, 1995.
3 K. Marx, *Economic and Philosophical Manuscripts*, trans. T. B. Bottomore, in E. Fromm, *Marx's Concept of Man*, New York, Frederick Ungar, 1966, p. 98.
4 Marcuse, "Some Social Implications of Modern Technology," p. 161.
5 D. Harvey cited in J. Stallabrass, *Gargantua: Manufactured Mass Culture*, London, Verso, 1996, p. 7.
6 I. Berlin, *Karl Marx: His Life and Environment*, Oxford, Oxford University Press, 1996, p. 5.
7 F. Copleston, *A History of Philosophy*, vol. 7, New York, Image Books, 1985, p. 1.
8 K. Marx, "Contribution to a Critique of Hegel's Philosophy of Law," *Marx Engels Collected Works* (henceforth *MECW*), vol. 3, London, Lawrence and Wishart, 1975, p. 176.
9 Ibid.
10 H. Kohn, *The Mind of Germany*, New York, Harper Torchbooks, 1960, p. 17.
11 See A. Bestor, "The Evolution of the Socialist Vocabulary," *Journal of the History of Ideas*, vol. 9, 1948, pp. 259–302.
12 D. McLellan, *The Young Hegelians and Karl Marx*, London, Macmillan, 1969, p. 34.
13 Marx, *Economic and Philosophical Manuscripts*, p. 127.
14 K. Marx, *The German Ideology*, *MECW*, vol. 5, p. 29.
15 D. F. Strauss, *The Life of Jesus*, London, SCM Press, 1973, p. 780.
16 Letter from K. Marx to L. Feuerbach, 11 August 1844, *MECW*, vol. 3, p. 354.
17 L. Feuerbach, *The Essence of Christianity*, trans. G. Eliot, New York, Harper, 1957, p. 47.

18 C. Wilson, *Feuerbach and the Search for Otherness*, New York, Peter Lang, 1992, p. 394.
19 L. Feuerbach, *Gesammelte Werke*, vol. 8, ed. W. Schuffenhauer, Berlin, Akademie Verlage, 1970, p. 9.
20 L. Feuerbach, *Principles of the Philosophy of the Future*, trans. M. Vogel, Indianapolis, Hackett, 1986, p. 19.
21 Ibid. p. 52.
22 Ibid. p. 53.
23 Ibid. p. 61.
24 Cited in McLellan, *The Young Hegelians*, p. 100.
25 Feuerbach, *Gesammelte Werke*, vol. 18, p. 337.
26 Ibid. p. 441.
27 Marx, *The German Ideology*, p. 37.
28 *MECW*, vol. 3, p. 271.
29 Ibid. p. 272.
30 Ibid. p. 274.
31 Ibid. p. 275: "Certainly eating, drinking, procreating, etc., are also genuinely human functions. But taken abstractly, separated from the sphere of all other human activity and turned into sole and ultimate ends, they are animal functions."
32 Ibid.
33 Ibid.
34 Marx, *Economic and Philosophical Manuscripts*, p. 165.
35 Ibid. p. 127.
36 Cornell West, *The American Evasion of Philosophy*, Madison, University of Wisconsin Press, 1989, p. 1.
37 K. Marx, "Letter to Ruge," *MECW*, vol. 3, p. 142.

2 THE TWENTIETH-CENTURY RECEPTION

1 M. Horkheimer, "The Authoritarian State," in A. Arato and E. Gebhardt (eds), *The Essential Frankfurt School Reader*, New York, Continuum, 1982, p. 108.
2 F. Engels, *Ludwig Feuerbach and the Outcome of Classical German Philosophy*, New York, International Publishers, 1996 edition, p. 47.
3 See J. Ortega y Gasset, *The Revolt of the Masses*, New York, Mentor Books, 1950.
4 D. McLellan, *Karl Marx: His Life and Thought*, Frogmore, Paladin, 1976, p. 187.
5 K. Marx, *The Communist Manifesto*, London and New York, Verso, 1998, p. 47.
6 Ibid. p. 51.
7 R. Wiggershaus, *The Frankfurt School*, trans. M. Robertson, Cambridge, MA, MIT Press, 1995, p. 33.
8 Bernstein cited in Lucio Coletti, "Bernstein and the Marxism of the Second International," *From Rousseau to Lenin*, trans. J. Merrington and J. White, New York, Monthly Review Press, 1974, p. 49.
9 Bernstein cited in Sidney Hook, *Marx and the Marxists*, New York, D. Van Nostrand, 1955, p. 179.
10 F. Engels, cited in Coletti, "Bernstein," p. 48.
11 Colletti, "Bernstein," p. 52.
12 Marx, *The Communist Manifesto*, p. 86.
13 V. I. Lenin, "Karl Marx," entry for *Granats Lexicon* (1913), Beijing, Verlag fuer Fremdsprachige Literatur, 1974.
14 See "The Attitude to the 'Socialist' Currents and to the Berne Conference," in *Theses, Resolutions and Manifestos of the First Four Congresses of the Third International*, London, Pluto Press, 1983, pp. 23–4.

15 Colletti, "Bernstein", pp. 219–20.

16 Marcuse cited in Wiggershaus, *The Frankfurt School*, p. 612.

17 Kautsky cited in Hook, *Marx and the Marxists*, pp. 203–4.

18 See R. Pipes, *A Concise History of the Russian Revolution*, New York, Vintage, 1995, p. 394.

19 L. Trotsky, "Theses on the Admission to the Communist International," *Theses, Resolutions and Manifestos of the First Four Congresses of the Third International*, p. 95.

20 V. I. Lenin, "Statutes of the Communist International," ibid. p. 124.

21 "Beyond Dialogue: A Letter from Seventeen Roman Catholic Bishops of the Third World Interpreting *Populorum Progressio*," in P. Oestreicher (ed.), *The Christian Marxist Dialogue*, London, Macmillan, 1969, p. 233.

22 C. Rodriguez, "Lenin and the Colonial Question," *New International*, vol. 1, no. 1, 1983, p. 94.

23 T. Borge, "The FSLN and the Nicaraguan Revolution," *The New International*, vol. 1, no. 3, 1984, p. 137.

24 F. Fanon, *The Wretched of the Earth*, trans. C. Farrington, New York, Grove Press, 1963, p. 86.

25 Ibid. p. 175.

26 Ibid. p. 139.

27 A good place to begin would be the chapter on "Western Marxism" in Maurice Merleau-Ponty, *The Adventures of the Dialectic*, trans. J. Bien, Evanston, Ill., Northwestern University Press, 1973, pp. 30–58.

28 M. Horkheimer, "The End of Reason," in *The Essential Frankfurt School Reader*, p. 28.

29 Horkheimer, "The Authoritarian State," p. 108.

30 H. Marcuse, "Some Social Implications of Modern Technology," in *The Essential Frankfurt School Reader*, p. 146.

31 T. Adorno, "On the Fetish Character in Music and the Regression to Listening," in *The Essential Frankfurt School Reader*, p. 270.

32 Wiggershaus, *The Frankfurt School*, p. 1.

33 A. Adorno and M. Horkheimer, *The Dialectic of the Enlightenment*, trans. J. Cumming, London, Verso, 1992. See particularly the chapter, "Elements of Anti-Semitism," pp. 168–208.

34 Cited in Wiggershaus, *The Frankfurt School*, pp. 275, 309.

35 Adorno and Horkheimer, *The Dialectic of the Enlightenment*, p. 3.

36 Ibid. p. 163.

37 Ibid. p. 167.

38 Ibid. p. 211.

39 A. Adorno, *Minima Moralia*, trans. E. F. N. Jephcott, London, Verso, 1978, p. 155.

40 *Nouvel Observateur*, quoted on the cover of the Sphere Books 1968 edition of *One Dimensional Man*.

41 H. Marcuse, *One Dimensional Man*, London, Sphere Books, 1968, p. 10.

42 Cited in Wiggershaus, *The Frankfurt School*, p. 103.

43 Marcuse, *One Dimensional Man*, p. 23.

44 Ibid.

45 Ibid. p. 26.

46 Ibid. p. 53.

47 Ibid. p. 24.

48 P. Collier and D. Horowitz, *The Destructive Generation: Second Thoughts about the 60s*, New York, Free Press, 1996, p. 14.

49 Marcuse, *One Dimensional Man*, p. 70.

50 See G. Anders, *Die Antiquiertheit des Menschen*, vol. 2, Munich, Beck, 1980, pp. 83–8.
51 K. Marx, "Letter to Ruge," *Marx Engels Collected Works*, vol. 3, London, Lawrence and Wishart, 1975, p. 159.
52 Ibid. "Political democracy is Christian since in it man, not merely one man but every man, ranks as sovereign, as the highest being, but it is man in his fortuitous existence, man just as he is, man as he has been corrupted by the whole organisation of our society, who has lost himself, been alienated, and handed over to the rule of inhuman conditions and elements—in short, man who is not yet a *real* species being."
53 Ibid. p. 163.
54 Ibid. p. 164.
55 Marx, *Economic and Philosophical Manuscripts*, trans. T. B. Bottomore, in E. Fromm, *Marx's Concept of Man*, New York, Frederick Ungar, 1966, p. 132.

3 POVERTY

1 World Bank data, online at http://www.worldbank.org/poverty/mission/up2.htm. There is much debate on the standards of measuring global poverty particularly given the wide differences of income and living costs among various countries. The World Bank tends to use two measurements (for under one and for under two dollars a day) but as its critics have pointed out, this is far too low to accommodate the millions of people in industrial countries who cannot survive on even 10 dollars a day. (See Michel Chossudovsky, "Global Falsehoods: How the World Bank and UNDP Distort the Figures on Global Poverty," online at http://www.transnational.org/features/chossu_worldbank.html.) Nonetheless, although the actual figure on global poverty would be higher than the one we cite if a higher minimum dollar threshold were used, the fact that even two dollars per day accounts for half of the world's population should sufficiently illustrate the scope of the problem.
2 B. Rowntree, *Poverty: A Study of Town Life*, New York, Howard Fertig, 1971, p. 117.
3 However, recent studies have shown that the research budget of pharmaceutical companies as a percentage of revenue is much smaller than commonly assumed. In the year 2000, two leading firms, GlaxoSmithKline and Bristol-Myers Squibb spent 14 per cent (versus profits of 28 per cent) and 11 per cent (versus profits of 26 per cent) respectively on research and development. This data, coupled with the fact that developing country manufacturers are able to produce the same drugs at a much lower cost, suggests that the Western conglomerates have a much greater capacity to lower prices on drugs than they generally acknowledge. See Melody Petersen, "Lifting the Curtain on the Real Costs of Making AIDS drugs," *New York Times*, 24 April 2001, C1/c10.
4 A. Sen, "Levels of Poverty, Policy and Change," *World Bank Staff Working Paper*, no. 401, Washington, DC, World Bank, July 1980, p. 1.
5 *World Bank Poverty Reduction Handbook*, Washington, DC, World Bank, 1993, p. 14.
6 Cited in S. MacPherson and R. Silburn, "The Meaning and Measurement of Poverty," in J. Dixon and D. Macarov (eds), *Poverty: A Persistent Global Reality*, London, Routledge, 1998.
7 A. Sen, *On Economic Inequality*, Oxford, Clarendon Press, 1997, p. 212–13.
8 K. Marx, *Value, Price, and Profit* (*The Marxists' Internet Archive*) online at http://www.marxists.org/archive/marx/works/1865-vpp.htm, p. 25.
9 Ibid. p. 45.

10 See J. Schwarz, *Illusions of Opportunity: The American Dream in Question*, New York, W. W. Norton, 1997, p. 114. Focusing on Afro-American teenage girls, Schwarz points out that often pregnancy is not accidental, but a conscious decision given that, unlike women from a higher-income stratum, they see few reasons to defer gratification of child-rearing until they have achieved certain professional goals. For similar conclusions, see also, Lee Rainwater, "The Problem of Lower-Class Culture and Poverty-War Strategy," in Daniel Patrick Moynihan (ed.), *On Understanding Poverty*, New York, Basic Books, 1969, pp. 229–59; Leon Dash, *When Children Want Children: An Inside Look at the Crisis of Teenage Parenthood*, New York, Penguin, 1989.

11 On the psychological aspects common to the poor, see O. Lewis, "The Culture of Poverty," in Moynihan, *On Understanding Poverty*, pp. 187–200. Lewis claims that the culture of poverty can be described "in terms of seventy interrelated social, economic and psychological traits" (p. 188).

12 Cited in C. Oman and G. Wignaraja, *The Postwar Evolution of Development Thinking*, London, Macmillan and OECD, 1991, p. 107.

13 P. Krugman, "Pursuing Happiness", *New York Times*, 28 March 2000, p. A29.

14 See S. Cullenberg, *The Falling Rate of Profit: Recasting the Marxian Debate*, London, Pluto, 1994, and D. Foley and T. Michl, *Growth and Distribution*, Cambridge, MA, Harvard University Press, 1999.

15 L. Althusser and E. Balibar, *Reading Capital*, trans. B. Brewster, London, Verso, 1997, p. 15.

16 F. Engels, Preface to K. Marx's *The Poverty of Philosophy*, New York, International Publishers, 1963, p. 12.

17 "Letter from Marx to J. B. Schweitzer," in *Marx, The Poverty of Philosophy* (appendix), p. 198.

18 See Gary Becker, *Human Capital*, Chicago, University of Chicago Press, 1993.

19 S. Fischer, R. Dornbusch, and R. Schmalensee, *Introduction to Microeconomics*, New York, McGraw-Hill, 1988, p. 287.

20 K. Marx, *The Holy Family*, in *Marx and Engels Collected Works*, London, Lawrence and Wishart, vol. IV, 1975, p. 33..

21 P. Sweezy, *Modern Capitalism and Other Essays*, New York, Monthly Review Press, 1972, p. 54.

22 Although recent literature on game theory, inequality, and growth, have partially addressed these weaknesses.

23 Cited in G. Hodgson, *Economics and Utopia*, London, Routledge, 1999, p. 117.

24 Marx, *Economic and Philosophical Manuscripts*, trans. T. B. Bottomore, in E. Fromm, *Marx's Concept of Man*, New York, Frederick Ungar, 1966, p. 98.

25 G. Simmel, *The Philosophy of Money*, trans. T. Bottomore and D. Frisby, London, Routledge, 1990, p. 427.

26 The comparative security of slaves to white unskilled wage labor was documented by early travelers to America. Willam Eddis in his *Letters from America* (1770) wrote: "Negroes being a property for life, the death of slaves, in the prime of youth or strength, is a material loss to the proprietor; they are therefore, almost in every instance, under more comfortable circumstances than the miserable European, over whom the rigid planter exercises an inflexible severity." Cited in Thomas R. Brooks, *Toil and Trouble: A History of American Labor*, New York, Dell, 1971, p. 7. Eddis's observation is fortified by the experiences of African-Americans following the Civil War. Despite all the lofty rhetoric that led to their emancipation, slaves, once released from the plantation, still needed to eat and clothe themselves. Most of them thus reverted to quasi-slavery in the form of sharecropping, paying rent for the use of land from the plantation to

scrape out an existence. The rest gravitated northward to supply the factories with their cheap labor.

27 Marx, *Value, Price and Profit*, p. 24.
28 Cited in the *Washington Post*, "A Tip of the Teamster Hat to Nader," Friday, 23 June 2000, A14.
29 Sweezy, *Modern Capitalism*, p. 141.
30 J. Winters, "Indonesia: On the Mostly Negative Role of Transnational Capital in Democratization," in L. E. Armijo (ed.), *Financial Globalization and Democracy in Emerging Markets*, New York, St Martin's Press, 1999, p. 246.
31 See "Sweating for Nike: A Report on Labor Conditions in the Sport Shoe Industry," Tim Connor and Jeff Atkinson, *Community Aid Abroad Briefing Paper*, no. 16, November, 1996, online at www.caa.org.au/campaigns/nike/sweating.html.
32 W. Adler, "A Job on the Line," *Mother Jones*, March/April 2000, pp. 44–7, 86–7.
33 P. Krugman, "In Praise of Cheap Labor: Bad Jobs at Bad Wages are Better than No Jobs at All," online at http://web.mit.edu/krugman/www/smokey.html.
34 Marx, *Value, Price and Profit*, p. 27.
35 J. K. Black cited in J. Marcet, *Conversations on Political Economy*, Boston, Bowles and Dearborn, 1828, p. 142.
36 Marx, *The Poverty of Philosophy*, p. 124.
37 This is presumably what Oscar Lewis has in mind when he writes: "When the poor become class conscious or active members of trade-union organizations or when they adopt an internationalist outlook on the world, they are no longer part of the culture of poverty although they may still be desperately poor. Any movement—be it religious, pacifist or revolutionary—that organizes and gives hope to the poor and effectively promotes solidarity and a sense of identification with larger groups destroys the psychological and social core of the culture of poverty." Lewis, "The Culture of Poverty," in Moynihan (ed.), *On Understanding Poverty*, p. 193.
38 Such lessons can be drawn from the milestones of the American labor movement such as the Haymarket Square incident. On 3 May 1886 some 3,000 lumberyard workers gathered at Chicago's Haymarket Square. A bomb went off, and killed some police officers. The police retaliated, killing several and wounding 200. In the aftermath, employers not only cracked down on strikers, they actually reversed some of the progressive legislation they had adopted. The effect of the bomb, noted Samuel Gompers, a leading American labor spokesman, "was that it not only killed the policemen, but it killed our eight-hour movement for a few years." See Brooks, *Toil and Trouble*, p. 70.
39 See Liz Featherstone and Doug Henwood, "Clothes Encounters: Activists and Economists Clash Over Sweatshops," *Linguafranca*, March 2001, pp. 26–33.
40 Louis Althusser, *The Future Lasts Forever*, trans. R. Veasey, New York, New Press, 1993, p. 225.
41 B. Geremek, *Poverty: A History*, trans. A. Kolakowska, Oxford, Blackwell, 1994, p. 55.
42 See Sen, "Levels of Poverty: Policy and Change."
43 F. Stewart, "Inequality, Technology and Payment Systems" in F. Stewart (ed.), *Work, Income and Inequality*, New York, St Martin's Press, 1983, p. 13.
44 M. ul-Haq, "Political systems and poverty," in *Social Reform and Poverty*, Washington, DC/New York, Inter-American Development Bank and the United Nations Development Program, 1993, p. 93.
45 A. Stukanov, "International Action for Global Poverty Eradication: The Case of the World Bank," *Scholarly Papers by IREX Alumni*, 8 March 1999, online at http://www.irex.org/publications/scholarpaper/ stukanov.htm.

46 World Bank mission statement, online at http://www.worldbank.org.
47 World Bank Policy Research Report, *Assessing Aid: What Works, What Doesn't and Why*, Washington, DC, World Bank, and Oxford University Press, 1998.
48 G. Hancock, *Lords of Poverty: The Power, Prestige and Corruption of the International Aid Business*, New York, Atlantic Monthly Press, 1989, pp. 44, 145.
49 Richard Robbins, *Global Problems and the Culture of Capitalism*, Boston, Allyn and Bacon, 1999, p. 103.
50 According to Joseph Stiglitz, former Chief Economist of the World Bank, the real problem with radical economists is not that they use emotionally charged words such as "exploitation" in their analysis, it is rather, "in their implicit or explicit policy prescriptions that radical economists fail to make their case." "Post-Walrasian and Post-Marxian Economics," *Journal of Economic Perspectives*, vol. 7, no. 1, 1993, p. 112.
51 Author interviews with anti-World Bank/IMF protesters, April 2000.
52 Robbins, *Global Problems*, p. 107.
53 F. Stewart, "Structural Adjustment Policies and the Poor in Africa: An Analysis of the 1980s," in F. Stewart (ed.), *Adjustment and Poverty*, London, Routledge, 1995, p. 142.
54 World Bank, *Poverty Reduction Handbook*, Washington, DC, World Bank, 1993, p. 291.
55 World Bank, *World Development Report: Workers in an Integrating World*, New York, Oxford University Press, 1995, p. 75.
56 J. Bernstein and J. Schmitt, "Making Work Pay: The Impact of the 1996–1997 Minimum Wage Increases" (Executive Summary), Washington, DC, Economic Policy Institute Study, 1998. See also David Carr and Allan Krueger, *Myth and Measurement: The New Economics of the Minimum Wage*, Princeton, NJ, Princeton University Press, 1995.
57 World Bank Internal Document, 2001.
58 Cited in Hal Draper, *Karl Marx's Theory of Revolution*, New York, Monthly Review Press, 1990, p. 44.
59 World Bank, *Poverty Reduction Handbook*, p. 44.
60 Cited in A. B. Atkinson, *The Economics of Inequality*, Oxford, Clarendon Press, 1975, p. 80. For a technical discussion of human capital theory, see pp. 79–86.
61 Gary Becker, *Human Capital*, Chicago, University of Chicago Press, 1993 (3rd edition).
62 Cited in Michael Harrington's *The Twilight of Capitalism*, New York, Touchstone, 1976, p. 272.
63 Ibid. p. 23.
64 Marx, *Value, Price and Profit*, p. 27.

4 CORRUPTION

1 K. Marx, "Letter to Ruge," in *Marx Engels Collected Works* (henceforth *MECW*), vol. 5, London, Lawrence and Wishart, vol. 1, 1975, p. 400.
2 Much recent literature has focused on the role of institutional culture in building legitimate democratic structures in transition economies. See D. Stark and L. Bruszt, "Remaking the Political Field in Hungary," *Journal of International Affairs*, vol. 45, no. 1, pp. 201–46, and D. Woodruff, *Money Unmade: Barter and the Fate of Russian Capitalism*, Ithaca, NY, Cornell University Press, 1999. In contrast to research based on optimal policy designs, these works attempt to build alternative socio-political approaches to analyze the governance of institutional experiments.

3 G. W. F. Hegel, *The Philosophy of History*, New York, Dover, 1956, p. 412.
4 Ibid. p. 413, fn.
5 K. Marx, *The German Ideology*, *MECW*, vol. 5, p. 38.
6 See J. Conlin, *The American Radical Press*, vol. 1, London, Greenwood Press, 1974, p. 9.
7 C. Offe, *Modernity and the State*, Cambridge, MA, MIT Press, 1996, p. x.
8 See J. Williamson, "What Washington means by Policy Reform," in J. Williamson (ed.), *Latin American Adjustment: How Much Has Happened*, Washington, DC, Institute for International Economics, 1990, pp. 5–20.
9 Ibid.
10 See two studies from the International Monetary Fund *Economic Issues Series*: Paolo Mauro, "Why Worry About Corruption?" no. 6, 1997, and V. Tanzi and H. Davoodi, "Roads to Nowhere: How Corruption in Public Investment Hurts Growth," no. 12, 1998.
11 See P. Evans, "The State as Problem and Solution," in S. Haggard and R. Kaufman (eds), *The Politics of Economic Adjustment*, Princeton, NJ, Princeton University Press, 1992, p. 145.
12 For an overview of contemporary Marxist challenges to liberal democracy, see D. Held, *Models of Democracy*, Stanford, CA, Stanford University Press, 1996, pp. 284–91.
13 F. A. Hayek, *The Road to Serfdom*, Chicago, University of Chicago Press, 1994 (50th anniversary edition), pp. 155–6.
14 L. Kolakowski, *Freedom, Fame, Lying and Betrayal*, London, Penguin Books, 1999, pp. 95–103.
15 R. Dworkin, *Sovereign Virtues*, Cambridge, MA, Harvard University Press, 2000.
16 H. Mueller, *Bureaucracy, Education and Monopoly: Civil Service Reforms in Prussia and England*, Berkeley, University of California Press, 1984, p. 158.
17 H. Beck, *The Origins of the Authoritarian Welfare State: Conservatives, Bureaucracy and the Social Question, 1815–1870*, Ann Arbor, University of Michigan Press, 1995, p. viii.
18 J. Gillis, *The Prussian Bureaucracy in Crisis*, Stanford, CA, Stanford University Press, 1971, p. 16.
19 Cited in Marx, "Contribution to the Critique of Hegel's Philosophy of Right," *MECW*, vol. 3, p. 50.
20 Mueller, *Bureaucracy, Education and Monopoly*, p. 158.
21 K. Marx, "Justification of the Correspondent from the Mosel," *MECW*, vol. 3, p. 349.
22 K. Marx, "Contribution to the Critique of Hegel's Philosophy of Right," *MECW*, vol. 3, p. 46.
23 Ibid. p. 47.
24 K. Marx, "On the Jewish Question," *MECW*, vol. 3, p. 164.
25 Ibid. p. 169.
26 Ibid. p. 157.
27 Ibid. p. 174.
28 Ibid. p. 187.
29 Ibid.
30 Cited in R. Tucker, "Marx as a Political Theorist" in Shlomo Avineri (ed.), *Marx's Socialism*, New York, Lieber-Atherton, 1973, p. 176.
31 Cited in M. Albrow, *Bureaucracy*, New York, Praeger, 1970, p. 19.
32 For an in-depth analysis of all eleven references to "the dictatorship of the proletariat," see R. Hunt, *The Political Ideas of Marx and Engels*, vol. 2, Pittsburgh, University of Pittsburgh Press, 1984, pp. 284–336.

33 See R. Miliband's entry on "The State" in T. Bottomore (ed.), *A Dictionary of Marxist Thought*, Oxford, Blackwell, 1991, p. 524.

34 See Robert Tucker, "Marx as a Political Theorist" and Ralph Miliband, "Marx and the State," in Avineri, *Marx's Socialism.*

35 K. Marx, *The Poverty of Philosophy*, New York, International Publishers, 1963, p. 174.

36 In fact, Engels, in "The Critique of the Gotha Program" alluded to the need for a surrogate by suggesting that "State" be replaced with *Gemeinwesen* (communal being). See Tucker, "Marx as a Political Theorist," p. 150.

37 See the transcript from the *Journal of Democracy* panel discussion on "Alexis de Toqueville and the Future of Democracy," online at http://www.ned.org/jod/panel.htm, p. 7.

38 J. Mukum Mbaku, *Corruption and the Crisis of Institutional Reforms in Africa*, Lewiston, NY, E. Mellen Press, 1998, p. xiii. For an overview on mechanisms applied by state authorities to preserve and perpetuate their power, see also Evans, "The State as the Problem and Solution."

39 See F. Gibney Jr., "A Tale of Two Worlds: Foreign Investment Soars and Cities Prosper, but Vietnam's New Wealth Has Yet to Enrich the Vast, Desperate Countryside" *Time*, 5 February 1996, vol. 147, no. 6.

40 World Bank, *Poverty Reduction Handbook*, Washington, DC, World Bank, 1993, p. 66.

41 K. Phillips, *Arrogant Capital: The Frustration of American Politics*, New York, Little, Brown and Company, 1995, p. 6.

42 D. Bell, *The Cultural Contradictions of Capitalism*, New York, Basic Books, 1996 (twentieth anniversary edition), p. 334.

43 H. Marcuse, "Repressive Tolerance," in P. Bacharach (ed.), *Political Elites in a Democracy*, New York, Atherton Press, 1971, p. 165.

44 V. Pareto, *Sociological Writings*, trans. D. Merfin, Totowa, NJ, Rowman and Littlefield, 1976, p. 270.

45 Ibid. p. 140.

46 See Ibid. p. 270: "The uses and abuses of power will be more considerable the greater the intervention of government in private affairs. As exploitable material increases, so do potential gains." More modern critics echo this view with reference to recent history in the Third World. See Mbaku, "Bureaucratic and Political Corruption in Africa," in Mbaku, *Corruption and the Crisis of Institutional Reforms in Africa*, pp. 47, 77 and D. Kaufmann, "Anticorruption Strategies: Starting Afresh? Unconventional Lessons from Comparative Analysis," in R. Stapenhurst and S. Kpundeh (eds), *Curbing Corruption*, Washington, DC, World Bank, 1999, p. 47.

47 G. Mosca, "The Final Version of the Theory of the Ruling Class," in J. Meisel (ed.), *The Myth of the Ruling Class*, Westport, Conn., Greenwood Press, 1980, p. 12.

48 P. Mauro, "Why Worry About Corruption?" *Economic Issues*, vol. 6, International Monetary Fund, 1997.

49 Kaufman, "Anticorruption Strategies," pp. 47–9.

50 See, for example, the response of Patricio Meller, a Chilean economist, to Williamson's seminal Washington Consensus article on the benefits of privitization in Williamson, *Latin American Adjustment*, p. 35. Meller makes three key points. 1) Latin American states, and developing countries in general, have few social safety nets to begin with. To divest the state from these nets while they are in the stages of construction is, therefore, often counterproductive. 2) Latin America has had bad experience with unregulated financial markets. The volatility

of speculative capital flowing in and out has had a damaging effect on macro-economic stability. 3) The private sector is an untrustworthy ally to which to delegate former state responsibilities. In these countries, it tends to shift easily from "productive to speculative to fugitive (capital flight) behavior."

51 J. Nellis, "So Far So Good? A Privatization Update," transition newsletter, The World Bank Group, November/December 1996, p. 7, online at: www.worldbank.org/html/prddr/trans/novdec96/doc5.htm.

52 D. Nelken and M. Levi, "The Corruption of Politics and the Politics of Corruption: An Overview" in D. Nelken and M. Levi (eds), *The Corruption of Politics and the Politics of Corruption*, Oxford, Blackwell, 1996, p. 2.

53 And some IMF economists have acknowledged that the analysis of corruption is often endogenous to unique political cultures, and may not always lend itself to economic paradigms of analysis. Instead, they have drawn upon non-economic methodologies such as the sociology of organized crime and gangs to understand better how, for example, patterns of allegiance develop in a "predatory hierarchy." See J. Charap and C. Harm, "Institutionalized Corruption and the Kleptocratic State," *IMF Working Paper*, Washington, DC, International Monetary Fund, July 1999.

54 See D. Della Porta and A. Pizzorno, "The Business Politicians: Reflections from a Study of Political Corruption," in Levi and Nelken, *The Corruption of Politics*, p. 88.

55 See M. Boycko, A. Shleifer and R. Vishny, *Privatizing Russia*, Cambridge, MA, MIT Press, 1995, p. 11: "The political influence over economic life (in Russia) was the fundamental cause of economic inefficiency, and the principal objective of reform was, therefore, to depoliticize economic life."

56 S. Holmes, "What Russia Teaches Us Now: How Weak States Threaten Freedom," *The American Prospect*, no. 33 (July–August 1997), pp. 30–9, online at http://www.epn.org/prospect/33/33holmf.html, p. 5.

57 J. Gray, *False Dawn: The Delusions of Global Capitalism*, New York, The New Press, 1998, p. 147.

58 In this respect, the naïveté of leading privatizers such as Boycko and Shleifer was particularly striking. "The experience of Russian privatization," they wrote, "demonstrated how misguided the Gorbachev and Western Sovietologists were, and how clearly the Russians revealed themselves as 'economic men.'" See Boycko, Shleifer and Vishny, *Privatizing Russia*, p. 10.

59 A. Faiola, "Some Latin American Countries Look Back to the Good Old Days of Dictators," *International Herald Tribune*, 1 June 1998, p. 10.

60 H. Mayo, *Introduction to Marxist Theory*, Oxford, Oxford University Press, 1960, p. 271.

61 See M. Johnston, "Fighting Systemic Corruption: Social Foundations for Institutional Reform," in Nelken and Levi, *The Corruption of Politics*, pp. 85–104.

62 See R. Teixera, "The Tax Cut Nobody Wants," *The American Prospect*, 5 June 2000, pp. 17–19.

63 E. Olson, "Swiss Charge Dictator's Ally in Plundering Nigeria," *New York Times*, 5 April 2000, p. A9.

64 *Transparency International*, online at http://www.transparency.de/contact/media_faq.html, p. 5.

65 R. Kanth, *Capitalism and Social Theory*, Armonk, NY, M. E. Sharpe, 1992, p. xx.

66 Karl Kautsky, *Marxism and Bolshevism: Democracy and Dictatorship*, 1934, p. 4, online at http://www.marxists.org/archive/kautsky/works/1930s/bolsh.htm.

5 BANALITY

1 G. Lukács, "The Old Culture and the New Culture," in *Marxism and Human Liberation*, New York, Dell Publishing, 1973, p. 18.
2 Cited in R. Monk, *Wittgenstein*, London, Penguin, p. 20.
3 Lukács, "The Old Culture and the New Culture," p. 4.
4 K. Marx, *Value, Price and Profit* (*The Marxists' Internet Archive*) online at http://www.marxists.org/archive/marx/works/1865-vpp.htm, p. 23.
5 Cited in G. MacLennan, "Documentary Philosophy: The Aesthetic Dimension," online at http://www.raggedclaws.com/criticalrealism/archive/gmac_dp.html, p. 1.
6 K. Marx, *Economic and Philosophical Manuscripts*, trans. T. B. Bottomore, in E. Fromm, *Marx's Concept of Man*, New York, Frederick Ungar, 1966, p. 179.
7 See P. Kain, *Schiller, Hegel, and Marx: State, Society, and the Aesthetic Ideal of Ancient Greece*, Kingston and Montreal, McGill-Queen's University Press, 1982.
8 D. Bell, "The 'Rediscovery' of Alienation" in S. Avineri (ed.) *Marx's Socialism*, New York, Lieber-Atherton, 1973, p. 61.
9 See D. Hodges, "The Young Marx—A Reappraisal," in Avineri, *Marx's Socialism*, who argues that "Marx was concerned not with the sources of social pathology in general, but with the alienation of the worker in particular" (p. 28).
10 Marx, *Economic and Philosophical Manuscripts*, p. 168.
11 K. Marx, "The Fetishism of the Commodity and Its Secret" in *Das Capital*, vol. 1, New York, Vintage Books, 1977, pp. 163–77.
12 Lukács, *Marxism and Human Liberation*, p. 252.
13 G. Debord, *The Society of the Spectacle*, trans. Donald Nicholson-Smith, New York, Zone Books, 1995, p. 18.
14 W. Haug, *Critique of Commodity Aesthetics*, trans. R. Bock, Minneapolis, University of Minnesota Press, 1986, p. 52.
15 T. Judt, *Past Imperfect: French Intellectuals, 1944–1956*, Berkeley, University of California Press, 1992, p. 190.
16 Ibid.
17 Lukács, *Marxism and Human Liberation*, p. 6.
18 G. Simmel, *The Philosophy of Money*, trans. T. Bottomore and D. Frisby, London, Routledge, 1990, p. 404.
19 E. Mandel, *Late Capitalism*, trans. J. de Bres, Atlantic Highlands, NJ, Humanities Press, 1975, p. 406.
20 C. Lasch, *The Culture of Narcissism*, New York, W. W. Norton, 1991, p. 72.
21 Haug, *Critique of Commodity Aesthetics*, p. 129.
22 Lukács, *Marxism and Human Liberation*, p. 252.
23 J. Stallabrass, *Gargantua: Manufactured Mass Culture*, London, Verso, 1996, p. 4.
24 M. Goldberg, "Film Bytes: Will Digital Film-Making and the Net Leave Hollywood an Empty Set," *Silicon Valley Reporter*, October 1998, issue 18, pp. 28–38, 106.
25 F. Jameson, *Postmodernism, or the Cultural Logic of Capitalism*, Durham, NC, Duke University Press, 1991, p. 147.
26 See J. Curry, "The Dialectic of Knowledge-in-Production: Value Creation in Late Capitalism and the Rise of Knowledge-Centered Production," *Electronic Journal of Sociology*, vol. 2, no. 3, 1997, online at http://www.sociology.org.
27 Some comparative data is provided in B. Wallis, M. Weems and P. Yenawine (eds), *Art Matters: How the Culture Wars Changed America*, New York, New York University Press, 1999, p. 33. Based on public expenditure on the arts and

museums, in US dollars per person: Sweden, 45.6, Germany, 39.4, France, 35.1, Netherlands, 33.6, Canada, 28.5, United States, 3.3.

28 On the need for greater allocations toward pre-school education in the United States, see I. Harris, "Starting Small, Thinking Big," *The American Prospect*, online at http://www.prospect.org/archives/28/28harr.html, and J. Salmon and K. Grimsley, "More States Pick up the Tab for Preschool," *Washington Post*, 13 March 2000, pp. A1, A6.

BIBLIOGRAPHICAL ESSAY

As an icon of anti-capitalist protest over a span of 150 years, Marx's key texts were not only interpreted, they were also applied to an enormous range of topics from industrial relations to literary criticism. And, almost every decade since Marx's death has produced scores of monographs and essays seeking to modernize the canon in synch with the changing nature of capitalism. However, like biblical scholarship, much of the literature revolves around canonical nuances and arcane points of contention. Therefore, the uninitiated reader might best be served by starting with a biography. There are also many works in this category, but they can basically be broken down into two groups: there are those that provide an intellectual history of Marx based on core texts and thinkers—Leszek Kolakowksi's three-volume *Main Currents of Marxism* remains unsurpassed in this genre (translated by P. S. Falla, Oxford, Clarendon Press, 1978), but Isaiah Berlin's *Karl Marx: His Life and Environment* (Oxford, Oxford University Press, 1996) and David McLellan's *Karl Marx: His Life and Thought* (Frogmore, Paladin, 1976) are also excellent introductions; and there are those that focus more on a psychological portrait of Marx the man— Robert Payne's *Marx* (New York, Simon and Schuster, 1968) and more recently, Frank Manuel's *A Requiem for Karl Marx* (Cambridge, MA, Harvard University Press, 1995) and Francis Wheen's, *Karl Marx: A Life* (New York, Norton, 2000). The Wheen and Manuel works are particularly well written and provide rather harrowing accounts of Marx's persistent financial and medical problems.

Those who would like to sample the original texts of Marx and the Marxists could begin with Sidney Hook's anthology (with introductory essay), *Marx and the Marxists* (New York, Nostrand, 1955). However, today, readers can more conveniently access these online. Here, *The Marxists' Internet Archive* (httm://www.marxists.org) provides an indispensable service for both the reader and researcher. It not only provides over 200 selections of Marx's and Engels's original work, but it has also archived numerous essays and monographs by Marxists, critics of Marxism, and philosophers working, loosely defined, in the Marxist tradition.

As for the academic controversies surrounding Marx and the application of his ideas, many of these are now outdated. However, one controversy that remains current is the connection between the early philosophical Marx and the later economist Marx. This distinction is so important because Western Marxism—Marxism without a proletariat, so to speak—almost single-handedly drew upon the early Marx to counter the incendiary claims that the later Marx made on behalf of the proletariat. Iring Fetscher's essay, "The Young and Old Marx," in Shlomo Avineri,

Marx's Socialism (New York, Lieber-Atherton, 1973) provides one of the best overviews on this subject. Written in the late 1960s at a time when the distinction between the early and late Marx, between, in a way, cultural criticism and radical revolution, was very much in the forefront, Fetscher contends that the later work *Das Kapital* is simply a more elaborate critique of the "alienated social relations" which Marx identified in the *Economic and Philosophical Manuscripts*. To support his point, he provides a concise and ideologically neutral definition of the question Marx posed himself at the outset, and never deviated from. It can still be applied to capitalism and modern free-market economics today. As Fetscher formulates it (p. 42):

> How did it happen that the bourgeois revolution did not achieve its pro-claimed aims, and why, despite formally legalized freedoms, individuals came, in the course of the division of labor and modern market mecha-nism, to be dominated by social processes which prevailed behind their backs and prevented everybody from achieving a status of humanity which could have been realized in the light of the wealth of society that already existed?

Marx's economic theory and poverty

On Marx's economic thought in general, the best introductory surveys can be found in Ernest Mandel's *The Formation of the Economic Thought of Karl Marx* (translated by Brian Pearce, New York, Monthly Review Press, 1973) and the section on "Marx the Economist," in Joseph Schumpeter's classic *Capitalism, Socialism, and Democracy* (London, Unwin, 1987). Both provide a lucid exposition for the lay reader. For a serious study of Marx situated in the history of bourgeois economic thought, one might turn to Maurine Dobb's *Theories of Value and Distribution Since Adam Smith: Ideology and Economic Theory* (Cambridge, Cambridge University Press, 1973). De-spite the daunting title, it is a clearly argued account of a critical issue, namely how much of the debate within mainstream economics has been dictated by how value and prices are determined. From such technical discussions emerge all kinds of questions as to how to measure human productivity or the role of the state in counteracting market determinations of value for the sake of the greater good. Other detailed expositions on the labor theory of value can be found in Eugen von Böhm Bawerk's *Karl Marx and the The Close of the Marxian System* (available on *The Marx-ists' Internet Archive*) and Joan Robinson, *An Essay on Marxian Economics* (Philadel-phia, Orion Editions, 1966). Those interested in the broader application of Marx's economic ideas to contemporary capitalism might sample Paul Sweezy's *Modern Capitalism and Other Essays* (New York, Monthly Review Press, 1972) and Ernest Mandel's monumental, *Late Capitalism* (translated by Joris de Bres, Atlantic High-lands, NJ, Humanities Press, 1975).

Readers interested in the shortcomings of mainstream economics might well begin with an article in the *New Yorker*, "The Decline of Economics," by John Cassidy (2 December 1996, pp. 50–60). Arguing that the academic profession of economics has become overly insular, mathematical, and detached from social problems, Cassidy reaches the damning conclusion that, "even those economists who do concern themselves with practical subjects often tackle them on a level so abstract that their work has few policy implications and, in the end, sometimes appears to be part of a giant academic game." Geoffrey Hodgson's chapter on the "Universality of Mainstream Economics," in his *Economics and Utopia: Why the Learning Economy is not the End of History* (London, Routledge, 1999) also provides trenchant criticism of the universal assumptions of mainstream economics, and how they can hardly accommodate the heterogeneity of market relations.

On a more specific level, students of economics will be interested in Stephen Resnick's and Richard Wolff's article, "A Marxian Reconceptualization of Income and its Distribution," in Stephen Resnick and Richard Wolff (eds) *Rethinking Marxism: Struggles in Marxist Theory: Essays for Harry Magdoff and Paul Sweezy* (Brooklyn, NY, Autononmedia, 1985, pp. 319–44) to study the contrasts between Marxist and mainstream or neoclassical theories of income. In their view, the mainstream argument reads (p. 322): "Personal preferences regarding final goods and regarding the supply of the given endowments of different factors and marginal productivity of those factors determine different incomes and their distribution in society." Thus, the distribution of income is based on varying endowments and individual preferences either to work hard or not. Marxian theory, on the other hand, begins from the opposite standpoint: not individual preferences, but the dynamic relationship between wage and profit in the manufacturing process. It begins with a theory of exploitation, or the appropriation of surplus labor. Thus, the schools of thought arrive at two very different views of eliminating relative poverty. For the mainstream economist it is about maximizing one's outcomes, which means either working harder or saving more (p. 324: "Work hard and be thrifty is the motto of the neoclassical view of capitalist society"). For the Marxist, it is about acquiring the means to earn a higher wage.

On the whole, it can be said that the discipline of economics *can* be socially relevant when it dispassionately exposes weaknesses and contradictions in the reigning mainstream orthodoxy (without the inflammatory rhetoric that taints much of protest scholarship). Here, David Carr's and Allan Krueger's *Myth and Measurement: The New Economics of the Minimum Wage* (Princeton, NJ, Princeton University Press, 1995), and Jared Bernstein's and John Schmitt's *Making Work Pay: The Impact of the 1996–1997 Minimum Wage Increases* (Washington, DC, Economic Policy Institute, 1998), both on the relatively benign impact of minimum wage hikes on unemployment, are notable contributions to that project.

Within the vast literature on poverty, there are countless literary, historical, theological, or sociological treatments. Bronislaw Geremek's *Poverty: A History* (translated by Agniesza Kolakowska, Oxford, Blackwell, 1994) does a particularly good job in chronicling the evolution of *perceptions* of poverty—from an exhalted Christian virtue, i.e., the renunciation of worldly goods, to a structural problem with technocratic solutions. If one were to limit oneself to poverty in a capitalist context, a good beginning would be Friedrich Engels's *The Condition of the Working-Class in England* (*Marx Engels Collected Works*, London, Lawrence and Wishart, 1975, vol. 4, pp. 295–597). Even those wary of Engels's politics will find in these pages a sobering and historically vivid portrait of the working poor in mid-nineteenth-century England. The interesting theme here is not just the Dickensian conditions of the poor, but also the apathetic response of factory-owners to these conditions in the absence of political pressure and widespread insurrection. Based on this work, one will begin to realize that the radical center of Marx's and Engels's agenda was as much based on a well-grounded disillusionment with contemporary political responses toward the working poor, as it was on a larger philosophical premises. However, for all its merits, Engels's account is somewhat journalistic and descriptive.

A more serious study of poverty can be found in Benjamin Rowntree's *Poverty: A Study of Town Life* (first published in 1901, reissued by Howard Fertig, New York 1971). Based on surveys with over 11,000 families in the northern English city of York, it applied what he called an "intensive" method—fieldwork as opposed to a country-wide extensive statistical approach—to explore both the structure and causes of poverty in a mid-sized industrial town. Part of the beauty of this work, aside from its period details (e.g., the precise food items purchased by a poor family with its weekly budget), is how it illustrates, in an earlier form, many of the working methods for effective poverty research that still apply today. These would include: a) detailed house-to-house surveys to acquire an accurate understanding of living conditions in poor areas. By interacting with the women who managed the household budget while their husbands were at work, Rowntree was particularly effective in getting a break-down on the consumption and saving patterns (or lack thereof) of the working poor; b) the significant effect, either positive or negative, of the provision of public services on the perpetuation of poverty. Here he showed particularly how inadequate sewage systems affected health conditions in the poor areas; c) the utility of establishing numerous gradations of poverty or so-called poverty lines under a general classification of poverty. As Rowntree demonstrates, this method allows one to explore subtle shifts in the quality-of-life changes, particularly increases or decreases in the food budget, that have knock-on effects on overall welfare.

A more modern classic of poverty scholarship can be found in Daniel Moynihan's excellent edited collection of essays, *On Understanding Poverty: Perspectives from the Social Sciences* (New York, Basic Books, 1968). Written at the height of US President Johnson's so-called War on Poverty, it provides a useful survey of the psychological and cultural dimensions of poverty, particularly as they affect individuals confronting their fate. In this volume, the essay by Oscar Lewis, "The Culture of Poverty," is particularly worth mentioning. It provides an anthropologist's account of the more subtle side-effects of poverty and shows that even when the causes of poverty may vary enormously, the side-effects—domestic violence, drug abuse, and a whole set of problems which discourage social participation—are often quite similar across geographical boundaries. Lewis's essay draws many of the same conclusions as Marx about the culture of poverty, without explicitly saying so. Like Marx, he affirms that one of the greatest obstacles to exiting from poverty is the culture of poverty itself. It is as much, if not more, debilitating than the absence or short supply of income.

A similar approach, with an almost opposite political message, is taken by the Peruvian Hernando de Soto, in his seminal work, *The Other Path: The Invisible Revolution in the Third World* (New York, Harper & Row, 1989). A best-seller at the height of Latin America's embrace of neoclassical economic policies, it shows that beneath the dismal poverty statistics, particularly on rural migrants to the cities, lies a high-energy informal sector teeming with optimistic and hard-working entrepreneurs. The argument draws from a detailed inquiry into the development of informal markets in Lima, and how they operate outside the normal boundaries of state intervention and taxation. More recently, de Soto has published the provocatively titled, *The Mystery of Capital: Why Capitalism Triumphs in the West and Fails Everywhere Else* (New York, Basic Books, 2000). Based on extensive fieldwork, it argues that an exit strategy for the poor lies in transforming their assets from dead into liquid capital, particularly by introducing the legal structure of property and property rights that exists in the West. It is an appealing thesis, particularly given the millions of disenfranchised slum-dwellers who are not able to use their property as collateral to expand their entrepreneurial activities. The problem is that the thesis rather cavalierly ignores the fact that many of the poor do not own the property they occupy, and could not seize ownership without creating widespread social instability.

Nonetheless, studies like de Soto's reflect two verities about the modern understanding of poverty, which partly contradict one another. 1) Contrary to vulgar leftist criticism, there are cases where the free market does provide the best means for the able-bodied working poor to improve their quality of life. 2) These cases, like all cases of poverty, often afford little scope for generalization. Poverty and the appropriate policies for its alleviation are often country specific. In terms of Item 1, readers might also wish to sample the subject of microcredit. By empowering the poor to apply their skills on the free market (yet by borrowing from institutions that would not otherwise lend to them), microcredit programs represent a mixture of grassroots populism, free-market libertarianism, and left-wing paternalism, and provide an interesting example of how capital can encourage growth if access to it is properly democratized. A good introduction is provided in Shahidur R. Khandker's *Fighting Poverty with Microcredit: Experience in Bangladesh* (Oxford, Oxford University Press for the World Bank, 1998). The work is fittingly based on the case of Bangladesh whose Grameen Bank provided one of the first success cases of microcredit programs. Those interested in policy prescriptions for poverty, particularly on a case-by-case basis, will find a wealth of material in the chapter, "Poverty and Policy," by Michael Lipton and Martin Ravallion (a leading World Bank poverty economist) in J. Behrman and T. N. Srinivasan (eds) *Handbook of Development Economics*, vol. III (Amsterdam, Elsevier Science BV, 1995). Those interested in case studies which challenge neoclassical linkages between income growth and poverty alleviation should consult Gary Fields's *Poverty, Inequality and Development* (Cambridge, Cambridge University Press, 1980), particularly Chapter 6, "Development Progress and Growth Strategies: Case Studies."

For the larger theoretical debates about income growth and development, readers may want to start with the works of Amartya Sen. These attack across a broad front the narrow utility-based definitions of well-being, and argue for a far broader conception, one that thinks more in terms of the development of capabilities rather than income. See Amartya Sen, *Commodities and Capabilities* (Amsterdam, Elsevier Science Publishers, BV 1985). The practical outgrowth of paradigm shifts concerning what constitutes development came to a head with the onslaught of criticism about IMF and World Bank structural adjustment programs in the 1980s. For a useful survey, see Frances Stewart, particularly her essay, "The Impact of Macroadjustment Policies on the Incomes of the Poor: A Review of Alternative Approaches," in Frances Stewart (ed) *Adjustment and Poverty: Options and Choices* (London, Routledge, 1995).

Marx's political theory and corruption

Chapter 4 explored a variety of themes, but one remained central: that traditional theories of liberal democracy cannot accommodate Marx's broader conception of human freedom, and unnecessarily try to divest the state from its responsibility to distribute access to the social surplus equitably. Here, there is a wealth of literature, but a few works can be suggested for further reading. Though they have a different emphasis, both Karl Polanyi's *The Great Transformation* (Boston, Beacon Press, 1957) and Christian Bay's, *Strategies of Political Emancipation* (South Bend, Ind., University of Notre Dame Press, 1981) provide a credible challenge to the permanence of the market economy. Polanyi, in particular, advances the intriguing thesis that the so-called primordial status of unregulated markets was in fact a political legacy of nineteenth-century elites. Both authors present the broader conception of freedom as an evolution from primitive, anarchic to more civilized forms of social organization. It is natural, they argue, that our basic needs evolve, and to satisfy them some measure of planning is required. Thus, institutions are required to provide direction and order to the otherwise volatile and arbitrary swings of the market economy.

For other vigorous challenges to the anti-statist bias of liberalism, readers should also consider Alexander Gershenkron's classic, *Economic Backwardness in Historical Perspective* (Cambridge, MA, Harvard University Press, 1962) which presents the case that no Western state has successfully modernized without a good degree of state intervention; and on its application to the Washington Consensus, Ute Pieper and Lance Taylor, "The Revival of the Liberal Creed: The IMF, the World Bank, and Inequality in a Globalized Economy" (New York, New School for Social Research, CEPA Working Paper, no. 4, January 1998). Finally, in the crowded arena of neoliberal discontent, John Gray's *False Dawn: The Delusions of Global Capitalism* (New York, The New Press, 1998) is an excellent contribution. A former adviser to the Thatcher administration and New Right ideologue, he has since converted, and provides here an eloquent testimony on the social costs and chaos of over-zealously divesting the state from the marketplace.

In terms of the specific categories of Marx's political thought, the role of the state remains ambivalent. Even though Marx primarily saw the state as a vehicle for class interests, the broad definition of freedom that he endorsed could not be possible without certain institutions or state-surrogates regulating the distribution of public goods. But if we consider this broader definition of freedom as central to the evolution of Western society in general, then a particularly vexing question rises to the fore: to what extent did Marx endorse the mechanisms of representative democracy to achieve these aims? Two articles that shed light on this can be found in Avineri's *Marx's Socialism* (cited above). Both Robert Tucker ("Marx as a Political Theorist") and Ralph Miliband ("Marx and the State") address the degree to which Marx endorsed the electoral process as a means of attaining social justice. Tucker concludes that, although for a brief period in the early 1870s Marx, along with the social democrats, did hold out hope for reform through the parliamentary system, he gradually lost faith in the possibility of a non-authoritarian revolution. Tucker also unequivocally endorses the notion that Marx had no place whatsoever for the state in his system. It was by its very nature allied to the ruling class. At best, it could only put its institutional tools at the disposal of a revolution in the early stages, then to be abandoned, once full communism set in. Miliband follows a similar tack, arguing that Marx's work on the state is pervaded by "a powerful anti-authoritarian and anti-bureaucratic bias." While denying the often uncompromising idea which Marx held about the proletariat's seizure of power, these essays are, however, partially constrained by their historical context. They were trying to disassociate Marx from

178

the common wisdom that linked "the dictatorship of the proletariat," with authoritarian Stalinism and totalitarianism in general. Now that, in the wake of communism, Marx has become more disembodied from concrete political contexts, there are grounds to present a more balanced perspective of his view of the state. Along these lines, readers might consult Claus Offe's *Modernity and the State* (Cambridge, MA, MIT Press, 1996) and David Held's review of contemporary Marxist critiques of liberal democracy in *Models of Democracy* (Stanford, CA, Stanford University Press, 1996, pp. 284–91). Both present a vibrant civil society as a key ingredient for holding democratic states accountable to the aims they profess. In particular, Marxist theorists such as Alex Callinicos and Norberto Bobbio, notes Held, see the failure of liberal democracy, among other things, in the "substantial structural constraints on state action" posed by tax evasion, and capital flight.

Marx's culture theory and banality

As for the major themes addressed in Chapter 5, there is an enormous range of literature on the meaning of authentic culture, on the meltdown in distinctions between highbrow and lowbrow, the role of technology in daily life, and the impact of simulation and reproduction on the contemporary art and music scene, not all of it from a Marxian framework. Some positions taken against the decline in modern culture are Christian in nature (which might include a general antipathy toward contemporary nihilism), others draw upon a more agnostic conservative elitism. Yet others offer sociological treatments of phenomena such as suburbanization that, though in the Marxian framework might otherwise be taken as a symptom of alienation, receive under their scrutiny a more value-neutral judgment. Such trends, however much market-driven, are seen as historical processes with both affirmative and negative characteristics. Two classic works along these lines are Christopher Lasch's *The Culture of Narcissism* (New York, Norton, 1991) and Daniel Bell's *Cultural Contradictions of Capitalism* (New York, Basic Books, 1996).

As for a more Marxist perspective, Fredric Jameson's *Postmodernism, or the Cultural Logic of Late Capitalism* (Durham, NC, Duke University Press, 1991) is a seminal work. In terms of its breadth and thoroughness, it is a fitting complement in the realm of culture to what Ernest Mandel in *Late Capitalism* achieved in the realm of economics. Although Jameson's views in *Postmodernism* can be easily sampled in terms of categories—architecture, art, film—a more accessible and compact treatment is provided in his essay collection, *The Cultural Turn: Selected Writings on the Postmodern, 1983–1998* (Verso, London, 1998). Particularly the essays "Postmodernism and Consumer Society," "Marxism and the Postmodern," and "Transformation of the Image in Postmodernity" provide an overview of the most pressing issues about late capitalist culture—the problematic nature of the individual art work where culture is ubiquitous, the difficulty of subversiveness when aesthetic criteria have been decentered, and ultimately, the elusiveness of beauty and meaning when all forms of cultural production seem to be held hostage by the need to manipulate the cultural consumer. Guy Debord's classic *The Society of the Spectacle*, published on the eve of, and made famous by, the 1968 uprisings (translated by Donald Nicholson-Smith, New York, Zone Books, 1995) visits many of the same themes as Jameson but in a more conventional philosophical style. In a structured argument based on over 200 theses, it presents the Spectacle as an all-consuming metaphor for the infectious spread of capitalism. The work elucidates many key Marxian themes that have a bearing on culture—such as commodity fetishism—as well as meditating on the role of commodity production in fragmenting and disembodying the self in modern society. It is well worth sampling. It offers up many intriguing observations, or in the Marxist vein, contradictions, such as the way that capitalism condescends towards workers in the workplace and yet grovels to them in a state of leisure, i.e., the seduction techniques employed by advertisement that reinforce, if not create, a false sense of autonomy among the working poor. It is in many ways an optimal work of Marxist philosophy in that it not only addresses fundamental questions of the human condition in the context of a concrete social reality, but also makes a persuasive case that such questions can only be raised in that context. However, the work advances certain positions that do not seem clearly thought through. For example, adopting a stance characteristic of Adorno, Debord claims that all commodities—from cars to television—under the guise of providing greater freedom "reinforce the isolation of 'the lonely crowd.'" As we discussed in Chapter 5, this statement—though a hallmark of the Marxist idiom—is tenuous at best, and would require a far more rigorous defense than Debord offers. Lefebvre's *Critique of Everyday Life* (translated by John Moore, London, Verso, 1991) though intended primarily as a work of sociology, is equally adamant in its faith that a true philosophy must be engaged in and critically illuminate the trivia of everyday life. In that sense, it is a classic example of how sociology and philosophy blur together to create a contemporary form of philosophizing. Philosophy remains the "search for the discovery of a 'conception of the world, of a living totality'" but it is "no longer speculative, separated from action and life, abstract, contemplative."

Finally, to understand the most recent currents of leftist discourse, four works can be recommended. Perry Anderson, editor of the opinion-shaping *New Left Review*, provides a thorough and useful assessment on the challenges facing the left at the dawn of the new millennium (Perry Anderson, "Renewals," *New Left Review*, January/February 2000). In the course of an overview of the most promising new areas of inquiries, he also laments the disconnect between leftist academic discourse and radical action. Citing a number of prominent critics of the liberal capitalist orthodoxy such as Habermas, Derrida, Stiglitz, Sen, and Dasgupta, he concludes, "the result is typically a spectacle of impressive theoretical energy and productivity, whose social sum is significantly less than its intellectual parts." The "social sum" refers to the political engagement, or significant lack thereof, of leading theorists on the left. Their renunciation of activism, and grand social transformation in favor of their own theoretical agenda, Anderson argues, has left the pro-market theorists, with an unchallenged field in which to trumpet the global spread of capitalism. These and other themes are taken up in a recent exchange of ideas between three leading leftist theorists, Judith Butler, Ernesto Laclau, and Slavoj Žižek, *Contingency, Hegemony, Universality: Contemporary Dialogues on the Left* (London, Verso, 2000). Slavoj Žižek, particularly in his essay "Class Struggle or Postmodernism? Yes, please!" rigorously articulates how postmodernism and its "irreducible plurality of stuggles," have unfortunately undermined a co-ordinated "essentialist" protest against capitalism. The recent wave of protests against international financial institutions and G8 summits has started to rouse the academic left from their political apathy. Antonio Negri and Michael Hardt's *Empire* (Cambridge, MA, Harvard University Press,

2001) is a sprawlingly ambitious neo-Marxist attempt to reconfigure democracy in an era of liquid boundaries and hybrid identities. But it suffers from an overly naïve perception both of grassroots movements and of the advantages of decentralizing power, particularly when viable alternatives are only vaguely articulated. And, for a work purportedly challenging twenty-first century capitalism, it is rather weak on rigorous economic thinking. Nonetheless, it has rapidly become a must-read among leftists intellectuals and anti-capitalist discontents longing for a theoretical manifesto for "democratic globalization." Finally, those who may doubt that leftist discourse has little to say about the capitalism of the twenty-first century, should look no further than Julian Stallabrass's outstanding work, *Gargantua: Manufactured Mass Culture* (London, Verso, 1996). It not only updates familiar Frankfurt School criticisms on the icons of consumer culture—e.g., advertising, media, mass-produced art—it also has many wise and troubling things to say about the creeping synergy between capitalism, cyberspace, and human behavior.

INDEX